The Visionary Moment

THE SUNY SERIES IN
POSTMODERN CULTURE

Joseph Natoli, *Editor*

The Visionary Moment

A Postmodern Critique

Paul Maltby

State University of New York Press

Published by
State University of New York Press, Albany

© 2002 State University of New York

For information, address State University of New York Press,
90 State Street, Suite 700, Albany, NY 12207

Production by Dana Foote
Marketing by Patrick Durocher

Library of Congress Cataloging-in-Publication Data

Maltby, Paul.
The visionary moment : a postmodern critique / Paul Maltby.
p. cm.—(SUNY series in postmodern culture)
Includes bibliographical references (p.) and index.
ISBN 0-7914-5413-4 (alk. paper)—ISBN 0-7914-5414-2 (pbk. : alk. paper)
1. American fiction—20th century—History and criticism. 2. Postmodernism
(Literature)—United States. 3. Visions in literature. I. Title. II. Series.

PS374.P64 M35 2002
813'.509113—dc21
2002017729

10 9 8 7 6 5 4 3 2 1

for Shirley

Mystical explanations are considered deep.
The truth is that they are not even superficial.
—Friedrich Nietzsche, *The Gay Science*

Contents

Acknowledgments

Portions of this book, subsequently revised and expanded, were first published in journals. Chapter 4, "The Romantic Metaphysics of Don DeLillo," originally appeared in *Contemporary Literature,* Volume 37, Number 2, Summer 1996, published by the University of Wisconsin Press. Parts of chapters 1, 2, and 3 originally appeared in *The Centennial Review,* Volume XLI, Number 1, Winter 1997, published by Michigan State University Press. I wish to thank Tim Newcomb of the University of Illinois, Bob Fletcher of West Chester University, and Christian Moraru of the University of North Carolina, who reviewed sections of this study and made helpful suggestions on how to improve them. Thanks are due to James Peltz, managing editor of SUNY Press, and Dana Foote, production editor, for their valuable assistance through the stages of the book's production. I am also grateful to Shirley, my wife, for the moral and intellectual support she gave me while I worked on this book.

Introduction

[A]nd suddenly . . . he pronounced, "Mon Dieu! How the time passes!" Nothing could have been more commonplace than this remark; but its utterance coincided for me with a moment of vision. It's extraordinary how we go through life with eyes half shut, with dull ears, with dormant thoughts. . . . Nevertheless, *there can be but few of us who had never known one of these rare moments of awakening when we see, hear, understand ever so much—everything—in a flash.* . . .

     —Joseph Conrad, *Lord Jim* 111, emphasis added

An old theory of truth still enchants us. According to this theory, truth, in the sense of "higher" spiritual knowledge, can be apprehended in an illuminating instant. The theory has a long history and today remains deeply inscribed in religious, literary, and colloquial discourse. I would surmise there are few among us who have not, at some time, believed in the possibility of the flash of insight that could deliver spiritually redeeming knowledge. Such a belief persists like folklore. Indeed, this theory of truth has survived in spite of wave after wave of antimetaphysical thinking (empiricism, dialectical materialism, Darwinism, psychoanalysis)—and the notion of the illuminating instant is essentially meta-physical. For example, when we recall that Reformed Theology was preoccupied with "the requirement of grace as an instantaneous illumination" (Pettit 13), the idea of the illuminating instant may be seen inter alia as a displaced expression of religious belief: a belief in knowledge whose purity and transcendence guarantees its power to transfigure the visionary subject.

  This belief is especially evident in much anglophone poetry and fiction of the last two hundred years—a literature haunted by the idea of the salvational moment. We encounter the belief in the common literary practice of plotting narratives around, or at least highlighting, what I shall designate as a "visionary moment." It is a familiar enough convention: the sudden enlightenment that, at a critical juncture in the life of the protagonist, dramatically raises spiritual aware-ness to the level of a transcendent and redemptive order of knowledge. To illustrate the extent to which this convention pervades poetry and fiction, I shall quote three of the four authors of the hitherto only published monographs on the topic.[1] (All four have adopted the term "epiphany," a term whose limitations I shall discuss in chapter 1.) In *The Poetics of Epiphany* (1987), Ashton Nichols identifies epiphany as "a defining characteristic of twentieth-century fiction," a convention, moreover, that served as "a standard means of organizing lyric poems during the nineteenth century" (1, 5; see also McGowan, "From Pater" 417). In *Patterns of Epiphany* (1997), Martin Bidney writes, "[B]eginning with the Romantic movement, epiphanies have been crucial organizing principles of modern poetry and imaginative prose" (1). And in *Epiphany in the Modern Novel* (1971), Morris Beja remarks on "the astonishing frequency with which sudden moments of intuitive insight appear in twentieth-century fiction" (18; see also 46). In fact, by the late fifties, it was already clear to Richard Ellmann that epiphany was "the technique which has now become a commonplace of modern fiction" (88). Therefore, it comes as a surprise to find that there has been no sustained critique of this convention. For example, the criticism of Beja, Bidney, and Nichols typifies this field of scholarship insofar as it ignores the ideological implications of the convention and does not question its metaphysical presuppositions. Rather, but for a few brief and isolated interrogations, which bear almost no resemblance to the critique advanced here (see e.g. Saltzman 8–28; McGowan "From Pater"), commentary on the epiphany/visionary moment—divided and contentious as it may be—generally adopts the perspectives of a formalist poetics or literary-historical survey. For example, Bidney, who adopts a "neo-Bachelardian approach" (16), aims "to show, first, that epiphanies tend to be composed primarily of *elements, motions, and/or shapes . . .* [and] [s]econd, . . . that any given epiphany maker is likely to present a distinctive, recognizable, *recurrent combination* of one or more elements, motions, and/or shapes. . . . (5).[2] And Nichols's aim is to "provide a comprehensive discussion of the origins and defining characteristics of the new literary epiphany . . . , [its] Romantic origins . . ., its development by the Victorians, and its role as a precursor of twentieth-century literary techniques" (*Poetics* 4).

My concern here is to extend the line of inquiry in the light of questions raised by postmodern critique. For, with very few exceptions,[3] the convention of the visionary moment has been neglected by scholars trained in postmodern epistemology. Consider, for instance, the most recent publication in this field: *Moments of Moment: Aspects of the Literary Epiphany* (ed. Tigges, 1999). Of the twenty-four essays collected in this anthology, just seven demonstrate an awareness of postmodern theory (see Boheemen-Saaf, Chapman, Dutoit, Henke, Losey, Nichols, Parke), and only four (Chapman, Dutoit, Henke, Losey) mount arguments that depend on it.[4] And even here, but for the two essays (Chapman and Henke) in which female writers are read, from a Kristevan perspective, as countering a phallocentric bias in the conventional use of epiphany, neither the metaphysical preconceptions nor the ideological characteristics of the literary epiphany are *questioned* in the light of postmodern critique. (Emphatically, this is not to suggest that these and the other essays in Tigges's anthology are in any way deficient, but only to point out the virtual absence of any postmodern interrogation of this literary convention.)

The case for a critique of the literary visionary moment is that it is enmeshed in metaphysical and ideological assumptions—assumptions that, by the standards of postmodern critique, are theoretically untenable and that, in most contexts, are irreconcilable with progressive political thinking. And given the widespread practice of organizing fictional narratives by means of this convention, the moment serves as an effective vehicle for perpetuating these assumptions. Where there is discussion of the visionary moment—which typically focuses on its use by Romantic, Victorian, or high-modernist writers—it is usually in ways that the writers themselves would endorse; that is to say, novelists and poets who employ the convention of the moment are generally taken on their own terms. Commentators may debate the precise narrative function of a writer's visionary moments or their structure or the consistency with which a writer uses them (issues persistently raised, for example, in discussions of Joyce's "epiphanies" or Wordsworth's "spots of time" [see e.g. Bowen; Hendry Chayes; Bidney; Langbaum]). However, other significant questions have yet to be addressed. In particular, we need to examine how the ways in which this convention is mobilized and the premises that underlie it may be construed as politically suspect and epistemologically unsound. In other words, commentary generally stops short of problematizing the visionary moment. Yet, the moment is susceptible to several forms of critique: positivist, psychoanalytic, materialist. The principal aim of this study is to examine the literary visionary moment from perspectives opened up by postmodern critique. For the moment is premised on assumptions about the nature of truth, cognition, and subjectivity, which are vulnerable to the demystifying and deconstructive impetus of this critique. Furthermore, the rhetoricity of the moment often encodes a conservative ideology and a logic of disempowerment (a diminished sense of political agency and historical identity), conditions that also make the moment an appropriate target for postmodern critique.

Insofar as visionary moments typically embody claims to (a) transcendent knowledge, (b) the mediation of occult faculties (e.g. "insight") in the attainment of that knowledge, (c) the instantaneous reception of the knowledge (e.g. the "flash" of insight), and (d) the proximity of redemption by virtue of the transfiguring truth ascribed to that knowledge, we may say they epitomize the pretensions of traditional forms of mystical narrative. Indeed, the literary visionary moment will be seen to stand in a synecdochal relation to the truth claims of mystical experience in its general (nonliterary) forms. Thus, the postmodern challenge to the visionary moment as a credible mode of cognition will also serve as an abbreviated and allegorical way of addressing the larger question of the credibility of mystical truth claims in general. I take the latter to be a legitimate target, especially at present, given the publishing boom in pop spirituality and New Age mysticism: this is the time of Deepak Chopra's vacuous pronouncements on the life of the soul, of shamanistic and millennial cults, of a burgeoning of belief in the supernatural.[5]

This study will also pursue the postmodern interest in the conditions under which meaning is sustained and sanctioned, which, in this case, calls for attention to the configurations of knowledge and the institutional forces that validate the visionary moment as a source of signification. Accordingly, I shall discuss, among other things, the remarkable persistence of the Puritan model of redemption; the Romantic legacy of a nonrational cognitive faculty; the endorsements supplied by literature itself *qua* prestigious institutional practice; and the ratifying force of bourgeois ideology. At issue here is the legitimation of the metaphysical truth claims implicit in the visionary moment.

Inquiry will, with just a few exceptions, focus on texts by North American writers active since 1945, with special reference to fiction by Don DeLillo, Jack Kerouac, Saul Bellow, Alice Walker, Paule Marshall, Flannery O'Connor, and Raymond Carver.[6] This choice of writers is largely guided by the opportunity each affords to explore the literary visionary moment in a distinctive context. For example, the implications of the use of this convention vary between a postmodern writer like DeLillo and a Beat writer like Kerouac and black women writers like Walker and Marshall. Moreover, the post-1945 time frame is significant, for the convention of the visionary moment in American fiction since Faulkner has been virtually ignored. One reason for this lack of critical attention is what we might call the Wordsworth/Joyce axis of scholarship. Here, under the rubric "epiphany," is where the discussion of the poetics and history of the visionary moment is concentrated. After all, critics maintain (and with good reason) that the literary epiphany originated in Wordsworth's poetry and was developed by Joyce into a formalized aesthetics (see e.g. Nichols, *Poetics* 12; Langbaum 34; Beja 32–33). Moreover, widely recognized as the most accomplished practitioners of the convention, Wordsworth and Joyce have been canonized as the exemplars of epiphanic literature. Where the discussion of the literary epiphany does branch out, it is largely along the lines of this axis, hence the focus on the English Romantics or the anglophone high-modernist novelists (see e.g. Abrams 385–90, 418–27; Langbaum 33–57; see also Beja; Bidney; Nichols *Poetics;* McGowan, "From Pater" *passim*).

The literary use of visionary moments became a convention in England during the initial phase of industrialization (roughly, 1780–1840), the expansive surge of modernization that radically transformed social relations, cultural practices, and much of the landscape. In particular, *The Prelude,* composed between 1799 and 1805, has been identified as inaugurating the formal and systematic use of the literary moment (see e.g. Langbaum 34; Bidney 25): its autobiographical narrative is frequently punctuated by moments of illumination, which Wordsworth called "spots of time" (12.208). The periodization is important, for the historical premise, to be explored later, is that, as a literary convention, the visionary moment emerges in tension with the most aggressive phase in the development of the forces of production. Subsequently, concurrent with the unremitting process of modernization, the convention has persisted as a defining feature of Victorian and modernist poetry (see e.g. Nichols *Poetics;* Bidney), of the anglophone high-modernist novel (see e.g. Beja) and, as we shall see, of American fiction since 1945. Moreover, in the context of what we may conveniently enumerate as the four *As* of capitalist modernization—Alienation, Anomie, Atomization, Angst—the visionary moment can be read as encoding the fantasy or hope of a whole and spiritually centered life (as intimated in the flash of transcendent and redemptive knowledge). In short, modernization sets the stage for the production and reception of this convention; it is the conjunctural force field that makes the option to write in this visionary mode seem such a compelling one and that makes the public and critical response to it such a sympathetic one.

The literary visionary moment will be seen to perform numerous ideological functions ("ideological," suffice to say here, in that visionary moments naturalize purely individualist models of human change and knowledge, thereby concealing the political constraints and socio-historical limits of change and knowledge). But it is important to stress that any political analysis of the moment that focused exclusively on its ideological implications would be skewed and one-sided. For we shall see how the literary visionary moment is also mobilized on behalf of a progressive politics; how it can perform a critical function by invoking the image of a postalienated and postanomic subject. Indeed, a key factor in its persistent appeal as a literary convention is its adversarial and utopian potential. Moreover, insofar as visionary moments may affirm or imply utopian ideals, their mystifications of knowledge and temporality are readily embraced. Thus, one and the same visionary moment may be at one and the same time ideological and critical/ utopian in character.[7] Accordingly, in several places (notably, in discussions of Kerouac and Walker), I shall try to give due weight to the critical function behind the use of literary visionary moments. However, my principal interest lies in exploring the ideological dimension of this convention and, in particular, in showing how it embodies a paradigm of knowledge pregnant with ideological implications.

The visionary moment promotes the influential myth that there is a "higher" order of knowledge that can "save" or transfigure the individual by virtue of its singular attributes—that is, knowledge as inter alia intuitive, instantaneous, pure, permanent, and universal. This amounts to a paradigm of knowledge that implicitly downgrades "worldly" forms of knowledge that have real transformative potential. The paradigm also assumes the model of a self-sufficient (or atomistic) subject as the private source of knowledge. Ideological effects follow from these assumptions. Thus, in dissociating knowledge from public life and interiorizing it, the paradigm occludes understanding of the socially constituted nature of knowledge. Furthermore, it obscures the role of knowledge in constructing the positions from which the subject makes sense of his or her place in the world. In short, the political implications of knowledge are effaced. The literary visionary moment also perpetuates the common assumption that knowledge acquired in an instant is likely to be pure and coherent, for instantaneousness suggests the bypassing of the contaminating and obfuscating effects of worldly mediation. Or, to put it another way, the visionary moment presupposes the ideal of a flawless channel of communication, free of the culture's "noise," insulated against the distortions of entropy.

It is in relation to the visionary moment as a paradigm of knowledge that I shall introduce my use of postmodern critique as a counterparadigm. But first, in recognition of a precept of this mode of critique, I must take the preliminary step of a self-positioning.

A protocol of postmodern critique is the inclusion of a statement of its own theoretical limits. By this reflexive gesture, it presents itself as an intervention rather than a voice speaking from outside of theory, a perspective rather than a panoptic judgment. These remarks apply not only to my focus on the convention of the visionary moment (already perspectivized as postmodern critique) but also to what I am calling "postmodern critique." After all, the latter is necessarily a construction, since this or any critique has no existence prior to its theorization. And to say this is not to suggest that there is anything idiosyncratic or contentious about my construction (which is, roughly, a mainstream, almost consensual model) but only that there can be no definitive account of what constitutes postmodern critique; depending on the disciplinary and ideological position of the theorist, the construction will, unavoidably, be selective and interested. Thus, I speak from within the critical-pedagogical enclave of the academy, where educators work to connect learning to the process of social change (of which more later) and where their curricula must reckon with a pervasive neoconservative hostility to "theory" as a desecrating and disruptive force. Moreover, it need hardly be said, this study is made possible largely by virtue of those cross-fertilizing inputs from inter alia poststructuralist theory, narratology, and cultural studies, which, since the mid-seventies, have animated literary-critical practice.

By "postmodern critique," I mean a mode of critique that is largely elaborated from the ideas of neo-Nietzschean thinkers (notably Foucault, Derrida, and Lyotard) and deployed against hegemonic discourses and practices with the aim of contesting and undermining their authority. Though not always conceived as a mission that translates into a clear agenda for political action, this mode of critique aims to demystify and delegitimize assumptions about, for example, "Truth," "Reason," the "Self," "History," "Culture," language, and gender—assumptions on which bourgeois, Eurocentric, patriarchal, and other ideologies and practices are said to be premised.[8] Postmodern critique makes no pretence of "disinterested" contemplation of its object; typically, it seeks to effect a radical change within the epistemological field (including the institutional structures that transmit knowledge) in the name of freedom from mystification and ideology. Among the strategies employed to this end (individualized here at the risk of some overlap and expounded at the risk of shifting to a pedagogic register) are

1. *Particularization.* The universalizing and totalizing claims of hegemonic discourse and practice are contested with the use of particularizing concepts, such as difference, perspectivism, ethnicity, and locality. Thus, in opposition to such undifferentiated concepts as Truth or Self, this critique posits (respectively) perspectives and subject positions.

2. *Denaturalization.* Against discourse or practice that masquerades as natural, postmodern critique will stress its socially and historically constituted character, its grounds of possibility. The "natural" discourse/practice is revealed to be a cultural construct.

3. *Delegitimation.* Proceeding from the premise that the legitimacy of a body of knowledge does not depend on its truth content or its provenance in some putative subject of reason, postmodern critique examines the role of institutional forces and disciplinary matrices in the production and authorization of knowledge.

4. *Textualization.* We are reminded that no discourse can escape the condition of its own textuality; hence, the incessant and differential "play" of signs (i.e., the ever-shifting intertextual fields in which signifiers acquire provisional meanings) is seen to deny any discourse the final meaning on which its authority depends.

5. *Defiguration.* Here the strategy is to expose how rhetorical force is deployed in the service of truth claims. The truth of a discourse is revealed to be substantially dependent on tropes, figures, and other techniques of persuasion.

6. *Decentering.* Where the "Self" is conceived in liberal-humanist terms as an autotelic, autonomous, and unitary being, it is "decentered" by postmodern critique, which reconceives it as an aggregate of discursively constituted and contradictory "subject positions." Given this plurality of positions, there can be no appeal to an ultimate or prior self as the validation for the "truth" of an experience.

7. *Stressing contingency.* Postmodern critique cogently articulates its sense of the contingent. It explains human experience not as the necessary outcome of some metaphysical principle operating beyond the reach of change and chance (e.g., Design or Telos), but in terms of the variability and diversity of historical, local, and random forces.

8. *Stressing contamination.* This desacralizing strategy undermines the authority derived from the (fundamentalist) belief in the possibility of a pure, pristine, and original text/language. The latter's enmeshment in extraneous meaning systems is revealed as inevitable through Derridean concepts such as "différance" and "supplementarity."[9]

These strategies account for much of this book's methodology. Some Marxist concepts also inform this critique. And, it must be said at once that, contrary to popular impressions, postmodern critique is, in many respects, far from postmarxist in its disposition. To be sure, Marxism—assailed for its "productivist logic" and "metanarrative" stance—was a principal target of much postmodern critique of the sixties and seventies and, in some respects, depending on how one chooses to theorize postmodern critique or Marxism, the two remain separated by irreconcilable differences. Yet, Marxist categories continue to have a ubiquitous presence in currents of this critique (for example, in much new historicist and postcolonial theory). Vincent Leitch, in a discussion of Fredric Jameson, observes, "By adding the concepts of hegemony and residual and emergent forms to the model of the mode of production, Jameson, *like other contemporary theorists,* postmodernizes Marxist historiography" (127, emphasis added). Capitalism and class remain as prominent and indispensable concepts, even if they are not assigned foundationalist status. (Given a social field reconceived as the site of *multiple* antagonisms, "capitalism" and "class" are no longer privileged as the governing terms in a final vocabulary, but as two among other primary vectors of power.) The category of ideology persists but, in its postmodern formulation, ideology is seen to emerge not just from within a class-based system of differences but also from within institutionalized differences of gender, race, ethnicity and so on.[10] Others have reconceptualized ideology as "master narrative" or even "discourse." And for Gayatri Spivak, "materialist"—a term still used in postmodern theory—functions as an "alibi word" for Marxism ("New Historicism" 285). Even if one concedes that there are problems with Marxism's *meta*narrative claims—its teleological conception of History, its projection of the working class as the necessary agent of emancipation—it still has *mega*narrative value as the theory of how "the constant revolutionising of production" structures key domains of social experience. In particular, the concept of capitalist modernization has proved vital to this study. The consequences of modernization—"uninterrupted disturbance of all social conditions, everlasting uncertainty and agitation" (Marx and Engels 52)—apply with no less force now than when Marx and Engels were writing and largely define the social space in which the literary visionary moment flourishes as a convention.[11]

A particular idea of human regeneration is crucial to the visionary-moment paradigm of knowledge. Almost invariably, this regeneration is conceived in the metaphysical context of a redemption which, moreover, is assumed to be a private, interior and, thus, entirely individualistic affair. The psyche is understood as the primary locus of the change and valued as where change most matters. It is a familiar and popular model of regeneration, whose validity is widely taken as granted. However, from the standpoint of postmodern critique, this model, as we shall see, raises awkward epistemological and ideological questions. But, for now, I want to highlight my own commitment to a political model of human regeneration. This model which, unlike the visionary model, I judge to be tenable, deeply informs my construction and use of postmodern critique. A guiding premise of this counterparadigm is that any viable and *sustainable* regeneration of the individual—be it moral, intellectual, or *spiritual*—is contingent upon prior transformations at the social (institutional and macrostructural) level of existence. (I stress "sustainable" to suggest a regeneration that amounts to more than just a phase of altered consciousness.) For this order of transformation to be possible, the individual must first be educated to a level of "critical literacy" in order to live as a "critical citizen." (These are concepts that I borrow from critical pedagogy, a current of education theory that explicitly identifies itself as postmodern. [See e.g., Giroux *Postmodernism;* Lankshear.] In consequence, as a practice, this pedagogy employs most of the postmodern strategies enumerated above.) Critical literacy enables us to question the institutional practices that use knowledge as a means of constituting subjects in subordinate and docile positions. It enables us to resist the sanctioned forms of literacy that disengage us from self-understanding as social, political, and culturally diverse subjects. With this practical competency, we can operate as critical citizens in the public sphere: debate and evaluate social policy, and cross cultural borders and open our minds to the diverse experience of others. In these ways, we are better able to serve as participants in the struggle for a radical-democratic transformation of the social order (cf. Giroux, "Literacy" 1). And I invoke democracy here partly in response to the visionary-moment model of regeneration, which may all too easily be read to imply that only an elect few— the spiritually redeemable—are eligible for this order of change. In short, this demystifying and deconstructive encounter with the convention of the visionary moment is, to a significant degree, animated by a commitment to uphold a political ideal of human change.[12]

Finally, authors in general do not depend on the visionary moment merely as a convenient narrative device. Indeed, it will be evident from the discussion of nonliterary sources (notably, interviews with, and essays by, the authors in question) that these authors work from deeply held personal philosophies in relation to which the visionary moment may be read as an expressive instance, an integral part. They believe in the visionary mode of understanding. Put another way, the moment is rarely an isolated expression of a writer's metaphysical outlook; rather, it tends to be just the most visible sign of an extensive metaphysics that permeates his or her oeuvre. Furthermore, the remarkable persistence of the visionary moment—as a literary convention it is now over two hundred years old—is testimony to its perceived value as a paradigm of knowledge. And, insofar as innumerable authors work with the convention, its knowledge paradigm is widely disseminated. (Suffice to note here that nearly all the authors discussed in this study have a prominent place in high school and college curricula and have a significant extracurricular readership.) Of course, there are other knowledge paradigms that need to be confronted but what makes this one an especially insidious paradigm is that it exists in the culture at large as common sense. However, postmodern critique has the resources to challenge this paradigm; they will serve in the name of a countervailing epistemology whose strategies aim for demystification and disenchantment.

I

Modalities of the Visionary Moment

The Concept of Epiphany

While ready-to-hand as an established designation, "epiphany" has, through its indelible association with Joyce's work, acquired a sedimentation of meaning that makes it inappropriate as a standard term for the convention examined here. Instead, I have opted for the less encumbered term, "visionary moment," which has its pedigree in near-identical terms used (but with less fanfare) by Joseph Conrad and Thomas Hardy, respectively, "moment of vision" and "moments of vision."[1]

Although writing in the "epiphanic mode" may have originated with Wordsworth (Langbaum 34; Nichols, *Poetics* xi; Johnson 7, 56), the convention of the literary epiphany is widely understood in the terms in which it was expounded and practiced by Joyce. When, around 1900, he transplanted "epiphany" from its theological context into his secular aesthetic, there were already several other terms that might equally well have served to designate the convention of the sudden and momentary illumination: Wordsworth's "spots of time," Conrad's "moment of vision" or, simply, "the Moment," as variously invoked by, among others, Shelley, Browning, and Pater (cf. Nichols ix; Abrams 385–90; 418–27; McGowan, "From Pater" 417–25). However, it was "epiphany" that beat out the contenders. Among the evaluative processes that enabled the ascendancy of this term, we should note the canonical reception of Joyce, starting in the early forties, from the standpoint of a formalist appreciation of his technical innovations: namely, his use of stream-of-consciousness, mythically patterned narratives, and the epiphany. In 1941, Harry Levin had identified the importance of the epiphany in Joyce's writing (28–37, *passim*), after which followed a spate of articles on the subject.[2] Moreover, it is noteworthy that several of the leading Joyce scholars of the fifties, notably Richard Ellmann and Hugh Kenner, were key players in the codification of modernism—an enterprise that defined literary value largely in terms that reflected Joyce's aesthetics (cf. Perloff 158). Then, in addition to scholarly endorsements of epiphany as an exemplary instance of modernist writing, we must also note the popularization of the term through general education courses, whose literature anthologies typically include a story from *Dubliners* in tandem with an expository account of the epiphany concept (see e.g., Hunt 223–24; Vesterman 6; Meyer 511). Finally, there is an interest in the selection of epiphany over kindred terms:

in spite of its resolutely secular usage, the term can invest a spiritual insight with the charismatic authority and drama of a religious experience. (Recall that, in its Christian usage, the term refers to the manifestation of Christ to the Magi.) Accordingly, Levin finds in Joyce's use of epiphanies, "attempts to create a literary substitute for the revelations of religion" (29).

"Epiphany," then, is the term most often used to designate what, in this study, I am calling a "visionary moment." However, "epiphany" cannot adequately signify forms of sudden and momentary illumination that diverge from Joyce's restrictive definition of the term. Indeed, it would be more accurate to think of the Joycean epiphany as one type of visionary moment, even though it is loosely applied to represent all types. (I shall sometimes use "epiphany, rather than "visionary moment," if that is the term used by the writer under discussion.)

An initial difficulty with "epiphany" is that the term acquired various meanings within Joyce's evolving oeuvre (cf. Walzl 153) and, in particular, his use of the convention shifted from the serious to the ironic. Between 1900 and 1904, Joyce wrote over seventy prose miniatures (Mahaffey 208 n.5; Scholes 152), which he called "epiphanies," and which were posthumously published under the same name. They were, for the most part, meticulously observed moments of street life, often in the form of snatches of overheard conversation, trivial exchanges, which (presumably) resonated with significance for Joyce.[3] But these epiphanies are quite different from the visionary "set-piece-of-prose" epiphanies (Gabler 218), which we find in *A Portrait of the Artist as a Young Man,* and where, moreover, the term "epiphany" is not even used. Vicki Mahaffey observes how in *Stephen Hero* (the earlier version of *A Portrait*), "Joyce uses 'epiphany' *both* to describe his records of moments that blend triviality with significance *and* to designate the revelatory climax of aesthetic apprehension" (190, emphasis added). Accordingly, Joyce's narrator recounts a brief and inconsequential flirtatious exchange between a young couple, "a fragment of colloquy out of which [Stephen] received an impression keen enough to afflict his sensitiveness very severely" (*Stephen Hero* 211). The experience inspires the following project:

> This triviality made him think of collecting many such moments together in a book of epiphanies. By an epiphany he meant a sudden spiritual manifestation, whether in the vulgarity of speech or of gesture or in a memorable phase of the mind itself. He believed it was for the man of letters to record these epiphanies with extreme care, seeing that they themselves are the most delicate and evanescent of moments. (211)

And from this passage the standard, aphoristic definition of the literary epiphany has emerged: "a sudden spiritual manifestation," which, moreover, is generally triggered by a mundane, insignificant stimulus. However, Joyce actually uses examples of commonplace objects—a clock in *Stephen Hero,* a basket in *A Portrait*—to illustrate this experience. Proceeding from the aesthetics of Aquinas, he proposes that the "*claritas*" (or radiance) of an object lies in the perception of its "*quidditas*" (or specific "whatness") (*Stephen Hero* 213; *A Portrait* 212–13). Hence he explains the process of epiphany: "[A] spiritual eye . . . seeks to adjust its vision to an exact focus. The moment the focus is reached the object is epiphanised." And "Its [the object's] soul, its whatness, leaps to us from the vestment of its appearance. The soul of the commonest object, the structure of which is so adjusted, seems to us radiant. The object achieves its epiphany" (*Stephen Hero* 211, 213; cf. *A Portrait* 213).

There are several epiphanies in *A Portrait*. However, while in *Stephen Hero* Joyce appears to be in earnest about the spiritual truth value of epiphanies, in *A Portrait,* the language of the epiphanies suggests the excesses of Stephen Dedalus' romantic sensibility (165–66, 211–12, 218–20). We sense an undertow of irony in the effusive rhetoric of the epiphanies and in the almost ludicrous artistic pretensions they inspire in Stephen: "forge in the smithy of my soul the uncreated conscience of my race" (247); "a prophecy of the end he had been born to serve . . . the artist forging anew in his workshop out of the sluggish matter of the earth a new soaring impalpable imperishable being" (163). Thus, Zack Bowen has felt prompted to ask: "Are the epiphanies really revelations of truth or character, or do they merely appear to be truth to the consciousness which experiences them?" (104). His answer is that "all epiphanies, some more subtly than others, are really, even if unstated, the epiphanies of the characters themselves. In every case [e.g. the boy in "Araby," Gabriel Conroy in "The Dead"], the language of the epiphany is the language of the character involved in its formulation . . . and Joyce remains somewhere behind the scenes paring his fingernails" (106; cf. *A Portrait* 209). Therefore, it comes as no surprise when, in *Ulysses,* Joyce has Stephen mockingly recollect the importance he, as a young aspiring artist, had once attached to his epiphanies:

> Remember your epiphanies on green oval leaves, deeply deep, copies to be sent if you died to all the great libraries of the world, including Alexandria? Someone was to read them there after a few thousand years, a mahamanvantara. Pico della Mirandola like. Ay, very like a whale. When one reads these strange pages of one long gone one feels that one is at one with one who once . . .(46)

There are several reasons why the limits within which Joyce defined epiphany make it inappropriate as the generic term for visionary moments. First, in general, the literary visionary moment, unlike the Joycean epiphany, is not dependent on the catalytic effect of a commonplace object or mundane gesture or snatch of conversation; typically, the stimulus for the visionary moment is a critical situation or incident that upsets a routine mindset. Second, it was an irreligious, anticlericist Joyce who coopted the Christian concept of epiphany for conspicuously, not to say provocatively, secular ends, that is, spiritually intense "esthetic apprehension" (*Stephen Hero* 212; *A Portrait* 209) or else a protagonist's recognition of his or her tragic flaw (as in the catastrophic insights that conclude "Araby" or "The Dead"). However, to insist on the secular status of the visionary moment is to exclude those moments that take the form of a sudden manifestation of the sacred (as in, say, the fiction of O'Connor or Kerouac, as in Raymond Carver's "Cathedral" or Alice Walker's "Everyday Use"). Third, to the extent that Joyce collected many epiphanies and enjoined the "man of letters" to record them, he assumes that, like Wordsworth's "spots of time," they are "scattered everywhere" (*Prelude* XII.224); they are certainly scattered throughout *A Portrait*. In contrast, the typical visionary moment is a singular and rare occurrence, and often a fictional narrative is built around it and the importance of the knowledge it conveys.

A conspicuous feature of commentary on the Joycean epiphany is the tendency to take the claims Joyce makes for epiphanic experience on his own terms. To be sure, the Joycean epiphany is a highly contested concept, but mostly only insofar as critics contest one another's interpretation of it (e.g., Scholes vs. Walzl; Langbaum vs. Scholes) or question the use Joyce makes of Aquinas' aesthetics (e.g. Noon; Beebe). But whether or not Joyce's theory of epiphany is actually valid is rarely raised as an issue. Take, for example, what, for convenience, we may call the *quidditas* doctrine: a specific object is "epiphanised" when "we recognise that it is *that* thing which it is. Its soul, its whatness, leaps to us from the vestment of its appearance" (*Stephen Hero* 213). The doctrine is invariably cited (e.g. Nichols, *Poetics* 11–12; Beja 77–78; Walzl 442–43; Hendry Chayes *passim*) but the extraordinary claim on which it is premised—the possibility of achieving an insight into the "whatness" of an object—goes unquestioned. And if the resources of postmodern critique may not have been available to many of those who have discussed Joyce's notion of epiphany, other kinds of critique were certainly ready-to-hand. For example, an obvious objection to the doctrine may be derived from Kant's limiting concept of the *noumenon:* the thing that can never be known in itself because of the intervening "regulative ideas" (causality, substance, etc.) that render the percept intelligible in *their* (aprioristic) terms. A second objection is possible when we reframe the epiphanic experience in psychoanalytic terms. Thus, what the doctrine mistakes as the "*claritas*" or "radiance" of the object *itself* (*Stephen Hero* 213; *A Portrait* 212–13) may be explained as the effect/affect of a libidinal investment, when a charge of psychical energy suddenly attaches itself to the object in question, thereby inflating its significance. In Freud's words, it would be a case of "object-cathexis" (*Introductory* 382). Third, as for an instance of postmodern critique, suffice to say at this point that, against any notion of a type of direct (prelinguistic) "insight" into the "intrinsic nature" of an object, we might reconceive the cognitive process as but the operation of an historically contingent language form, which *constructs a perspective* from which to "read" an object, but can never access its individual being. And here we might cite Richard Rorty, who cautions us "not [to] think of our 'intuitions' as . . . more than the habitual use of a certain repertoire of terms" (22). Finally, in an effort to establish a context for the *quidditas* doctrine, we must ask: why this concern with the epiphanisation of objects? (Joyce speaks of "the commonest object" [*Stephen Hero* 212–13] and cites the examples of a clock and basket.) In his analysis of the commodity structure, Georg Lukács observes how the reifying logic of "rational objectification conceals above all the immediate—qualitative and material—character of things as things." He proceeds to quote Marx: "'Private property alienates not only the *individuality* of men, but also of *things*'" (92, emphases added). Thus, in an age characterized by the universal commodification of the object-world, market exchange-value divests objects of their individual qualities; henceforth, they are understood quantitatively insofar as they must be exchanged on the basis of an abstract medium of equivalence, that is, money. Under these conditions, one can understand the desire for "the commonest objects" to reveal or epiphanise their individual being, their "*quiddity.*"[4]

Anatomy of the Visionary Moment

A visionary moment forms the climax of Flannery O'Connor's well-known story, "A Good Man Is Hard to Find" (1953). Recall that a grandmother, on vacation with her family in Georgia, encounters a gang of killers on the edge of some woods. The gang, led by "The Misfit," murders the family one by one, and the grandmother herself is just minutes away from becoming its last victim. At this point, she has a brief conversation with The Misfit, who confesses his spiritual turmoil as one who has struggled with the moral consequences of the possibility that Christ did not raise the dead. For,

> "If He did what He said, then it's nothing for you to do but throw away everything and follow Him, and if He didn't, then it's nothing for you to do but enjoy the few minutes you got left the best way you can—by killing somebody or burning down his house. . . ."
> "Maybe He didn't raise the dead," the old lady mumbled. . . .
> "If I had of been there I would of known and I wouldn't be like I am now." His voice seemed about to crack and the grandmother's head cleared for an instant. She saw the man's face twisted close to her own as if he were going to cry and she murmured, "Why you're one of my babies. You're one of my own children!" She reached out and touched him on the shoulder. The Misfit sprang back as if a snake had bitten him and shot her three times through the chest. . . .
> . . . [She] half sat and half lay in a puddle of blood with her legs crossed under her like a child's and her face smiling up at the cloudless sky. (*Complete Stories* 132)

The grandmother's visionary moment has a number of features that are common to literary representations of this experience:

1. The visionary moment is invariably distinguished by the suddenness of its occurrence. Hence, the grandmother is not prepared for her spiritual transformation.

2. The visionary moment is, precisely, a momentary experience. Accordingly, we read that "the grandmother's head cleared for an instant."

3. The visionary moment has a precarious existence; it cannot be summoned or prolonged at will. Therefore, O'Connor plots her story so that her protagonist is shot at the very instant of illumination, which is her means of securing the otherwise elusive vision.

4. The visionary moment signifies that a spiritual rebirth either has occurred or will occur. The grandmother has a Christian vision of spiritual kinship with her own murderer—"'You're one of my own children!'" she declares. It is a vision O'Connor invites us to understand as a sign of redemption.

5. The visionary moment is often validated in the name of a transcendent power or force: Grace in the grandmother's case.[5]

Next, consider Tommy Wilhelm's visionary moment in Saul Bellow's *Seize the Day* (1956). On his "day of reckoning"—when, among other things, he has been rejected by his father and cheated of all his money by a friend-cum-father-figure—Wilhelm reflects on the redemptive potential of a mystical experience in a subway a few days earlier. Preceded by the observation that "the real soul says plain and understandable things to everyone" (84), the following experience is recounted:

And in the dark tunnel, in the haste, heat, and darkness which disfigure and make freaks and fragments of nose and eyes and teeth, all of a sudden, unsought, a general love for all these imperfect and lurid-looking people burst out in Wilhelm's breast. He loved them. One and all, he passionately loved them. They were his brothers and his sisters. . . . [H]e was united with them by this blaze of love. . . .

So what did it matter how many languages there were . . . ? Or matter that a few minutes later he didn't feel anything like a brother toward the man who sold him the tickets?

. . . [P]eople were bound to have such involuntary feelings. It was only another one of those subway things. Like having a hard-on at random. But today, his day of reckoning, he consulted his memory again and thought, I must go back to that. That's the right clue and may do me the most good. Something very big. Truth, like. (84–85)

Bellow's account of a visionary moment closely corresponds with O'Connor's. Hence, we can note its sudden occurrence, its transient and precarious existence. Hence, it promises spiritual rebirth. Wilhelm's recognition of a profound kinship with others prefigures and prepares the way for the novel's final scene where his tears for a dead man he never knew carry him, in the closing words of the book, "toward the consummation of his heart's ultimate need" (118). And finally, as in O'Connor, a transcendent force is invoked to validate the experience. Thus, Wilhelm grasps the significance of his experience as "Something very big. Truth, like," something, that is, spoken by "the real soul [which] says plain and understandable things to everyone."

Our third visionary moment belongs to Jack Kerouac's *On the Road* (1957). Sal Paradise, the narrator/protagonist, reports the following experience on a crowded street in San Francisco:

> And for just a moment I had reached the point of ecstasy that I always wanted to reach, which was the complete step across chronological time into timeless shadows . . . , and myself hurrying to a plank where all the angels dove off and flew into the holy void of uncreated emptiness, the potent and inconceivable radiances shining in bright Mind Essence, innumerable lotus-lands falling open in the magic mothswarm of heaven. I could hear an indescribable seething roar which wasn't in my ear but everywhere and had nothing to do with sounds. I realized that I had died and been reborn numberless times but just didn't remember especially because the transitions from life to death and back to life are so ghostly easy, a magical action for naught . . . I realized it was only because of the stability of the intrinsic Mind that these ripples of birth and death took place. . . . (173)

Once more, we can observe features common to the literary visionary moment: its transient nature, the idea of rebirth, and its validation in the name of a transcendent power, that is, "Mind Essence." Moreover, Paradise's account incorporates other properties typical of visionary experience, including feelings of ecstasy and the sense of being outside of chronological time. The passage quoted is an instance of Beat soul exploration inspired by Zen mysticism and the Gnostic-Romantic writings of William Blake and Ralph Waldo Emerson.

The visionary moment is not to be confused with what we might call the "auratic moment." The visionary moment is experienced as a moment of actual, impending, or potential enlightenment, that is to say, a moment whose knowledge can or could be articulated. The auratic moment is experienced as a rich emanation of feeling, a sudden diffusion of affect. The following excerpt from F. Scott Fitzgerald's *Tender Is the Night* may be read as an example of an auratic moment:

> There were fireflies riding on the dark air and a dog baying on some low and far-away ledge of the cliff. The table seemed to have risen a little toward the

sky like a mechanical dancing platform, giving the people around it a sense of being alone with each other in the dark universe, nourished by its only food, warmed by its only lights. And, as if a curious hushed laugh from Mrs. McKisco were a signal that such a detachment from the world had been attained, the two Divers began suddenly to warm and glow and expand. . . . Just for a moment they seemed to speak to every one at the table, singly and together, assuring them of their friendliness, their affection. And for a moment the faces turned up toward them were like the faces of poor children at a Christmas tree. Then abruptly the table broke up—the moment when the guests had been daringly lifted above conviviality into the rarer atmosphere of sentiment, was over before it could be irreverently breathed, before they had half realized it was there.

But the diffused magic of the hot sweet South had withdrawn into them—the soft-pawed night and the ghostly wash of the Mediterranean far below—the magic left these things and melted into the two Divers and became part of them. (33–34)[6]

Auratic moments may be commonplace, as in the aestheticized perception typical of characters in high-modernist narratives, for example, Faulkner's Quentin Compson in *The Sound and the Fury* or Thomas Wolfe's Eugene Gant in *Look Homeward, Angel.* This mode of perception is also evident in Henry James's fiction: think of Lambert Strether in *The Ambassadors* or Isabel Archer in *The Portrait of a Lady.* Strether's way of seeing can, for example, transform a stretch of French countryside into a painting—"a certain small Lambinet that had charmed him, long years before, at a Boston dealer's" (341); it can transform people, like the sculptor Gloriani, into objets d'art (126). Hence, in a discussion of the aesthetic vision of Jamesian heroes, who have the capacity to convert perceptions of the ordinary into art, Richard Poirier observes:

> Having, by the very nature of the imaginations that engendered them, only a tangential relation to what is really going on, these moments needn't be *made* into anything else, needn't be organic . . . with anything but the creative vision itself. They are, as it were, pure art in being freed from the pressure of any environment but that of the mind from which they issue. (127–28)

And these remarks should remind us of the striking parallel between James's pursuit of enhanced aesthetic perception and Walter Pater's notion of *aesthesis,* as expounded in his famous "Conclusion" to *The Renaissance.*[7] Pater privileged the "moment" purely for its own sake—that is, for its exquisiteness, vitality, and intensity—and repudiated any *use* for art, in particular, placing it in the service of truth or knowledge. Art is to be valued because it "comes to you proposing frankly to give nothing but the highest quality to your moments as they pass, and simply for those moments' sake" (qtd. in McGowan, "From Pater" 420). Such moments are conceived as isolated, atomistic, divorced from social history. In short, the auratic moment lacks significant propositional content; it is a source of precious feeling rather than articulable knowledge.

We also need to distinguish the literary visionary moment from conventional forms of mystical experience. Several distinctions will be noted later in this chapter, but there are three that merit attention here. If we may limit the discussion of mysticism to the terms by which it is understood within traditional Christian gnosis, we should begin by noting the three stages in the ascension to spiritual perfection: (a) the purification of the intellect (*via purgativa*); (b) exhaustive knowledge of the noetical world as achieved through contemplation (*via contemplativa* or *illuminativa*); (c) union with God by virtue of his saving grace (*via unitiva*) (see Keller 75, 81). Proceeding from this schema, we should note that, unlike the literary visionary moment in which illumination is effortlessly achieved, the mystic typically achieves illumination only by way of arduous contemplation. Moreover, conventional mystical experience assumes the form of the revelation of something sacred: it is, to borrow Mircea Eliade's term, either "hierophanic" (a manifestation of the sacred in an ordinary object) or theophanic. In either case, the revelation is understood to be the work of divine agency. However, while some visionary moments may be hierophanic or theophanic—as in the fiction of O'Connor or the poetry of Gerard Manley Hopkins[8]—most moments are not premised on the external force of divine revelation; their spirituality is of a secular type and the source of their visionary power lies within the psyche. And from these distinctions it also follows that union with God, which is the ultimate stage of the mystical ascension, is rarely the outcome, or even the orientation, of the typical visionary moment. Finally, in the visions of the religious mystics, for example, the "shewings" or apparitions experienced by Julian of Norwich or Margery Kempe, nothing is physically sensed; the source of the vision is purely internal and sometimes physically induced by bodily abuse (starvation or flagellation) or illness. On the other hand, the literary moment may be triggered by an external stimulus; for example, an overheard comment, as in Katherine Mansfield's "Miss Brill," or a smell, as in Katherine Anne Porter's "The Grave."

Last, we need to distinguish between two types of visionary moment, what I shall call "redemptive" and "catastrophic" moments. To be sure, both types have properties in common: they occur suddenly and unannounced; they are of instantaneous duration; they are premised on the mediation of an occult faculty ("insight," "intuition"); they claim the communication of pure and transcendent knowledge. However, while the redemptive visionary moment signifies a transfiguration or regeneration of the subject (although often the change is intimated only as impending rather than accomplished within the time frame of the narrative), the catastrophic moment is marked by a sense of spiritual desolation. The latter may be seen as a descendant of the Aristotelian recognition (*anagnorisis*), that is, the protagonist's discovery of a flaw in his or her character that has or will have a tragic or destructive outcome. Typically, the epiphanies in Joyce's *Dubliners* (but not in *A Portrait*) are catastrophic visionary moments. Take, for example, Gabriel Conroy, in "The Dead," who suddenly "saw himself as a ludicrous figure . . . idealizing his own clownish lusts," a perception that leaves him with a sense of a moribund soul, a sense of his "own identity . . . fading out into a grey impalpable world" (179, 182). Or think of John Marcher's tragic recognition, in Henry James's "The Beast in the Jungle": "he had been the man of his time, *the* man, to whom nothing on earth was to have happened" ("The Beast" 282). Neither Conroy nor Marcher will recover from the devastating self-insight.[9] Unless otherwise stated, all visionary moments discussed in this study are of the redemptive type, which is by far the more common of the two.

The Extratextualized Visionary Moment

As a literary convention, the visionary moment derives much of its credibility from the common belief that such moments are experienced in real life. Indeed, this belief is surely a factor in the survival of a convention which, from a postmodern perspective, looks so archaic. Thus, as a preliminary step in the critique of the use and implications of the moment as a literary convention, we must probe the assumption on which that convention partly rests: Are visionary moments experienceable outside of literature?

It should be said at once that the sudden "insights" that have played such a crucial role in scientific discovery cannot be identified as visionary; in this context, insight entails neither claims to transcendent and redemptive knowledge nor to the operation of some occult or supernatural agency in the acquisition of that knowledge.[10] Neither should we confuse the sudden self-insight—"So this is who I really am!", the "click! of recognition" (Brereton 108)—with the absolute or transcendent self-knowledge typical of literary visionary moments. While a literary character may be privileged with a sudden insight that locates his/her existence within an overarching cosmic scheme (like Ruby Turpin in Flannery O'Connor's "Revelation" [*Complete Stories* 508] or Sal Paradise in *On the Road* [173]), there are good reasons—postmodern and otherwise—to contest the notion that real-life insight could ever yield the equivalent in absolute self-knowledge. The objections to the notion of a knowledge that fully defines "the self" (i.e., that which is said to lie beyond the local and contingent manifestations of character) require only nominal mention here. Thus, we must reckon with the volatile logic of "différance," in consequence of which there is said to be no stable vocabulary in which self-knowledge can be grasped. We must also reckon with the postmodern dissolution of the self as a biologically given and unitary entity and its redefinition as an aggregate of historically constituted and contradictory subject positions. From this standpoint, self-knowledge could only ever amount to the privileging of one among many subjectivities as *the* Self. Furthermore, we must reckon with the limits and distortions of self-knowledge that may stem from ideological misrecognition or from unconscious resistance.

One might appeal to experiences reported by mystics as evidence for the credibility of real-life visionary moments. However, we must distinguish between the mystic's suddenly altered state of consciousness (which confers an unfamiliar angle of vision and which resonates with fresh, expansive, and profound meaning) and the mystic's interpretation of that consciousness as visionary by virtue of claims about what type of meaning is experienced and the medium of its delivery. To clarify this distinction, consider an autobiographical account of a visionary moment by Wayne Teasdale, an ecospiritualist:

> I remember sitting on a hill somewhere in Sri Lanka watching the wind stirring the trees, and suddenly I realized something, an intuition triggered by the movement of the trees as they received the breezes of the wind. It was as if the wind, like hands, was plucking a harp, the trees. It was then that I understood the relationship of the cosmos to God, that is, the cosmos as His mediated presence. This insight is an example of the Cosmic or Primordial Revelation, and so is an ontological perception of a nature-mysticism, an instance, if you will, of theophanic consciousness. (221, emphases added)

That Teasdale experienced such a phase of consciousness is not in doubt. However, within the radically antimetaphysical terms of postmodern thought, it cannot be admitted that he has been the beneficiary of "the Cosmic or Primordial Revelation" or "theophanic consciousness," or that the experience testifies to the workings of "intuition" or "insight." The deep spirituality of his experience may be freely acknowledged as long as we avoid any sense of spirituality that entails claims to transcendent knowledge, omniscience, redeemability, and supernatural agency.

An examination of Teasdale's visionary moment can reveal the process whereby a mental event acquires visionary status. This is to say that the moment is not intrinsically visionary but, rather, is constituted as such (and not, for example, as aberrant or nonsensical). First, insofar as the moment occurs unannounced ("suddenly I realized"), it is as if it was *received,* its knowledge communicated from a source beyond the subject. Under these conditions, the "revealed" knowledge acquires a kind of oracular or sacred authority. As tradition has it, knowledge delivered in this instantaneous fashion must be highly significant rather than trivial.

Second, the natural phenomenon observed by Teasdale is interpreted as the effect of God's "mediated presence." The phenomenon—"it was as if the wind, like hands, was plucking a harp, the trees"—is read as a fragment from some universal narrative of "the relationship of the cosmos to God." However, the process of interpretation is occluded. The moment seems to speak for itself, to announce its own significance to a passive (noninterpreting) subject. But the moment is always-already interpreted because it is "read" by an institutionally and ideologically positioned subject. Thus, one would expect an ecospiritualist like Teasdale to encounter his experience in visionary terms. On the other hand, a timber merchant, "sitting on a hill . . . in Sri Lanka watching the wind stirring the trees" is more likely to have "suddenly realized" the value of Sri Lankan lumber.

Third, we are most often acquainted with real-life visionary moments in narrated form. That is to say, we know them less through direct personal experience than through their narration by "visionary" subjects. And just as studies of conversion narratives are often premised on the distinction between the conversion experience and its narration (see e.g., Brereton 14–27; Stromberg 1–16), so we must also reckon with the distortions and secondary elaborations that occur when an experience must (a) submit to the dynamics of the genre in which it is reported and (b) conform to the ideology of the institution or formation within which the "visionary" subject writes. Thus, a formally narrated visionary moment will acquire a high level of coherence and interestedness. Accordingly, Teasdale recounts the story of a pure theophany, an experience which, as told, was remarkably and altogether free of irrelevant and contradictory, ambiguous and ambivalent, thoughts. And his narration promotes the ecospiritualist creed of God's immanence in nature. Indeed, it is a construction of nature as benign, where the wind gently stirs the trees "like hands . . . plucking a harp." That the wind can also ravage trees, that all the planet's ecosystems could be destroyed by a single bolide impact, are facts banished from the narrative by Teasdale's ecospiritualist subjectivity.

The above points describe some of the factors involved in the process whereby a mental event is (without conscious intention) transformed into a visionary moment. A look at another autobiographical account of a visionary moment can enlarge the postmodern perspective on this process. In an interview, given to the *Paris Review* in 1965, Allen Ginsberg recalled a spiritual experience during his student days (he gives the date as 1948), when he lived in a sublet apartment in East Harlem:

> I came [i.e., ejaculated] . . . with a Blake book on my lap . . . and *suddenly I realized* that the poem was talking about me. "Ah, Sun-flower! [sic] weary of time, / Who countest the steps of the sun; / Seeking after that sweet golden clime, / Where the traveller's journey is done" . . . [T]he sweet golden clime, *I suddenly realized* that this existence was it! And, that I was born in order to experience up to this very moment that I was having this experience, to realize what this was all about—in other words that this was the moment I was born for. This initiation. Or this vision or this consciousness, of being alive unto myself, alive myself unto the Creator. As the son of the Creator—who loved me. . . .
>
>   . . . [A]nd a sense of cosmic consciousness, vibrations, understanding, awe, and wonder and surprise. And it was *a sudden awakening* into a totally deeper real universe than I'd been existing in. (302–304, emphases added.)

A radical alteration of consciousness was induced, it seems, by a reading of a poem by William Blake and encountered as a visionary moment. In particular, we should note Ginsberg's dependence on the words *suddenly* and *sudden,* which in the space of barely two pages he uses ten times. This usage works to suggest that his experience was unmediated by the process and constitutive role of interpretation and that, instead, the moment arrived replete with its *own* visionary meaning. It is a condition, moreover, that seems to guarantee the truth of that meaning since it leaves no space for fallible human judgment.

Ginsberg illustrates the account of his experience with so many references to Blake, so many allusions to and quotations from *Songs of Innocence and of Experience* and the prophetic books, that he renders the experience intelligible first and foremost as a Blakean vision. Indeed, elsewhere in the interview, he speaks of his "Blake visions" (291, 311, 317). We must also consider the possibility that, in the telling (of 1965), the original experience (of 1948) has been inflated by a counter-cultural rhetoric, which privileges Blakean visionary consciousness for its anti-hegemonic value.[11] As Theodore Roszak writes in *The Making of a Counter Culture,* "[Ginsberg's] protest does not run back to Marx; it reaches out, instead, to the ecstatic radicalism of Blake" (126). What Ginsberg gives us is a sixties recounting of a forties experience.

Consider a sample of the terms with which Ginsberg recollects the above and other visionary moments: "The total consciousness . . . of the complete universe" (305); "the experience was . . . blissful" (306); "infinite self" (309); "total being" (310); "cosmical awareness" (311). This is the language with which mystics commonly describe the feelings of omniscience and omnipotence and the feelings of ecstasy that frequently accompany mystical experience.[12] And these are feelings that are so readily understood in psychodynamic terms as having their source in a sudden incursion of psychical energy, which floods and overstimulates the mental apparatus and cathects itself on the visionary thought-process. In this way, we may speculate that the entire experience is charged with libidinal affect, a condition that could explain both Ginsberg's massively inflated self-image and the immediately compelling, almost overwhelming force of the idea-complex.[13]

It is not surprising, then, that the mystical subject should presume to have visionary powers and feel himself/herself to be in the presence of Truth. In the experiences reported by Ginsberg and Teasdale we can identify the production of an imaginary self, one that is gratifyingly centered in relation to the cosmos— whence Ginsberg's "this was the moment I was born for," and Teasdale's confident assumption of "theophanic consciousness" in a world he sees as graced by "His mediated presence."

We may conclude, then, that spiritual experience is one thing, the truth claims made on its behalf quite another; in particular the claim that such experience amounts to a visionary moment, that it communicates transcendent or redemptive knowledge or confers omniscience or is enabled by some occult faculty such as insight. To be sure, many visionary moments (autobiographical or literary) are not as fully crystallized or presumptuous of cosmic awareness as those reported by Teasdale and Ginsberg. However, even where the moment only takes the tenuous form of an intimation or fragment, it is, typically, an intimation or fragment of "higher" knowledge; for, whatever the degree of its narrative elaboration, the visionary moment is generally oriented toward the transcendent and the redemptive.

All this is to say that it is a category-mistake to think of a "real-life visionary moment" as a type of spiritual experience; rather, it is a way of understanding one. If the moment is visionary, it is so only after the fact and in particular, by force of ideological and narrative construction. After all, while one can actually experience awe, wonder, or some other spiritual state, one cannot actually experience transcendent knowledge or the omniscient viewpoint; one can only claim to. The alternative is to believe that an individual, even Allen Ginsberg, can step beyond the historically available configurations of knowledge and thus attain a cosmic knowledge of existence or of one's place in the Creation. Put another way, to believe in the possibility of authentic visionary moments is to believe, contrary to the conventionalist terms of postmodern epistemology, that there is a presocial order of knowledge, which has always existed in some dimensionless realm. And it is to believe that the subject can acquire this knowledge by virtue of some occult mode of cognition, a channel of understanding—"insight" or "intuition"—that has instantaneous and direct access to the Truth.

Thus, while literary visionary moments are generally offered to the reader as real occurrences (unless the author is mocking the convention, in which case we are to understand that the "visionary" character is deluded), "real-life visionary moments" appear, in postmodern terms, as narrative and ideological elaborations of a subjective experience. And, ironically, while Conrad and other authors may in part justify their literary use of visionary moments by appealing to our belief in the real-life visionary moment, we may well speculate that it is our belief in the real-life moment that is largely derived from the widespread practice of using visionary moments in fiction. For, as I shall argue later, we must reckon with the possibility that literature itself supplies the forms that enable us to encode certain subjective experiences as visionary.[14]

The Visionary Moment as a Literary Convention

Visionary moments are represented in fiction as if they could have an extratextual basis, as if we should believe in the real-life possibility of a privileged order of knowledge ("insight," "intuition," "illumination"). Yet these representations are premised on assumptions about the nature of truth, cognition, and the subject that appear highly questionable in the light of postmodern theory. An initial postmodern response must be an insistence on the modality of the visionary moment as first and foremost a literary convention.

If we think of the visionary moment as a convention that readers have naturalized as common sense, one means of reaffirming its conventionality is to highlight how literary representations of the visionary moment change in response to the emergence of new literary norms. For example, in two major currents of American fiction in the post-1945 era, broadly speaking, we can identify a break with high-modernist norms: notably, in the renewed mimetic impulse of the "late" realists (e.g., Carver, Bellow, and Updike) and in the radically self-reflexive, anti-totalizing strategies of the postmodernists (e.g. Pynchon, Abish, and Barthelme). Here we shall see how, in the light of Carver's late realism and Pynchon's postmodernism, the high-modernist representation of the visionary moment no longer appears natural.

The visionary moment is the showpiece of the literary aesthetics of anglophone high modernism. Joyce, Woolf, Faulkner, and others crafted a prose whose emotional and lyric intensity was commensurate with the impact of visionary experience on their characters. In contrast, visionary moments in American fiction of the post-1945 period tend to be formulated in a prose almost devoid of affect. Consider the difference between a visionary moment authored by Virginia Woolf in *Mrs Dalloway* (1925) and one by Raymond Carver in "Cathedral" (1983). The mystical cast of Woolf's language frames Clarissa Dalloway's intuition of her (repressed) lesbian identity as an encounter with an elusive spiritual truth: a fleeting intimation of the healing, transfigurative power of some ultimate ("farthest verge") Self:

> [S]he did undoubtedly then feel what men felt. Only for a moment; but it was enough. It was a sudden revelation, a tinge like a blush which one tried to check and then, as it spread, one yielded to its expansion, and rushed to the farthest verge and there quivered and felt the world come closer, swollen with some astonishing significance, some pressure of rapture, which split its thin skin and gushed and poured with an extraordinary alleviation over the cracks and sores. Then, for that moment, she had seen an illumination; a match burning in a crocus; an inner meaning almost expressed. (36)

In Carver's story, the narrator—a self-confessed atheist (372)—has failed to describe a cathedral to his blind houseguest, Robert, though he mentions that men built cathedrals to be "close to God" (372). Robert suggests they draw a cathedral together. He instructs the narrator to close his eyes and, with his hand resting on the narrator's drawing hand, silently communicates the *meaning* of a cathedral, bringing his host close to God. The narrator declares, "It was like nothing in my life up to now" (374) and the story ends with these lines:

> "Well?" [Robert] said. "Are you looking?"
> My eyes were still closed. I was in my house. I knew that. But I didn't feel like I was inside anything.

"It's really something," I said. (375)

" 'It's really something' "—no wonder they call Carver a "minimalist."[15]

The drama of Woolf's visionary moment (and, indeed, the moments of other high modernists [cf. Joyce, *Portrait* 211; Faulkner *Sound* 81–82]) derives partly from its narrative viewpoint—that is, the impression of experiential immediacy as conveyed by the use of interior monologue—and partly from its Symbolist use of rhythm and richly resonant (e.g., sexually charged) language. By comparison, the language of Carver's visionary moment does not register the momentousness of the experience described. Where Woolf suggests the texture of the experience itself, Carver conveys only the notion of such an experience (an approach all the more evident in that he depends on two clichés of mystical writing for this purpose: the blindness/insight motif and the de-differentiation of inside/outside to suggest transcendence). And, following Carver, much the same could be said of the representation of visionary moments by the other post-1945 authors discussed in this study, including Don DeLillo, Saul Bellow, Flannery O'Connor, and Alice Walker. Their moments are rendered in largely denotative terms, with a minimal use of literary artifice.

One factor behind this attenuated representation of visionary moments is the recoil of many postwar writers from what (in a rather one-sided reading) they perceive as high modernism's near solipsistic inwardness and excessive mediation of literary technique: tendencies seen as erecting a barrier between the writer and the world. Hence, if I may generalize still further, the (re-) emergence of a major current of fiction that strives for a less private, more objectively focused viewpoint. Thus, in contradistinction to the Symbolist character of much high-modernist prose (the predilection for allusive and "evocative" writing), the writers I discuss (excepting Kerouac) have purposefully adopted a nonimpressionistic language. Carver has stated: "I'm drawn to traditional (some would call it old-fashioned) methods of storytelling: . . . I believe in the efficacy of the concrete word, be it noun or verb, as opposed to the abstract or arbitrary or slippery word." He maintains: "For the details to be concrete and convey meaning, the language must be accurate and precisely given. The words may be so precise they may even sound flat, but they can still carry . . ." (qtd. in Lehman 50). Similarly, DeLillo has spoken of his search for a prose of "sun-cut precision," a prose defined by its "clarity and accuracy" ("Outsider" 60). In short, to write under the sway of such criteria is to eschew the kind of allusive, mystically resonant language that animates the high-modernist visionary moment.

The post-1945 type of visionary moment must also be seen as emerging from a historical conjuncture in which the artist's sense of cultural placement is different from that of his or her high-modernist predecessor. The conditions for this change may be hastily summarized. The massive and successful expansion of central government power, necessary for mobilizing an entire nation and its resources for war, paved the way for the hypertrophied bureaucracy of the postwar period. This is the period of the "administered society," of (following Marcuse and Lefebvre) the technical-bureaucratic organization of production and consumption, which leads to the perception of society as a highly regulated "system." This is, moreover, a paranoid type of perception, qualitatively different from the modernists' sense of the oppressive rule and ambience of bourgeois values. It is a perception which, as Tony Tanner has persuasively argued, vitally informs the North American fiction of the postwar era. Tanner's reading is guided by the premise of "the American writer's dread of all conditioning forces to the point of paranoia" (16). Put in slightly different terms, the post-1945 writer is haunted by a profound sense of acculturation: the sense that if almost all social practices, including artistic production, are culturally conditioned or institutionalized, then that "semi-autonomous" space, which the modernists could still assume for their art, has been significantly eroded. Under these circumstances, the writer is less likely to assume the confident posture of one speaking from the guaranteed vantage point of a transcendent poetic consciousness; less likely to think of art as a suprasocial activity. Rather, he or she adopts the "worldly" voice of one on the same plane as the reader. Thus, on the one hand, postwar writers follow the high modernists in assigning a crucial place to the transcendent "moment, in which things come together" (Woolf, *Mrs Dalloway* 168). On the other hand, the tempered language in which such moments are recounted may be read as symptomatic of the writer's feeling that he or she is speaking from an unprivileged, culturally grounded position.

The survival of the visionary moment as a literary practice, its persistence even in the postmodern period, prompts the question: What are the immediately practical advantages of adopting this convention? First, the visionary moment can serve as a *structural device,* that is, a way of organizing a narrative around an incisively defined endpoint. Such a climax can conclusively resolve the complications of the preceding action and supply the narrative with a dramatically decisive destination. Many of O'Connor's stories offer an exemplary instance of this device. Second, the visionary moment can serve as an *antiproairetic device.* By this I mean that the moment often substitutes for action, for a narrative plotted around events. In this respect, the use of visionary moments, from around 1890 onward, reflects that tendency in stories and novels, and in particular high-modernist fiction, to achieve the effect of a lyric poem. Thus, Robert Langbaum has remarked on the "lyrical structure" and "lyrical stasis" of the "epiphanic poem or story," in which very little happens; which is "devoted to intensifying an object into radiance rather than to telling a story with a beginning, a middle, and an end." He concludes that "the modern short story is plotless and apparently pointless in order that it may be epiphanic" (42–43). Third, the visionary moment can serve as a *narrational device,* that is, a way of accelerating or facilitating the story of a character's development. Psychological change is generally a slow, protracted, and uneven process, and if represented as such in fiction would result in cumbersome, unshapely narratives. The visionary moment is one solution to this problem; the process of change is compressed into precisely a moment, hence it invariably occurs "suddenly." Moreover, the suddenness of the change has the effect of dramatizing the character's break with a routine or restricted mindset. Fourth, the visionary moment can serve as an *aesthetic device;* that is, it offers creative latitude in recounting the cognitive processes of a transfigured consciousness; it offers opportunities for releasing language from semantic or syntactic norms. Recall, for instance, Kerouac's "innumerable lotus-lands falling open in the magic mothswarm of heaven." The Beats and high modernists have eminently exploited the aesthetic potential of the visionary moment (while late realists, like Carver and Bellow, have not). Finally, the visionary moment can serve as a *rhetorical device* for forcefully promoting a code of ethics or system of ideas alternative to those that prevail. Thanks to this device, authors need not sermonize or propagandize on behalf of their beliefs. Rather, through the swift, economical gesture of the visionary moment—coming as it often does at the climax of the narrative—an author can all the more effectively dramatize the redemptive or admonitory value of his or her philosophy.

It seems evident, then, that as a convention, the visionary moment finds a measure of legitimacy simply on the grounds of its usefulness, not to say indispensability, as a multipurpose literary device. And it is precisely fiction's dependence on literary devices that is exposed and questioned by the self-reflexiveness that characterizes postmodernist fiction. No longer is the author seen either as the high-modernists' godlike artificer or as the naturalists' documenting observer. Rather, he or she is seen as a crafty manipulator of techniques, a legerdemainist who, far from reflecting reality, conjures up reality-effects. By parodying or flagrantly subverting the processes of narrating, plotting, troping, naming, and *enlightenment,* postmodern self-reflexive writers, like John Barth, Grace Paley, Thomas Pynchon, and Kurt Vonnegut, draw attention to fiction as a *set of conventions* and thereby undermine its pretensions to mimesis (specifically, the pretensions of those writing in the naturalist or classical realist traditions). This, then, is a tendency in relation to which the visionary moment is susceptible to exposure as essentially a literary convention—contrary to its implicit claim to represent a credible, real-life experience.

Thomas Pynchon's *The Crying of Lot 49* (1966) is a postmodern self-reflexive text that may be read as a parody of the practice of organizing narratives around visionary moments: it ironically exposes the visionary moment as a literary convention. Oedipa Maas, the novel's protagonist, is continually tantalized by "some promise of hierophany" (31), by the sense that "a revelation . . . trembled just past the threshold of her understanding . . . [as if she were] at the centre of an odd, religious instant" (24). Throughout the story, she encounters signs that seem to promise revelation but, perversely, the more she probes their significance, the more their possible meanings multiply. Pynchon has contrived a situation that thwarts the possibility of a final illumination. His plotting reverses the conventional narrative process, in which the clues to a mystery are pursued until the climactic moment of its resolution. And, of course, the reader is also teased as Pynchon mocks our expectation of a revelation that will close the narrative. Like Oedipa, we are "waiting, as if to be illuminated" (152).

Edward Mendelson has discussed how *Lot 49* exploits the metaphor of Pentecost. He reminds us that Pentecost was the day when the Apostles became "filled with the Holy Spirit and began to speak in other tongues" (Acts 2:4), and that "Pentecost" derives from the Greek for "fiftieth." Accordingly, of the novel's closing scene, he observes, "The crying—the auctioneer's calling—of the forty-ninth lot is the moment *before* a Pentecostal revelation, the end of the period in which the miracle is in a state of potential, not yet manifest" (207–208, emphasis added). The novel ends just as that final cry that may prove all-enlightening— "the direct, epileptic Word, the cry that might abolish the night" (*Lot 49* 118)—is about to be uttered. But, within the terms of the novel's postmodern epistemology, the cry *cannot* be uttered because an all-enlightening "Word" is judged to be inconceivable.[16]

To sum up, at the self-reflexive level, *Lot 49* may be read as an extended parody of how we see reality through perspectives inherited from fiction: Oedipa's quest is largely directed by her literary sense of plot, metaphor, and final en-lightenment.

2

Validations of the Visionary Moment

Further to its interest in the conditions of knowledge production, postmodern critique explores the processes by which a discourse acquires validation as "knowledge"; the processes by which it becomes naturalized or legitimized as "science" or "common sense." Foucault's "genealogical" research into the power apparatuses behind the accreditation of knowledge as "scientific" or Barthes's investigation of how realism rests not on reality but on the institutionalization of culturally specific writing and reading practices (e.g., the mastery of literary "codes" as discussed in *S/Z*) are exemplary instances of this mode of inquiry. And if we take this approach we can ask: What cultural forces have served to underwrite or create the intellectual conditions for the acceptance of the visionary moment as a credible mode of cognition? The question is worth pursuing given the persistence of the visionary moment as a convention in post-1945 American fiction, a persistence all the more remarkable in an artistic and philosophical climate of demystification, where irony, parody, skepticism, and deconstruction have become the norm. At issue here is the legitimacy of the essentially mystical belief in a metaphysical medium of "higher" knowledge such as "insight," "intuition," or "the Heart." Although the sources of such a belief are numerous and moreover change over time, there are three that deserve particular attention for their part in contributing to the legitimacy of the visionary moment: (a) the prestige of the conversion narrative within the Western tradition of religious writing; (b) the Romantic exploration and promotion of a nonrational cognitive faculty; (c) the ideology of bourgeois individualism that encourages the view of salvation as a personal, *private* matter. For if the visionary moment survives and flourishes as a literary convention, it is not just because it serves as a useful narrative device; we must reckon with the force of ideological motivation and the cumulative history of religious, literary, and philosophical discourses that have served to institutionalize the moment as the expression of a valid form of knowledge, and to manufacture the terms in which it is understood.

Puritan and Romantic Paradigms

If we limit attention to the validating process of visionary moments in anglophone literature, we might begin by noting the authority of the Bible as a critical part of that process. To be sure, the books of the Old Testament are remarkable for their graphically detailed accounts of revelatory dreams and apocalyptic visions, as in Daniel 7 and 8 or Ezekiel 1. But, strictly speaking, this mode of visionary experience does not meet our criteria for defining the literary visionary moment. First, Old Testament illumination is an oculocentric matter of visions appearing before the eye or in dreams. Second, these visions are not momentary; whole chapters are required to recount their sequence of images. Rather, the Christian phenomenon of the conversion experience should be seen as the antecedent of the literary visionary moment.[1] In particular, recall the New Testament account of Paul's sudden conversion on the road to Damascus. In that famous episode, recounted in Acts (22:6–11), a distinctly Old Testament–style visual element persists in the form of the blinding light from heaven, yet, as Paul remarks, "Those who were with me saw the light but did not hear the voice of the one who was speaking to me" (22:9). Those words reframe the experience as a largely "interior" or private event, in which respect the episode prefigures that later trend toward the subjectivization of religious experience. Indeed, when we turn to what is probably the best-known conversion narrative in English literature, John Bunyan's *Grace Abounding to the Chief of Sinners* (1666), we cannot but be struck by the near absence of reference to the author's external circumstances: the drama is played out almost exclusively on the interior stage of the soul.

Grace Abounding chronicles the spiritual travails of its author, who continually alternates between the transports of conversion and the despair of "backsliding," as Satan strives to win back a former sinner. For example, while

> in the midst of a game of cat, . . . a voice did suddenly dart from heaven into my soul, which said, "Wilt thou leave thy sins and go to heaven, or have thy sins and go to hell?" At this I was put to an exceeding maze; . . . I looked up to heaven, and was as if I had, with the eyes of my understanding, seen the Lord Jesus looking down upon me, as being very hotly displeased with me. . . .
>
> . . . [And] suddenly this conclusion was fastened on my spirit . . . that I had been a great and grievous sinner, and that it was now too late for me to look after heaven; . . . [A]nd fearing lest it should be so, I felt my heart sink in despair. (Sections 22–23)

Here we find the defining features of the visionary moment as that which occurs "suddenly" and unbidden, and which is transient and yet has the power to profoundly unsettle or transfigure the visionary subject. But, above all, the feature of Bunyan's narrative that deserves attention is the pronounced "interiority" of its focus. The external world is occluded insofar as the vision bypasses the senses, namely that of hearing ("a voice did suddenly dart from heaven into my soul") and of sight ("and was as if I had, *with the eyes of my understanding*, seen the Lord Jesus").[2] Indeed, the terms in which Bunyan recounts his moment clearly reflect the Puritan tendency to subjectivize religious experience. Harry Levin, commenting on this very phenomenon, put the matter succinctly: "Revelation was no longer based upon dogma, but upon the mystical intuition or the poetic insight that could scrutinize the welter of appearances and discern the presence of hidden realities" (*The Power of Blackness,* 1958, qtd. in Reising 63).

Levin's observation might well have been supported with lines penned by the devotional poet and contemporary of Bunyan, Henry Vaughan, for whom, "Wise Nicodemus saw such light / As made him know his God by night" ("The Night" 1.5–6). For Vaughan's work, with its pervasive theme of religious conversion (precipitated by the poet's own conversion experience around 1648), is an exemplary instance of that Puritanic appeal to the authority of inner experience.[3] W. R. Johnson has discussed how in *Silex Scintillans* (1650; 1655), Vaughan broke with the public posture of the traditional lyric's "I-You" mode of address; the poet's rhetoric is marked by the absence of the standard "pronominal, *social* form" (Johnson qtd. in Halley 59). Instead, the poet, in his solitary contemplation, produces a "meditative" lyric, where piety is found in the "soul's calm retreat" ("The Night" 1.27).

The type of visionary experience that Bunyan and Vaughan describe with such intensive focus on their private, mental states ("private ejaculations" is the subtitle of *Silex Scintillans*), reflects that enhancement of individualism which, following Max Weber, has often been seen as a defining feature of Protestant culture. (It is, in part, a matter of Protestantism's "direct appeal to the heart of the individual believer as against traditional ceremonial processions and the miracle of the mass" [C.Hill 486].) The Protestant examination of conscience tended to promote a measure of self-consciousness, and the Puritans reinforced this tendency by affirming that no outward signs can ultimately prove the certainty of (inward) grace. In short, these were trends that pointed to the beginnings of an ideology of individualism, an ideology that, as we shall see, must surely be counted as a key condition of possibility of the visionary moment.

It is instructive to consider Cardinal Newman's words on the Protestant model of conversion insofar as they work to denaturalize the experience. Newman was at pains to distinguish his Augustinian Catholic mode of spiritual autobiography from the English Protestant mode. Writing as one "with [whose] *Apologia* the autobiography [became] self-conscious as a genre" (Peterson 312), he identified accounts of the conversion process in Protestant autobiography conspicuously in the terms of a narrative convention: "conviction of sin, terror, despair, news of the free and full salvation, apprehension of Christ, sense of pardon, assurance of salvation, joy and peace, and so on to final perseverance" (qtd. in Peterson 301). This scornfully schematic account has the calculated tone of one describing the format of a predictable plot line—the target being those spiritual autobiographies which, two centuries later, still respected *Grace Abounding* as the genre's paradigmatic form.

Romantic literature marks another significant stage in the evolution of representations of visionary experience. A Romantic epistemology, in large part founded on a conception of the imagination as a cognitive faculty (the "prime agent of all human perception," wrote Coleridge [*Biographia* 167]), supplied the basis for what were to become commonsense notions about the nature of visionary experience. This "faculty," to restate a familiar view, was defined in polar opposition to that of Reason.[4] Reason was precisely that which alienates us from Imagination: "Entering into the Reasoning Power, forsaking Imagination" (Blake, *Jerusalem* 74.7. See also 74.10–13). Enlightenment rationalism, which for William Blake meant the "Rational Power [of] . . . Bacon & Newton & Locke" (54.16–17), found endorsement to the extent that it coincided with the interests of a burgeoning and aggressive bourgeois class; for, insofar as its logical and empirical procedures undermined the claims to legitimacy of church, monarchy, and tradition, rationalism opposed precisely those institutional restraints on the expansion of industrial capital. (Blake explicitly links his trinity of rationalists to the progress of the Industrial Revolution [15.11–20].) And it was under the prestige and authority of rationalism, with "Abstract Philosophy warring in enmity against Imagination," that "Albion fled from the Divine Vision" (5.58, 57.12). In Blake's mythopoeia, Imagination is the conduit for perception of the Divine; indeed, Imagination *is* "The Divine Vision" and, hence, it is elevated above Reason as the sole organ of Truth.

Like Blake, Wordsworth exalted the Imagination as a cognitive faculty, superior by virtue of its visionary power to Reason. In book 12 of *The Prelude*, "Imagination and Taste, How Impaired and Restored," he observes that the "virtues" of the "natural graciousness of mind . . . could not stand / The open eye of Reason" (50, 66–67). That Reason should be figured in terms of an "open eye" suggests both the empiricist orientation of the dominant philosophy (the "new idolatry" [77]) and its repressive monitoring of other modes of cognition. Moreover, Wordsworth voices regrets about an earlier phase of his life that was marked by the tyranny of the visual over the visionary (i.e., "inner faculties"):

> When the bodily eye, in every stage of life
> The most despotic of our senses, gained
> Such strength in *me* as often held my mind
> In absolute dominion. . . .
> Still craving . . .
> wider empire for the sight,
> Proud of her own endowments, and rejoiced
> To lay the inner faculties to sleep. (12.128–31, 144–47)

It is this antipathy to what we might call oculocentrism that impels Wordsworth to extol the "inward eye" (149), to exalt insight as a mode of seeing superior to the inspecting eye of the empiricist. Indeed, insight *is* the defining virtue of the Imagination: "Imagination, which, in truth / Is but another name for absolute power / And clearest insight" (14.189–91). And,

Imagination— . . .
. . I now can say—
'I recognise thy glory:' in such strength
Of usurpation, when the light of sense
Goes out, but with a flash that has revealed
The invisible world, doth greatness make abode. (6.592, 598–601)

By the terms in which he privileged Imagination as the medium of truth, Wordsworth significantly helped to establish the criteria for the modern (and modernist) visionary moment. First, the way to truth is via a subjective process (the insight or intuitive perception of the Imagination). Second, this is necessarily a nonrational process insofar as it bypasses inductive or deductive procedures. A third criterion is precisely the momentariness of the vision, whence the "flash that has revealed / The invisible world," and "objects recognised / In flashes, and with glory not their own" (5.604–605). Indeed, Wordsworth invites us to read *The Prelude* as an autobiographical record of his illuminating "flashes," an ensemble of insightful visionary moments such as those experienced at the Simplon Pass (6.621–40) or during the ascent of Mount Snowdon (14.28–62), but most of all, during those "spots of time" when an "ordinary sight" suddenly radiates significance, like the "visionary dreariness" of a girl, with a pitcher on her head, walking on a windswept moor or a landscape with just a lone sheep and a blasted tree (12.208–335).

It is in Wordsworth, as many commentators have observed (e.g., Langbaum 33–57; Nichols, *Poetics* 35–69; Beja 32–35), that we find the origins of the literary epiphany. And without going so far as to trace the post-Romantic evolution of the visionary moment in literature, at least we can note that succeeding generations of anglophone writers—say, Hopkins, Tennyson, and Browning among the Victorians; Joyce, Woolf, and Faulkner among the high modernists— reinforced, each with his or her own modifications, those essential features of the visionary moment that crystallized in Wordsworth's work. Joyce, to restate only the most familiar case, explained his literary epiphany as "a sudden spiritual manifestation," which, moreover, is "the most delicate and evanescent of moments," and which is activated by insignificant, commonplace experiences (*Stephen Hero* 211)—all recognizable properties of Wordsworth's visionary moments. Joyce's celebrated examples of epiphany, in *Dubliners* and *A Portrait,* reinvigorated and further promoted the practice of plotting narratives around visionary moments, while an influential apparatus of Joyce scholarship has largely developed the terms in which post-Romantic literary visionary experience has come to be understood.

We can say, then, that literature itself, perhaps more than any other institution, has played a crucial role in legitimizing the visionary moment as a valid medium of knowledge. And contrary to those who would claim to have experienced visionary moments outside of literature, we may assume that literature has

been preeminent among textual mediations in supplying the forms and conceptual frames necessary to identify and construct such experience as, precisely,
visionary. To state the matter this way is to follow in the tracks of Bakhtin for
whom, "the genres of literature enrich our inner speech with new devices for the
conceptualiztion of reality" (134).

The convention of the visionary moment also finds a measure of legitimation in its capacity as an ideological construct. The terms in which visionary
moments are typically represented in fiction can be understood as reinforcing the
doxa that accommodate subjects to the needs of a class-based social system and
that blind them to a politically relevant understanding of that system. For example, we find that the redemption implicit in the visionary moments of *Seize the
Day* and "A Good Man Is Hard to Find" is represented only at the level of the
individual; it is an "interior," exclusively private affair, lacking any material,
institutional basis. A radical transformation of the external, social order is not
recognized as a precondition for individual salvation. And this focus on salvation
at the individual level may be understood as a type of false solution that follows
from a historical conjuncture where the balance of forces is weighted against
collectivist or class action. Furthermore, several characteristics of literary rendi-
tions of visionary moments, namely, their suddenness, momentariness, and pre-
cariousness, are themselves symptomatic of the doubt that such experiences could
actually be secured at this time in history; social evolution has not reached the
stage where the transfiguration of consciousness can be a guaranteed fact of life.
Nevertheless, the visionary moment is offered or received as a reassuring sign that
the subject as individual can surpass his or her limiting circumstances; the
restrictions—economic, political, cultural—that impede the subject's spiritual or
moral awakening can be transcended.

The appeal to the authority of inner experience, itself a feature of the literary
ethos of Puritan England, became still more pronounced among the Romantics
and their modernist successors. It is a commonplace that the Romantic and
modernist cultivation of private vision expresses alienation from the social reality
of capitalist modernization. But for a firmer grasp of the relation between capitalism and the individualist ideology on which the visionary moment is typically
premised, it is instructive to focus on the growth of that order of experience we call
"personal life." For at issue here is the need to trace the disposition of social forces
that have prompted the visionary moment's theme of *individualized* redemption
in a post-Puritan, secular age.

Industrial capitalism created a social basis for individualism within the
proletarian family. As Eli Zaretsky argues, "The family became the major sphere of
society in which the individual could be foremost—it was the only space that
proletarians 'owned.' Within it, a new sphere of social activity began to take shape:
personal life" (*Capitalism* 61). As a refuge from the alienating conditions of labor
(the social world of commodity production), the private sphere of the family is
where the "personal life" of meaning and purpose tends to be pursued. After all,

given capitalism's tendency to devalue, de-skill, and routinize labor, given the impersonal character of an increasingly "rationalized" labor process, the essentially social activity of work has been robbed of meaning (cf. Braverman 1974). Under these circumstances, privacy, rather than community, becomes the sphere of self-definition. And here it is appropriate to invoke Lukács' seminal concept of reification. In his analysis of the links between the increasing specialization of skills and the collective worldview, Lukács observed: "the [capitalist] division of labor disrupts every organically unified process of work and life and breaks it down into its components" (*History* 103). This condition of reification results, among other things, in "the destruction of every image of the whole" (103). It encourages a perception of people and everyday productive activities as discrete entities with no intrinsic connection—a perception that reinforces the tendency to seek meaning within the "personal" domain of existence.

Mass consumption, to say nothing of post-Fordist strategies of market-niching, has further promoted the cultivation of personal experience and increased the opportunities for highly individualized development. Among the more obvious reasons for this are that commodities are generally marketed in the name of personal satisfaction or fulfilment, and that most consumption takes place within the private enclosure of the home.

To draw attention to the individualistic implications of production and consumption under capitalism is not to lose sight of those contradictions (e.g., labor-management conflict, environmental degradation) that can generate collective thought and action. Nevertheless, the phenomenal enlargement of "personal life" is a defining feature of capitalism that cannot fail to have an impact on the literary imagination, and this seems especially evident in the visionary moment's theme of personal salvation.

Today, any argument for the *possibility* of visionary moments must reckon with the implications of the sociological model of the "Culture of the Simulacrum." According to this (somewhat hyperbolic) model, the defining feature of our postmodern culture is the prodigious expansion of the mass media to the point where signs have displaced their referents, where images of the Real have usurped the authority of the Real, hence subjectivity (so it is said) is but constituted by simulacra (Baudrillard *Simulations*). Accordingly, it would seem that under these "hyperreal" conditions, the visionary moment, far from revealing some supernal truth, could only reproduce the packaged messages of the mass media. Yet it also needs to be said that the persistence of the visionary moment as a convention in American fiction of the postmodern period (as, for example, in the work of DeLillo), may be explained as an indirect or unconscious critique of the degradation of public debate and information under late capitalism. That is to say, in response to the colonization of the public sphere by factoids, sound bites, talk-show prattle, propaganda, PR and marketing "hype," visionary experience is reinvested with the aura and authority of unmediated and unmanipulated truth. And, it should be added that, for those writing within a discursive field that is distinguished by its skepticism, irony, secularism, and pragmatism, the visionary moment—as a fleeting, precarious phenomenon—is the most credible form that visionary experience can take.

Philosophical Validations

Ashton Nichols explains that "the term 'epiphany' derives from the Greek *phainein* 'to show'. . . . The Greek forms *epiphainein* and *epiphaneia* mean respectively 'to manifest' and . . . 'manifestation.'" He adds that "Greek literature and religion commonly recorded appearances of gods and goddesses, which were described as 'epiphanies'" (*Poetics* 5–6). For "epiphany" carries the implication that whatever manifests itself is not readily or usually evident to the senses; originally, the term signified the unveiling of the supernatural in the realm of the natural. Accordingly, to take this point a step further, I would suggest that the concept of epiphany implies an aletheic model of truth, that is to say, truth as a process of disclosure. In his inquiry into the etymology of *alétheia* (the Greek for truth), Heidegger had emphasized the alpha-privative: a-letheia. In this way, he reminded us that the word embodies the original (pre-Platonic) experience of truth as "unconcealment" or "disclosure," rather than a conception of truth as correct judgment or correspondence between a proposition and its referent. And here it is worth briefly pursuing Heidegger's line of reasoning because it leads him to a notion of epiphany, to a conception of truth as a sudden inward unveiling. Moreover, if we were to seek a philosophical foundation for the literary epiphany, Heidegger's writing would seem on the face of it to be the first place to look.

Heidegger maintained that a precondition of any truth based on judgment or correspondence (*homoiosis*) is a *prior disclosure* of the very referent of judgment/correspondence (see e.g., Hatab; Visker). However, he insisted that this truth is not a matter of a transcendent subject apprehending an objective entity (an erroneous assumption that, says Heidegger, has marred the Western metaphysical tradition from Plato to Husserl and beyond). Rather, this argument rests on the hermeneutic idea of "pre-understanding": insofar as human existence is radically grounded ("bound-up") in a practical orientation to the material world, we already (or structurally) exist in a primordial relation to things by which they present themselves to us as "ready-to-hand" or encounterable. It is by virtue of this human mode of Being-in-the-world, which Heidegger calls *Dasein*, that the self-disclosure or "presencing" of objects is enabled. In short, to know an object in propositional terms is to presuppose a space ("clearing") of encounterability, where objects are always-already available to *Dasein*. And it is instructive to note Heidegger's lexicon of epiphanic terms for this condition of pre-understanding: "the lightning-flash of the truth of Being"; "the sudden flash of the truth of Being"; "insight"; "in-flashing" (*The Question* 45–47).

Consider the following passage from *Being and Time*, which illustrates Heidegger's idea of epiphanic pre-understanding:

[W]hen something ready-to-hand is found missing, though its everyday presence has been so obvious that we have never taken any notice of it, this makes a *break* in those referential contexts which circumspection discovers. Our circumspection comes up against emptiness, and now sees for the first time *what* the missing article was ready-to-hand *with,* and *what* it was ready-to-hand *for.* The environment announces itself afresh. What is thus lit up is not itself just one thing ready-to-hand among others . . . it is in the 'there' before anyone has observed or ascertained it. It is itself inaccessible to circumspection, so far as circumspection is always directed towards entities; but in each case it has already been disclosed for circumspection. (105)

However, the pre-understanding implicit here—"it is in the 'there' before anyone has observed or ascertained it"—is, from the postmodern standpoint, highly questionable. We are asked to believe in the precultural cognition (that moment of "lighting up") of some self-revealing "ready-to-hand" entity, when postmodernism enjoins us to keep in mind that we live in an always-already interpreted world: as Foucault puts it, "There is never an *interpretandum* which is not already an *interpretans*" (qtd. in MacCabe 10); any object, natural or manufactured, cannot but be culturally (e.g., ideologically or economically) coded. The notion that reality discloses or epiphanises itself in the medium of primordial Being is, within the conventionalist epistemology of postmodern thinking, simply untenable.

Beja and Nichols have also explored philosophical foundations of the literary epiphany. Beja singles out Henri Bergson for his "great influence" in "providing for the moment of illumination [a] new base to replace older, theological ones" (54). He notes Bergson's antirationalist concepts of "duration," understood as the inner experience of time that enables us to perceive the dynamic flux of reality, and "intuition," understood as the preanalytical, "intellectual sympathy" by which we achieve "absolute knowledge" of a thing (qtd. in Beja 55). (Indeed, a principal thesis of Bergson's metaphysics is that to think intuitively is to think in duration.) Alternatively, Nichols argues that the "radical empiricism" of Locke and Hume "became the prototype" for Wordsworth's model of the epiphanic subject. Locke had characterized mental life as "a train of ideas which constantly succeed one another" (Locke 144) and from this succession of discrete ideas we derive our sense of time (145). And this argument led to Hume's view of time as an imperceptible succession of "still" moments; "each moment, as it succeeds another, [is] perfectly single and indivisible" (qtd. in Nichols, *Poetics* 22). Hence, Nichols proposes, "This increased emphasis on experience as a series of independent moments is one of the root intuitions behind the new literary epiphany" (23).

To be sure, these accounts of the philosophical sources of epiphany are illuminating but, by the standards of postmodern theory, it is not enough to identify the philosophical "influence" or "prototype" behind the epiphany. We need to go a step further and examine the epistemological field in which the discourse of epiphany becomes possible. And for this purpose we should start by identifying a major rupture in the configuration of knowledge, which marks the transition to modernity in the late sixteenth and early seventeenth centuries. In this period, the perceived disjunctures between the world as represented in ecclesiastical and Latin texts and the world as experienced undermines the authority (the formerly inviolable *auctoritas*) of the book. As Hassan Melehy puts it:

> The world of books and the institution that has the charge of maintaining the closure of this world come under serious questioning: the written sign whose authority is presented as unquestionable shows itself to be flawed; written signs are no longer reliable, and a new ground for the foundation of knowledge must be found. And it is in this modern world that the space for the institution of the modern subject is cleared. (15)

In this modern world the individual subject becomes the new ground for the foundation of knowledge. This condition is best exemplified by Descartes' idea of the *cogito,* the insular personal consciousness that is understood to be the true locus of knowledge. No longer is knowledge located in the public domain of the *auctoritates,* but in the private domain of the *cogito.* Now, "the most certain routes to knowledge" are internalized in the "two methods" of "intuition" and "deduction" (Descartes 4). Intuition provides "the conception which an unclouded and attentive mind gives us so readily and distinctly that we are wholly freed from doubt about that which we understand." (4)

The foregoing points are raised not to suggest the influence of Descartes but rather to point to the epistemological break that enabled the conception of the "intuitive" epiphanic subject. Thus, about fifty years after Descartes had formulated his notion of intuition, it was possible even for the arch-empiricist Locke to write: "It is on . . . intuition that depends all the certainty and evidence of all our knowledge; which certainty everyone finds to be so great that he cannot imagine, and therefore not require, a greater" (326).

The Writer and Reader as Visionary Subjects

Another source of validation for the idea that the literary visionary moment is a credible representation of a real-life experience lies in the Romantic and high-modernist conception of the artist as visionary and genius. That is to say, the convention of the moment and, in particular, its claims to embody a higher order of truth, have credibility to the extent that we accept a model of the artist as someone endowed with special powers of insight. Raymond Williams has traced the evolution of this model and identified a "radical change" in ideas of the artist, of art, and of their relation to society in consequence of the political, social, and economic changes produced by industrialization (*Culture* 49). One such change (to pursue what has become a familiar line of argument) was the displacement of the system of patronage, in the late eighteenth century, by the market, which included the institution of commercial publishing. Art became subjected to the vagaries and impersonal workings of the marketplace; it came to be conceived as a specialized form of production and was reduced to commodity status. And in response to this enveloping market relationship the artist, in the spirit of professional protest, promoted him- or herself as a unique type of person. Hence, Williams observes: "At a time when the artist is being described as just one more producer of a commodity for the market, he is describing himself as a specially endowed person" (53). At this time, the word *art,* which, hitherto, had generally signified skill (from the Latin *ars*), now acquired a more exalted meaning:

> The emphasis on skill, in the word, was gradually replaced by an emphasis on sensibility; and this replacement was supported by the parallel changes in such words as *creative* . . . , *original* . . . , and *genius* (which, because of its root association with the idea of *inspiration,* had changed from 'characteristic disposition' to 'exalted special ability' . . .). (60)

This idealized notion of the artist as autonomous genius, someone to be "distinguished from other men" (Wordsworth 738), is given repeated emphasis in Wordsworth's writing. In *The Prelude,* he defines himself as "a *creative* soul" (12.207, Wordsworth's emphasis). He has "a mind sustained / By recognitions of transcendent power" (14.74–75). He is one of Nature's "higher minds" (14.90). The poet "drink[s] the visionary power" (2.3) and to him/her "the power of truth / Come[s] in revelation" (2.392–93). The poet is someone "possessed of more than usual organic sensibility" (735). And, famously, Wordsworth asks: "What is a Poet? . . . A man, it is true, endowed with more lively sensibility, more enthusiasm and tenderness, who has a greater knowledge of human nature, and a more comprehensive soul, than are supposed to be common among mankind" (737). In the light of these observations, we should think of Wordsworth's "spots of time"— those visionary "moments / [which] are scattered everywhere" (*Prelude* 12.208, 223–24), both in his life and poetry—as a strategic exhibition of the enhanced and "creative sensibility" (2.360) that separates the artist from other people. The "spots of time" serve as the most eloquent testimony to this sensibility: they are the purest and most compressed form of the artist's "visionary power." In short, the visionary moment is one literary practice through which the socially alienated writer may assert or promote him- or herself. But if it is the moment that affirms the artist's (self-proclaimed) difference from others, at the same time it is a measure of the extent to which the public has accepted the idea of the difference—i.e., the artist as "genius" or "creative soul"—and that idea serves to validate the literary practice of the visionary moment. We believe in visionary moments because we believe in the idea of the visionary artist who experiences them.

I have singled out Wordsworth for special attention since he is generally credited with the first (programmatic) use of the literary visionary moment. But the literary moments of subsequent writers have also been justified by appealing to that Romantic notion of the artist as a specially endowed person—the "creative soul." Thus, Joyce's perception of the artist was inextricably bound up with his idea of the artist's visionary ability to epiphanise. Recall these lines: "By an epiphany he meant a sudden spiritual manifestation . . . He believed it was for the man of letters to record these epiphanies with extreme care, seeing that they themselves are the most delicate and evanescent of moments" (*Stephen Hero* 211). And subsequently, in *A Portrait,* we find that the experience of epiphany often induces Stephen Dedalus to assert his identity as an artist. Hence, the wading-girl epiphany invokes his artist's destiny "to recreate life out of life" (166); the birds-in-flight epiphany is read as an "augury" of the impending exile necessary for his development as a writer (218–20); in the epiphany inspired by the sound of his name, his artistic vocation is revealed to him: "He would create proudly out of the freedom and power of his soul, as the great artificer whose name he bore, a living thing, new and soaring and beautiful, impalpable, imperishable" (163–64). Finally, in his semiautobiographical novel, *Of Time and the River,* Thomas Wolfe expounds his ideas on art through his portrait of a young artist, Eugene Gant. Gant traces the source of artistic creativity to "flashes of blind but powerful intuition" and affirms the artist's "intolerable desire to fix eternally in the patterns of an indestructible form a single moment of man's living, a single moment of life's beauty, passion, and unutterable eloquence, that passes, flames and goes" (qtd. in Beja 163).

These examples illustrate how the literary visionary moment finds a measure of validation in the self-serving and popular notion of the artist as one endowed with visionary powers. Yet this Romantic/high-modernist model of the artist has been decisively rejected by postmodern conceptions of the artist and artistic practice. One key function of the self-reflexiveness, which largely defines postmodern fiction, is to draw attention to the literary text as chiefly a set of well-worn and manipulative devices, such as plotting, troping, naming, character stereotyping, recycling myths and fairy tales. These devices are understood to produce effects—suspense effects, excitement effects, meaning effects—whereby the artist comes to be seen not as a visionary or a genius but as an illusionist or wirepuller. Robert Coover's *Pricksongs & Descants,* Thomas Pynchon's *V,* and John Barth's *Lost in the Funhouse* are all exemplary instances of writing that projects this model of the artist. Alternatively, the artist may be seen as a manufacturer of meaning, conspicuously building sense out of lexical units, as in the case of Walter Abish, who writes paragraphs and entire works in which words are ordered strictly by their sequence in the alphabet, and who constructs stories out of individually titled paragraphs or heads each paragraph with a word count (see e.g. *Alphabetical Africa* and *In the Future Perfect*). Postmodern fiction has also reconceptualized the artist as a pasticheur or bricoleur rather than an inspired originator; unconsciously or otherwise, he or she assembles texts from (recycled) fragments of the works of others, as famously highlighted by Kathy Acker in *Blood and Guts in High School.*

In short, the artist is seen as a fabricator, and as a manipulator of narrative ploys and codes. There are no visionary moments—nor can there be—in fiction predicated on such demystified conceptions of the artist; for the postmodern critic, the artist does not communicate Truth but stages truth-effects. Last, there is another current of postmodern art that projects a model of the artist as a saboteur of signification. Here one may cite the guerrilla semiotics of William Burroughs's cut-ups, designed to interject "noise" into the System's communications circuit (see Maltby), or the deconstructive impetus of Sherrie Levine's "rephotographs," which strategically reframe the iconic images of modernism in order to expose their ideological content. In such practices, the artist's primary aim is to subvert signs rather than organize them into a stable pattern of meaning. Such an agenda clearly will not accommodate the literary visionary moment which, like the lyric poem, must be counted among the most intensive ordering of signs; indeed, this minute and meticulous structuring of signs is a precondition for suggesting the preciousness and visionary power of the moment.

The idea that the literary visionary moment has an extratextual reality finds a further degree of validation in the belief that many moments can be vividly experienced in the act of reading them. (At least this reading experience was the goal of Romantic authors and, notably, Hopkins and Conrad.) Thus, Ashton Nichols observes:

> Any reader of a literary epiphany becomes a potential participant in the experience. . . . The claritas/quidditas of the object or image is available to the reader of an epiphanic poem or prose narrative in much the same way as it was to the author. The reader, in effect, is always able to complete the epiphany in his or her own mind. (*Poetics* 12; see also 31)

And Robert Langbaum asserts that "Wordsworth and Coleridge . . . create structures that produce epiphanies in the reader" (40; see also 50). Yet, it must remain open to question whether writers ever succeed in actually inducing epiphanic experiences in their readers; to believe that they do is to assume, in the manner of phenomenological criticism, that language is a perfectly transparent medium in which the reader has direct, unmediated access to the consciousness of the writer and can, therefore, reexperience the latter's states of awareness. Furthermore, to believe that writers can "work" a visionary moment on the page so as to produce one in the reader is to assume a level of control over the reading process that amounts to textual determinism. After all, it is one thing to acknowledge that reading a literary text may produce a profound spiritual experience; it is quite another to believe that (a) the reader's response has been strategically directed by the author so that it occurs at just that point when the visionary moment is encountered on the page and (b) the reader experiences the moment precisely on the author's terms. To believe that the author can reactivate a visionary moment in the mind of the reader is to assume a docile, readily "positionable" reader rather than one who "negotiates" a version of the text that is likely to reflect the perspectives of his or her interpretive conventions and the limits of his or her literary competence. We must also consider the determinations imposed on the sense of the text by the conjuncture of its reception, or the projections and transformations of meaning imposed by the psychodynamics of the reading process (as explored, for example, by Norman Holland through his "transactive" paradigm [see Holland]).

There is another sense in which the notion of an epiphanic reader might be questioned. The visionary moment is premised on a fundamentalist attachment to a linear reading process. Typically, an author plots the occurrence of a visionary moment with the expectation that the reader will pursue a strictly linear course through the text and thus encounter the moment at its strategically designated place (which is often at the climax of the narrative). However, the reader who reads the same narrative in hypertextual form, who "surfs" it via multiple reading paths, will encounter the moment in a semantic field of his or her own choosing; that is to say, a field that may undermine the moment's closural force. (See Landow)

Finally, in "The Secret," a poem published in 1964, Denise Levertov contributes to that decade's somewhat cynical, postmodern emphasis on the limits of art's effectivity. The poem registers the disjuncture between the author's diminished sense of literature's potential and the expectations of a largely pre-postmodern readership. Levertov makes some wry observations about that perennial dream of suddenly discovering "the secret of life" on a page of literature. (She also expresses nostalgia for this outdated ideal of the traditional reader.) Yet, as the poem argues, claims to have found "the secret" are highly suspect, for not only is the secret news to the author, but it cannot be repeated, cannot be recalled, and cannot even be traced back to its textual source. Hence, one is left to conclude that the very undisclosability of the secret is evidence that it had no real substance to begin with. (At best, the secret is a banality; it may be discovered "a thousand times" in other lines and then forgotten again.) Here in its entirety is the poem:

> Two girls discover
> the secret of life
> in a sudden line of
> poetry.
>
> I who don't know the
> secret wrote
> the line. They
> told me
>
> (through a third person)
> they had found it
> but not what it was
> not even

what line it was. No doubt
by now, more than a week
later, they have forgotten
the secret,

the line, the name of the poem. I love them
for finding what
I can't find,

and for loving me
for the line I wrote,
and for forgetting it
so that

a thousand times, till death
finds them, they may
discover it again, in other
lines

in other
happenings. And for
wanting to know it,
for

assuming there is
such a secret, yes,
for that
most of all.

3

Metaphysics of the Visionary Moment

The Poststructuralist Problematic

From the standpoint of postmodern thought, an expansive metaphysics is embedded in the literary visionary moment. That is to say, the moment is premised on assumptions about truth, cognition, and the self, which, in the light of postmodern accounts of language, discourse, and subjectivity, are open to charges of logocentrism and humanism.

A visionary moment has to be recognized as such. In each of the illustrations discussed earlier (see pages 15–17), the insight or revelation may appear to speak for itself, to announce its own meaning as if it were intrinsically significant. However, the visionary moment cannot but be discursively constituted. The moment is "visionary" only insofar as a particular discourse interprets it to be so. Although the experience is apparently unmediated—for insight always comes in a flash, revelation occurs all of a sudden—it takes one of a culture's institutionally privileged discourses, like that of Humanism or Christianity, to construct the experience as significant. If this construction operates instantaneously or (what amounts to the same thing) if the process of interpretation seems to have been bypassed, this effect occurs because the discourse in question has already constituted the field of subjectivity that "reads" the moment as visionary.

Although the visionary moment is essentially a discursive construct, the experience is understood in terms that assign it a metaphysical nature. Thus, in "A Good Man Is Hard to Find," we are to understand that it is Christian Grace that enables the grandmother to see the man who has killed her family and is about to kill her as her spiritual kinsman. In *Seize the Day,* Wilhelm's insight into his spiritual kinship with all humankind ("They were his brothers and his sisters") is represented as the "Truth" spoken by "the real soul [which] says plain and understandable things to everyone" (84). And this stress on "plain and understandable" suggests a direct or intuitive channel of understanding, which is to say a channel of understanding that is unmediated by language. (Recall that Wilhelm is given to ask: "So what did it matter how many languages there were?" (85)) Finally, in *On the Road,* Paradise's mystical illumination is premised on the assumption that he has reached the "*timeless*" domain of "bright Mind Essence" (173), a domain that (given the references to earlier rebirths and deaths) I take to be Kerouac's version of nirvana. In each of the above cases, the conditions of possibility of the visionary moment are clearly transhistorical insofar as the writers invoke, respectively, Grace, eternal Truth, and "Mind Essence," conditions that, it is implied, transcend the culturally privileged, and thus *historically specific*, discourses that, I propose, have constructed the moment as visionary.

The visionary moment in the fiction in question tends to be experienced or interpreted as complete, ultimate, and absolute in its truth; in its finality, it closes off other possible meanings that might be assigned to it. The soul that speaks to Tommy Wilhelm communicates "Something very big. Truth, like" (85). Sal Paradise's realizations—e.g., "I realized that I had died and been reborn numberless times"—are accorded the status of ultimate truth by virtue of the eternal "stability of the intrinsic Mind" (173). And for O'Connor's grandmother, it is nothing less than Grace—"the Divine life and our participation in it," as the author said of her story (*Mystery* 111)—that underwrites the absolute truth of the sudden revelation of her spiritual kinship with The Misfit. In each case, the visionary moment is read within the closural terms of a discourse that produces a single, univocal meaning for it, namely, Bellow's humanism, Kerouac's Zen mysticism, and O'Connor's Christianity. In Derridean terms, all three accounts of the visionary moment are premised on concepts that operate as transcendental signifieds, namely, "Soul," "Mind Essence," "Christ." These Final Meanings suppress the excess meanings disseminated by any signifier so that, as in the texts cited, the moment is autocratically encoded on Their terms as visionary and nothing but. In short, the representation of the visionary moment as if it embodied a final, fast-frozen truth amounts to a "logocentric" illusion; that is to say, the transient "meaning-effects" generated by the endless "disseminations" of language are mistaken for immutable meanings.

It should also be remarked that the meaning of the visionary moment appears to be, from a postmodern perspective, impossibly pure; there is nothing to suggest that this order of meaning is in any way hybrid, derivative, or counterfeit. Rather its significations are always pristine, immaculate, original. In other words, such meaning is assumed to exist, *as if in some transcendent realm*, outside the space of intertextuality. Indeed, from the standpoint of intertextuality—that is, the recognition that texts can only emerge from the reworkings of other texts—the text of the visionary moment could only ever be an adulterated and derivative product. This is especially evident in respect of Sal Paradise's visionary moment in which Kerouac recycles just about every cliché associated with mystical experience: invocations of "heaven," "rebirth," "ecstasy," "radiances," the "inconceivable," the "indescribable," the "magical." Moreover, the rhetoric of the passage as a whole reads like a stylistic synthesis of Blake's "prophetic" writing and textbook Zen mysticism. And in the case of Tommy Wilhelm's sudden sense of being "united" with those around him in a "blaze of love," we find Bellow peddling still more clichés about mystical experience: that the visionary subject feels "at one" with the world, that this feeling is necessarily the "Truth," and that it typically occurs in sordid or sinful circumstances (in this case, in a "dark tunnel". Cf. Roth 60). The condition of intertextuality should remind us that no meaning, visionary or otherwise, is self-authenticating or self-sufficient; that the meanings of texts are largely constituted within a force field of other texts, each of which is only intelligible in the light of another. In short, as Barthes has cogently argued, all meaning is mediated, never purely itself ("Death" 146).

The visionary moment invariably has the quality of ultimacy. It is not just that the subject is supposed to have apprehended some ultimate order of meaning but as a condition for, or as a consequence of, doing so, he or she has reached the ultimate stage of spiritual or moral development. The subject, as if in some divine state, can progress no further. Indeed, the possibility that the subject might progress further would not only imply that the visionary moment was less than conclusive, but that he or she was less than complete. Hence, implicit in the account of a visionary subject is the model of a fixed or nonprocessual subject, a subject no longer contradictorily "split" or self-divided. The rebirth theme of the literary visionary moment signifies the emergence of a unitary and immutable subject. The sudden perception of spiritual kinship with a mass murderer is intended to indicate that O'Connor's grandmother has attained the state of Grace—an all-or-nothing condition. That is to say, to be in a graced or "saved" state, an individual must be beyond the mutability and instability of the subject-in-process. (Recall the postmodern reconceptualization of the self as an aggregate of *transitional* identities, these said to be continually prone to restructuring insofar as the discourses that "narrate" them into being are always imbricated in the endless "play" or "productivity" of signification.) Similarly, the visionary experience of Bellow's Tommy Wilhelm implies the subject's ultimate or totalized spiritual development. Thus, in respect of the visionary moment that concludes *Seize the Day* (and that essentially repeats the perception of spiritual kinship of the earlier visionary moment [84]), we read that Wilhelm "sank deeper than sorrow . . . toward the consummation of his heart's ultimate need" (118). To "consummate" is "to bring to a state of completion or perfection" (*Webster's*). Moreover, insofar as "heart" is Bellow's Pascalian term for soul (a usage evident in the novel aptly titled *Herzog*), he is evidently informing us of Wilhelm's elevation to the final, irreversible, and perfected stage of his development. In other words, Wilhelm is about to cease being a subject-in-process.

Bellow, writing within a Romantic-Humanist configuration of knowledge, assumes a sovereign or autonomous human essence ("soul" or "heart") as the self-sufficient foundation of understanding. Hence, in a society he identifies by its Babel of languages ("Every other man spoke a language entirely his own" [83]), and where empiricist induction is seen as crass epistemology ("You do not go from simple *a* and simple *b* to the great *x* and *y*" [84]), it is "the real soul [that] says plain and understandable things to everyone" (84). This "soul" *can* speak to everyone precisely insofar as it is privileged as the origin, locus, and guarantor of a *pure* ("plain and understandable") and primordial truth. Moreover, implied here is the subject's transcendent vantage point in relation to the visionary moment. For the knowledge that the moment conveys is always apprehended in its totality; there is no current of its meaning that escapes or exceeds this (implicitly) omnipotent consciousness. As if beyond the instabilities and surplus significations of language, the subject is assumed to be the sole legislator of meaning. (All of which is to say nothing of any *unconscious* investment in the meaning of the visionary moment.)

In general, for Bellow's Tommy Wilhelm, O'Connor's grandmother, and Kerouac's Sal Paradise, there is no question of having to consciously interpret the meaning (always singular, univocal) of their insights. Rather, those meanings are *immediately* experienced as plainly and unequivocally of visionary significance. And as a postmodernist counterexample of this situation, recall again the predicament of Pynchon's Oedipa Maas. She hopes that the mysterious posthorn emblem, which she frequently discovers in unexpected places, signifies the existence of an order of "transcendent meaning" (*Crying* 181) in a culture wasted by degraded communication. But the hope invested in that sign must coexist with a range of other interpretive options: hence (a) repetitions of the same sign may be a random occurrence, which, however, her imagination is patterning into significance or (b) the signs may be forgeries planted to deceive her or (c) they may be forgeries, when, however, there is no plot to deceive her, and so on. In short, one and the same sign appears to be informed with contradictory meanings, its significance mockingly ambiguous and indeterminate.

Finally, the visionary moment is premised on a depth model of subjectivity: "insight" implies *inner* seeing, "intuition" implies an interior (presensory) conduit to the truth—putative faculties which, like Bellow's cognizant "heart" or "soul," lie "furthest-in." At the other extreme, one could say that postmodern thinking has "dis-interiorized" subjectivity. Henceforth, it is but the nodal point of intersecting semiotic systems: for Baudrillard, "a terminal of multiple [media] networks" ("Ecstasy" 128), while for Barthes, the "I" is "already itself a plurality of other texts, of codes which are infinite. . . . [Hence] subjectivity has ultimately the generality of stereotypes" (*S/Z* 10). And, suffice to note here, in the postmodern fiction of Walter Abish (*How German*), Donald Barthelme (*Snow White*), and Robert Coover (*Pricksongs*), a depth model of subjectivity is conspicuously replaced by a model of it as but the construct of mass-media dreck and the culture's current clichés and platitudes.

In view of the foregoing points, it comes as no surprise to find that those fiction writers who foreground the textual limits of cognition actively resist the convention of the visionary moment. Indeed, almost any self-reflexive work of fiction will not accommodate this convention. Fiction by Jorge Luis Borges and Paul Auster will serve to illustrate the point.

One can read Borges's "The Library of Babel" as an angst-ridden parable of Derrida's dictum "there is nothing outside the text" (*Grammatology* 163). In this short story, which opens with the words "The universe (which others call the Library)" (51), the universe is imagined as a labyrinth of book-lined galleries extending to infinity. In their totality, the books of the library "register all the possible combinations of the twenty-odd orthographical symbols . . . : in other words, all that it is given to express, in all languages" (54; see also 57). The librarians spend their melancholic lives wandering from one gallery to the next in search of the book that will vindicate, or illuminate the meaning of, their existence. Of particular interest here is the search for "the catalogue of catalogues" (52) or for "a book which is the formula and perfect compendium *of all the rest*" (56). For, as a metaphor of interminable textuality, Borges's library suggests that such questing is futile; after all, there can be no terminal text when every text is seen to generate its countertext, which, in the case of the catalogue, will be "the demonstration of the fallacy of the true catalogue" (54). In fact, the librarians are shown to be trapped in a *mise-en-abîme* of textuality: "thousands and thousands of false catalogues" (54); "several hundred thousand imperfect facsimiles: works which differ only in a letter or comma" (56). Moreover, we are told that "the Library is unending" and that it exists "*ab aeterno*" (52). And, apart from connecting stairways, each gallery is surrounded by vast fathomless airshafts (51, 52)—the void, one might say, of the *hors-texte*. Accordingly, there can be no metalinguistic vantage point beyond the endless dynamic of text/countertext; no secure ground, beyond the "play" of textuality, from which the subject can speak with complete certainty. In Borges's infinite web of textual affiliations, there can be no privileged center: "*The Library is a sphere whose exact center is any one of its hexagons and whose circumference is inaccessible*" (52).

Borges' library repeats the confusion of Babel with its "senseless cacophonies, verbal jumbles and incoherences" (53). The logocentric belief in "the catalogue of catalogues" is but the dream of forlorn librarians, who must live in a world of unending and uncontrollable textuality; a world in which there can never be a final illumination or moment of truth. It is a story that may serve as the prototype for that current of postmodern fiction, which in highlighting the infinite play of textuality rigorously excludes the metatextual possibility of the visionary moment.

In *City of Glass,* Paul Auster critiques the classical detective story as a source for vindicating the empiricist faith in representation: insofar as clues obligingly disclose the nature of crimes, it would seem that we live in an eminently revealable world, where signifiers (clues) tightly coalesce with signifieds (crimes).[1] It is the burden of Auster's narrative to undermine this premise. Consider, for example, one character's response to the protagonist's name—Quinn:

> "I see many possibilities for this word, this Quinn, this . . . quintessence . . . of quiddity. Quick, for example. And quill. And quack. And quirk. Hmmm. Rhymes with grin. Not to speak of kin. . . . And win. And fin. And din. And gin. And pin. And tin. And bin. . . . I like your name enormously, Mr. Quinn. It flies off in so many directions at once." (90)

The passage may serve as an illustration of the infinite and differential "play" of signifiers (see Derrida, *Writing* 280, 289): their ungovernable dissemination of meaning, their overrunning of determinate limits. Hence, there is no quintessence of Quinn, that is to say, no identity whose meaning is independent of the multi-directional and anarchic play of signification. This point is emphasized by Quinn's experience of himself as a "triad of selves" (6): he writes detective novels under the pen name of William Wilson but identifies with the voice of his private-eye narrator, Max Work. Later, as writer-turned-private eye, Quinn will adopt the name of "Paul Auster" (12) while "living in the grip of [a] pun," whereby "private eye" signifies investigator, private I, and inner eye (9–10). Indeed, in the absence of stable signifiers, which would make for cohesive (self-) representation, Quinn's identity gradually dissolves so that, by the end of the novel, there is no one to claim the words he speaks: "He felt that his words had been severed from him, that now they were a part of the world at large, as real and specific as a stone, or a lake, or a flower. They no longer had anything to do with him" (156). Here, the "materiality" (the autonomous productivity) of language is made evident as Quinn's sense of self finally disperses into chains of signifiers.

Formerly, Quinn had "demand[ed] that the world reveal itself to him" (10), yet, insofar as understanding is said to be mediated through signifiers—which as signifiers are polysemic, volatile, unanchored—his demand will not be met. Clearly, the absolutist truth claims of revelation (itself necessarily a signifying process) cannot survive on the slippery ground of unending wordplay. Therefore, it is understandable that Quinn should become absorbed in the research of the man, one Peter Stillman, Sr., whom he has been hired to investigate. Stillman, a deranged scholar of Puritan texts, is inspired and obsessed with the millenarian mission to recover the first language of Adam. This is language before the Fall, when "words had not been merely appended to things . . . [but] had *revealed their essences*" (52, emphasis added). Stillman's mission amounts to a logocentric quest for a pure, original and above all, revelationary language—language before it degenerated into an unruly mass of arbitrary signs. (His search induces him to lock his baby son in a dark room *incommunicado* for nine years, on the assumption that the boy would spontaneously develop prelapsarian speech.)

"The detective," says Auster's narrator, "is one who looks, who listens, who moves through this morass of objects and events in search of the thought, the idea that will pull all these things together and make sense of them" (9). But Quinn's investigation yields no such revelationary thought or idea: "[H]e knew nothing, he knew that he knew nothing" (124; cf. *Ghosts* 202). The narrative ends without the traditional disclosure of the detective story: "At this point the story grows obscure. The information has run out, and the events that follow this last sentence [in Quinn's notebook] will never be known. It would be foolish even to hazard a guess" (157). A clear and conclusive revelation would assume a terminal point in the incessant play of signification; in effect, it would be an exit from textuality. However, early on, we are warned to expect no such exit: "What interested

[Quinn] about the stories he wrote was not their relation to the world but their relation to other stories" (8). Moreover, in this characteristically self-reflexive gesture, Auster draws attention not only to the intertextual nature of his own story, *City of Glass* (whose intertexts include *Through the Looking Glass, Don Quixote, Paradise Lost, The Narrative of Arthur Gordon Pym*), but also to the textual limits of all narrative.

Of course, not all writers resist the metaphysics of the visionary moment in the name of textuality. For example, visionary moments are occluded from the work of Samuel Beckett by virtue of the latter's (late-modernist) absurdist philosophy. His characters inhabit a universe conspicuously indifferent to the human presence: life promises nothing, all enterprise is ultimately futile, and existence is debased by a chronic state of ignorance. Ideas do not link up in an absurd universe, hence the silences that punctuate the dialogue in *Waiting for Godot.* The protagonists' frequent regression to cliché and proverbs illustrates a failure to arrive at any understanding of their situation. Godot, the hoped-for voice of illumination, never arrives and so Beckett's vagrants are not one whit wiser by the end of the play. Clearly, their predicament cries out for a visionary moment but no such salvational knowledge is forthcoming in an absurd world. Moreover, the problem is compounded by Beckett's perception of language as exhausted; for him, the issue is not a surplus of meaning but a deficit, and (elsewhere) his characters anticipate "the time when words must fail" (*Happy Days* 25). Language is in the grip of entropy and has no revelationary power. Hence, Ed Jewinski has discussed how Beckett, under the "anxiety" of Joyce's "influence," mapped out his place in literature in an antithetical position to his precursor precisely on the question of epiphanic writing. Thus, where Joyce believed in "the apotheosis of the word" (qtd. in Jewinski 166), that is, in the power of language to reveal reality, "for Beckett, language is not capable of an 'apotheosis.' Beckettian language—especially the word—will remain opaque, impenetrable, unredeeming. No transcendence is allowed with or through or by language" (167). Thus, Jewinski reads Beckett as essentially a practitioner of nonepiphanic language, a writer whose words "accumulate" but never "illuminate" (171).

Finally, to assume that one and the same visionary moment would have the same significance, embody the same abiding truth, for the same person at different stages of his or her life is, of course, to assume a nonhistorical, nonprocessual subject. And, again, we can turn to Beckett to see this very assumption satirized. In *Krapp's Last Tape,* a one-act tragicomedy, the sixty-nine-year-old Krapp listens to himself speaking on a tape he recorded thirty years ealier, in which he recounts a personal visionary moment. However, the bitter and hopeless old man feels altogether estranged from his enthusiastic younger self, the latter encountered almost as another incarnation. Thus, the reported moment is now perceived not only as comically irrelevant but futile—so much hot air. In this excerpt from the tape, Krapp's cynical perspective is indicated by the parenthetical and italicized stage directions:

Spiritually a year of profound gloom and indigence until that memorable night in March, at the end of the jetty, in the howling wind, never to be forgotten, when suddenly I saw the whole thing. The vision at last. This I fancy is what I have chiefly to record this evening, against the day when my work will be done and perhaps no place left in my memory, warm or cold, for the miracle that . . . (*hesitates*) for the fire that set it alight. What I suddenly saw then was this, that the belief I had been going on all my life, namely—(KRAPP *switches off impatiently, winds tape forward, switches on again*)—great granite rocks the foam flying up in the light of the lighthouse and the wind-guage spinning like a propeller, clear to me at last that the dark I have always struggled to keep under is in reality my most—(KRAPP *curses, switches off, winds tape forward, switches on again*)—unshatterable association until my dissolution of storm and night with the light of the understanding and the fire—(KRAPP *curses louder, switches off, winds tape forward, switches on again*). . . . (15–16)

Krapp persistently interrupts the recorded reflections of his thirty-nine and twenty-eight-year-old selves; he winds the tapes forward and backward or changes them. Thus, we are given just an aggregate of incongruous and incommensurate fragments, which do not add up to a gratifyingly coherent life narrative. The premise is cogent and uncompromising: there is no stable and unitary identity to guarantee the durability of a visionary "truth."

Of Abstractions and Particulars

The knowledge conveyed by the visionary moment is necessarily on the scale and elevation of a grand abstraction; anything less, that is, knowledge at the level of temporal or local existence, would not qualify as visionary. By definition, the literary visionary moment transcends the particular and everyday limits yet, para-doxically, it is precisely this generalized and expansive focus that works to reduce rather than enrich (the reader's) understanding of human experience. The broader a generalization, the thinner its content; it removes from consideration that which is distinctive of and specific to the visionary subject's situation. And "situation" is the pivotal term here, the term that postmodernism invokes to deflate and subvert the pretensions to transcendent vision. After all, to make a familiar point, subjec-tivity is always situated. It is situated by the way of life enabled by the mode of production and by ethnicity and place. It is situated by the vectors of power—gender, class, race, and so on —and by the episteme, which limits what can be thought. However, insofar as the visionary moment is conceived as transcending "situatedness," it projects knowledge that is distorted by exclusions and stereotyp-ing, and marked by vacuous generalization. V. S. Naipaul's *A Bend in the River* (1979) offers a vivid illustration of this problem.

The protagonist, Salim, has been raised in a prosperous family of Indo-Muslim merchants in a tradition-bound community on the coast of East Africa. However, his settled life is upset by political instability and violence, which force him to migrate into Central Africa. His new home is unspecified but we infer from the presence of expatriate Belgians and from references to the tyranny of the "Big Man" in the capital (and to his invented tribal traditions and Africanization program) that Salim is in Mobutu Sese Seko's Congo,[2] some time in the mid-sixties. Here, he takes over a relative's general goods store in a remote town in the bush. A part of the narrative recounts efforts by a Belgian missionary-priest and other Europeans to bring "civilization" to the region. However, these efforts are repeatedly wrecked by indigenous forces (i.e., the "Liberation Army" and Mobutu's henchmen) motivated by the belief that Africa's salvation lies in the recovery of its precolonial cultures (see e.g., 214, 219). Furthermore, with allusions to *Heart of Darkness,* there are suggestions that barbarism and evil are intrinsic to the African wilderness (see e.g., 14). Ultimately, amidst growing violence, Salim is forced to flee the country and we are left with the familiar modernist image of the alienated and homeless subject.

Taking Naipaul exactly on his own terms, commentators typically read Salim's predicament as emblematic of our dislocation in (no less than) "the modern world." Thus, for Richard West, *A Bend in River* is "more than a true and powerful book about Africa. It is . . . one of those books that make you question many assumptions about *the world today*" (18, emphasis added). For Bernard Levin, writing in the *Sunday Times,* "Mr Naipaul is our greatest war-reporter from the front line of *the modern world's* Kulturkampf" (qtd. in Naipaul dust jacket, emphasis added). For Claire Tomalin, also writing in the *Sunday Times,* "V. S. Naipaul uses Africa as a text to preach magnificently upon the sickness of *a world* losing touch with its past" (qtd. in Naipaul dust jacket, emphasis added). And, as if Naipaul has not removed us far enough from the specifics, that is, the precise sociopolitical dynamics of Mobutu's Congo, he extrapolates still further from Salim's experience in order to make a transhistorical judgment on humankind. Moreover, this judgment derives its authority through its articulation in the form of a (catastrophic) visionary moment:

> There came a moment, with the coming of the light, when suddenly the night became part of the past. . . . Out of my great pain, I had an illumination. It didn't come in words. . . . It seemed to me that men were born only to grow old, to live out their span, to acquire experience. Men lived to acquire experience; the quality of the experience was immaterial; pleasure and pain—and, above all, pain—had no meaning; to possess pain was as meaningless as to chase pleasure. (229)

And, to reinforce the centrality of this "moment" to the novel's overall argument, Salim reports a little later:

Then I remembered my illumination, about the need of men only to live, about the illusion of pain. . . . After a time I didn't have to call up the illumination. . . . It was there, beside me, that remote vision of the planet, of men lost in space and time, but dreadfully, pointlessly busy. (248; see also 252)

This "moment" marks the culmination of Salim's experience of the Congo; an accumulated knowledge that suddenly crystallizes into the form of a metaphysical insight. But we should note just how far removed it is from the particulars of life in an outlying Congolese province in the sixties:

Remove #1. As a nation-state, the Congo is a conspicuously political construct: an invention of European colonialism in conjunction with King Leopold II's guileful diplomacy (see Hochschild). A territory more than four times the size of France, its boundaries enclose over two hundred ethnically and linguistically diverse populations. Postcolonial Congo remains a mongrelized entity, weakened by intertribal struggles for control of mineral and energy resources. In short, "the Congo" is a political generalization, which cannot be said to "map" this culturally heterogeneous reality.

Remove #2. Naipaul uses the violence and instability of the Congo to exemplify (postcolonial) Africa in toto, which leaves him open to the same charge as that leveled against Conrad. Recall how, in *Heart of Darkness,* Conrad had also used the Congo as a microcosm of the continent, thus evoking Africa as a monolithic, undifferentiated whole (B. Fleming 90). Typically, Salim refers to the Congo (never specified by name) as Africa: "And I saw Africa in a way I had never seen it before" (108); "What illusions Africa gave to people who came from outside!" (238). But, granted many common features, the postcolonial experience of African states remains a varied one and any attempt at wholesale generalization can only repress the differences that crucially distinguish the history of Mobutu's Congo from that of, say, Nyerere's Tanzania or Khadafi's Libya or Nkrumah's Ghana.

Remove #3. Postcolonial Africa, in turn, serves as Naipaul's emblem of modernity; that is to say, a reality defined by radical dislocations, economic and political volatility, and loss of the past—"History was something dead and gone, part of the world of our grandfathers" (186; see also 147, 252). *A Bend in the River,* like *Heart of Darkness,* ends with the protagonist traveling down a river in darkness. Thus, Naipaul, like Conrad, concludes with a nondialectical image of humanity hopelessly adrift. This image is one of the novel's inflated abstractions, in which "African darkness" is generalized to signify the decay of "the modern world."

Remove #4. Finally, the visionary moment supplies the outermost frame, another bloated abstraction, which is "the human condition." Salim's illumination speaks for all humankind at all times: "men were born only to grow old. . . .

[P]leasure and pain had no meaning"; "that remote vision of *the planet,* of men lost in space and time" (emphasis added).

In outlining Naipaul's sequence of extrapolations, we can see how with each progressively larger generalization, the focus gets hazier: monoethnic province > multiethnic Congo > Africa > modern society > homo sapiens. But from the standpoint of postmodernism, which, as Lyotard puts it, "refines our sensitivity to differences" (xxv), Naipaul's abstractions miss the singularity of the events from which his totalizing inferences are made. How does he get from the sociopolitical experience of a region of the eastern Congo,[3] in the sixties, to a transhistorical judgment on humankind without distortion or loss of accuracy? Indeed, particularity has been occluded from the start, insofar as Naipaul leaves out (African) place names and the name of the "Big Man" (as if post-Independence Africa has known only despotic Mobutus and not the likes of Lumumba, Nkrumah, Nyerere, or Kaunda). Too much specificity will only impede his tendency to make overarching pronouncements about humanity. A more focused account of the colonial legacy of internecine tribal rivalry, of neocolonial economics,[4] of the political fragility of a state in the throes of modernization, would surely moderate his claims about the meaninglessness of human life. Such an account would counter the suggestion that the irrationality witnessed by his protagonist is inscribed in human nature with the suggestion that it is generated by the institutional deformations of a nation trapped in violent socioeconomic contradictions. In the end, the novel's argument finds its ultimate expression in a visionary moment whose metaphysical projections depoliticize the tensions of a specific conjuncture by obscuring the particulars of time and place.

To make the foregoing points is not to lose sight of the fact that a novelist cannot broadly comment on human experience without generalizing from particulars, without universalizing from the local. But given the postmodern valorization of difference and the disparate, this fundamental practice of fictional narrative can, at times, seem problematic and ideologically suspect. Moreover, the use of visionary moments can only reinforce the distortions that occur when novelists extrapolate from particulars. After all, insofar as some philosophical "insight" into "human nature" is *received* in the form of an illumination, it is invested with the authority of a "higher" truth. Neither the protagonist nor the reader is expected to contest a truth delivered in this form. The visionary moment legitimizes the knowledge it conveys. It is a convention whose rhetoric supports a novelist's metaphysical truth claims.

What Naipaul perceives as the meaninglessness of human life one can alternatively see as the amplified, drawn-out cry of that fraction of the bourgeoisie whose interests are threatened by postcolonial counterforces (e.g. "Africanization" or Communist guerrilla armies). Indeed, in this novel, humanity is chiefly represented as petit-bourgeois traders (notably, Salim the merchant) and, clearly, the "Liberation Army" is seen to pose a threat to the cosy hierarchical arrangement of colonial times: "They're going to kill all the masters and all the servants" (284). (Salim himself is a master accompanied by a family slave, Metty.)[5]

Finally, Christopher Wise reads in *A Bend in the River* a "neo-modernist" agenda for the regeneration of postcolonial Africa (62). He argues that Naipaul advocates "the wholesale liquidation of traditional cultures, so that a new or 'absolutely modern' Africa may come into being" (68). Hence Naipaul's rejection of "African" art and religion (especially the functions assigned to masks, sculptures, and fetishes) as the products of an irrational, moribund world of "simple magic" and "spirits" (*A Bend* 56, 70, 130). It is, therefore, ironic that "neomodernist" Naipaul should conspicuously rely on the convention of the visionary moment; that is to say, he works with the mystical belief—essentially no more advanced than belief in "simple magic" and "spirits"—that Truth arrives from some occult source in the form of an "illumination," whose meaning, moreover, can be comprehended in an instant.

In *The Space Between: Literary Epiphany in the Work of Annie Dillard*, Sandra Humble Johnson examines the pivotal importance of the literary epiphany to Dillard's autobiographical writings. She argues that "The sum total of [Dillard's] work—the [epiphanic] moments combined with the narrative supporting and leading up to them—is a treatise on illumination" (24). In what is unquestionably a sensitive and insightful study of the Pulitzer Prize–winning writer, Johnson nevertheless uncritically reproduces Dillard's epiphanic model of knowledge. (At the very least, for a monograph published by a university press in 1992, one might have expected a perfunctory acknowledgment of how postmodern theory could imperil Dillard's "neoromantic epistemology" [2].)

As a writer who works in the traditions of English Romanticism and American Transcendentalism (see Johnson, ch. 1 and 2), Dillard places a high premium on intuitive knowledge. For example, Dillard, in what amounts to an astounding non sequitur, argues from Heisenberg's Uncertainty Principle to vindicate epiphanic intuition. Given the ultimate imprecision of scientific measurement, it (supposedly) follows that (in Johnson's words), "illumination and intuition [become] the only method to catch a glimpse of what lies behind the 'veil'. . . . Intuition is always more accurate than culturally accumulated raw data or knowledge" (21). But while Heisenberg, at least, famously factored the problem of mediation into the process of inquiry (i.e., the observer always informs the nature of the observation), the problem of mediation is not perceived as an issue for Dillard's intuitive subject. As Johnson credulously puts it, "With the literary epiphany [Dillard] is able to experience divinity individually, without institutional mediation" (61)—as if faith in epiphanic experience and the concept of divinity were not themselves institutionally mediated. To illustrate this question of mediation in more detail, consider the account of an epiphany that Dillard gives in *Pilgrim at Tinker Creek* (1974):

I sit on a bridge as on Pisgah or Sinai, and I am both waiting becalmed in a cleft of the rock and banging with all my will, calling like a child beating on the door: Come on out! . . . I know you're there.

And then occasionally the mountains part. The tree with the lights in it appears, the mockingbird falls, and time unfurls across space like an oriflamme. (Qtd. in Johnson 58.)

Johnson introduces this epiphany by explaining that because Dillard "has wiped her slate clean of foregone conclusions, the moment of epiphany can show itself" (58; see also 28–29). Yet, the very rhetoric of Dillard's account betrays an intelligence formed from "foregone conclusions." Her key metaphors indicate a spiritual experience rendered intelligible in conspicuously Judaeo-Christian terms: the allusion to Pisgah, the mountain from whose summit Moses viewed the Promised Land (Deuteronomy 34:1–3); the self-indentification as a child, insofar as the child is revered as eminently redeemable (cf. Mark 10:15: "[W]hoever does not receive the Kingdom of God like a child shall not enter it"); the invocation of the exalted image of the oriflamme, that is, the sacred banner of the abbey of St. Denis, adopted as an inspirational standard by French kings. Dillard aims, says Johnson, to "rid . . . the mind of knowledge acquired by institutions and systems" (28). Johnson continues: "The denial of preconceived ideas is necessary for this romantic," who, we are told, seeks illuminating moments beyond "mortal knowledge" (29). However, the impetus of postmodern critique is to reverse such thrusts at transcendence and, in this case, "ground" Dillard's mind precisely within "institutions and systems." For example, she is a writer working *within* the conventions of "the American Transcendental and Muir-wilderness traditions" (53); a "neoromantic" with a historically peculiar "strong reliance on epiphany" (56). And it is in these respects that the subtitle of Johnson's monograph proves instructive. "Literary Epiphany in the Work of Annie Dillard" tells us that, in her autobiographical writings, Dillard encounters her spiritual experiences largely in literary (and, therefore, institutionalized) terms. The literary convention of the epiphany invests with a narrative structure experiences that might otherwise be encountered as incoherent or amorphous. Moreover, the literary writer is just one of a conjunction of institutional subject positions that define the limits of Dillard's knowledge. She also epiphanizes from her positions as a white, middle-class, unaffiliated Christian, raised in Pittsburgh, educated at Hollins College, living and writing in the United States in the seventies and eighties. It is *this* culturally and historically situated Annie Dillard who has spiritual experiences and invests them with meaning, not some abstract being beyond "institutions [and] systems," beyond "preconceived ideas" and "foregone conclusions."

In a 1978 interview, Dillard affirmed her belief in a "natural mind" or precultural mode of knowing (29). This premise is crucial to her epiphanist's notion that there are experiences whose meanings are not institutionally mediated.

This is to assume that meaning can exist independently of sign systems, rather than assume that it is the latter which render experiences meaningful in the first place. Moreover, the postulate of a precultural mode of knowing does not in itself amount to an argument for the existence of a *superior* type of cognition; the first proposition does not entail the second. Nevertheless, in *An American Childhood* (1987), Dillard develops this line of thought in her Romantic ideal of the child who "untainted by institutions" can "see into the heart of things" (34, Johnson's words). As Johson observes, "*American Childhood* is predicated on this 'innocent eye'" (34). And here it is instructive to quote Nietzsche's response to the familiar notion of the "innocent eye":

> [L]et us be on guard against the dangerous old conceptual fiction that posited a "pure, will-less, painless, timeless knowing subject"; let us guard against the snares of such contradictory concepts as "pure reason," "absolute spirituality," "knowledge in itself"; these always demand that we should think of an eye that is completely unthinkable, an eye turned in no particular direction, in which the active and interpreting forces, through which alone seeing becomes seeing *something,* are supposed to be lacking. . . . There is *only* a perspective seeing, *only* a perspective "knowing". . . . (*Genealogy* 119)

The perceiver is always and necessarily situated by virtue of "active and interpreting forces". There is no natural insight, no innocent eye.

The question of subject positions returns when Johnson (again, uncritically) paraphrases Dillard's views on the irrelevance of feminist perspectives vis-à-vis her personal epiphanies:

> If she were to accept the categorization as "woman writer" she would undermine the very heart of her material: Homo sapiens in touch with the merging of time and eternity, unpolitical, leaping beyond the idea of gender into the idea of the artist in touch with the infinite. She is artist above all, coming to eternity not as a political/cultural victim but as a mind expanded by the moment filled with light, the genderless moment of merging with God. (60–61)

Here we have a conspicuous instance of humanism's undifferentiated concept of "Homo sapiens." It should be remarked how, in this passage, we move from the relatively concrete subject position of "woman writer," to the less concrete position of genderless artist and finally, to the vaporous abstraction of "a mind expanded by the moment filled with light"—the mind, that is, of "Homo sapiens in touch with the merging of time and eternity." In other words, we are asked to accept the claim that the epiphanic visionary (in this case, Dillard herself) is unsituated as a gendered, political, and historical subject in a moment of pure transcendence. Yet, this claim is undermined by the historically contingent and ethnocentric assumptions that manifestly position the epiphanic subject. First, the very significance that Dillard attaches to her epiphanies is historically and culturally specific; that is to say, not all people at all times have, or will have, faith in the "illuminations" supplied by momentary intuitions. Indeed, as Johnson herself affirms, in a periodizing argument, Dillard's reliance on epiphanies makes her a "neoromantic" with roots in English Romanticism and American Transcendentalism. Second, it is evident in the passage quoted that the exalted terms in which Dillard conceives of herself as an artist are essentially Romantic. Furthermore, in what amounts to another periodizing (antitranscendent) observation, Johnson writes: "As an artist called to her work, a holy bard, she believes, like Wordsworth, that not all people are capable of the divine moment of inspiration or illumination" (37). And my purpose in highlighting this historical connection is to insist that "the artist" is a historically variable and culturally specific construct, not a transcendent identity. (Thinking within a postmodern episteme, fiction writers like Robert Coover and Walter Abish see themselves as manipulators of codes rather than "holy bards.") Third, that singular "God," with which Dillard as "inspired" artist "merges," is yet another historical and ethnocentric construct; after all, monotheism is not an eternal or universal given.

To raise the foregoing points is not to doubt that Dillard has had profound spiritual experiences. However, as we have seen, the very terms she and Johnson use implicitly undermine the claim that epiphanies are experienced from the universal elevation of "Homo sapiens." In a review of *Pilgrim at Tinker Creek,* Eudora Welty complained of Dillard presuming to be "a voice that is trying to speak to me out of a cloud instead of from a sociable, even answerable, distance on our same earth" (qtd. in Johnson 3). It is as socially rooted terrestrials that we have spiritual experiences, not as transcendent subjects.

Mystical Unions, Postmodern Disjunctures

In *Imagined Communities* (1983), Benedict Anderson examined the role of literature in the production of imaginary identifications of nationhood. He argued that the expansion of a supravernacular print capitalism—especially in the forms of popular novels and mass-circulating newspapers—provided its readers with a sense of belonging in the abstract form of a national community. This sense of belonging, moreover, became more significant as the processes of modernization weakened the face-to-face forms of affiliation derived from work or the family or neighbourhood. Here I want to proceed from Anderson's thesis to suggest the role of literature in the construction of another kind of "imagined community," that is, universal spiritual community. By this term, I mean either a sense of belonging to a community, which is said to transcend time, place, and material interests and to be inclusive of all humankind, or a sense of having an assured place (a *necessary* belonging) within some supposed cosmic scheme in which everything that exists is interconnected. Specifically, I want to identify the literary visionary moment as a narrative convention that often promotes notions of universal spiritual community. For typically the "reality" of such a community is intimated to a fictional character in a fleeting instant. It is as if the knowledge revealed is conceptualized as an order of truth so exalted, so remote from mundane experience, it can only be grasped through the medium of the visionary moment. (In contrast, nationhood can be experienced at almost any time through a profusion of tangible signifiers, such as coins, stamps, flags, or maps.) However, while ideas of universal spiritual community remain widely influential today, enjoying a measure of support even within academia, when seen from the perspectives of postmodern theory and in the light of the political experience of living in a postmodern culture, such ideas look fantastic and fallacious.

Thus, beyond a critique of the visionary moment in its capacity as a literary form and knowledge paradigm, there is a case for reflecting on its *propositional content,* the specific knowledge that such moments are said to convey. Indeed, the status of the visionary moment largely rests on its credibility as a source of "higher" knowledge, of which the postulate of a universal spiritual community may be taken as an instance.

The literary visionary moment frequently communicates a profound sense of spiritual connectedness. For example, early in *The Grapes of Wrath,* Steinbeck's apostate preacher, Jim Casy, recounts a mystical insight:

> "I figgered about the Holy Sperit and the Jesus road. I figgered, 'Why do we got to hang it on God or Jesus. Maybe,' I figgered, 'maybe it's all men an' all women we love; maybe that's the Holy Sperit—the human sperit—the whole shebang. Maybe all men got one big soul ever'body's a part of.' Now I sat there thinkin' it, an' all of a sudden—I knew it. I knew it so deep down that it was true, and I still know it." (31; see also 535, 537)

Recall that Steinbeck's novel chronicles the growth of class consciousness among farmers dispossesed of their land by private corporate interests. However, the emerging collectivity or "phalanx" brings more than just tactical advantage. It is valued as a preliminary phase in what Steinbeck believes to be a macroevolutionary movement toward universal spiritual community: a historically inevitable transformation "from 'I' to 'we'" (194) whereby, for instance, "twenty families became one family [and] the children were the children of all" (249). And accounts of intimate sharing—a breakfast shared among migrant workers (373–74), a woman breastfeeding a starving man (580–81)—are formulated in sacramental terms that suggest the experience of authentic spiritual community. Moreover, this stress on community is itself framed by Steinbeck's holistic mysticism, a mysticism communicated by Casy, for whom, "'There was the hills, an' there was me, an' we wasn't separate no more. We was one thing. An' that one thing was holy'" (105).[6]

A similar experience of mystical union is recounted in O'Neill's *Long Day's Journey into Night*. Edmund, the younger brother in the highly dysfunctional Tyrone family, who confesses, "'I will always be a stranger who never feels at home, . . . who can never belong'" (135), recalls a visionary moment at sea:

> "[A]nd for a moment I lost myself—actually lost my life. I was set free! I dissolved in the sea, became white sails and flying spray, became beauty and rhythm, became moonlight and the ship and the high dim-starred sky! I belonged, without past or future, within peace and unity and a wild joy, within something greater than my own life, or the life of Man, to Life itself! To God, if you want to put it that way." (134)

O'Neill's lines are in many respects reminiscent of the idea of nirvana, where the subject loses its individuality not simply through annihilation but (as the Buddhist saying goes) "as the dewdrop slips into the shining sea"—the immersion being a metaphor for merging with the universal life. (Cf. Kerouac, *Dharma* 241; W. James 410.) And, for good measure, here is a passage from *The Color Purple*, by Alice Walker, where Celie, in a letter to her sister, recounts a sudden experience of cosmic union as reported to her by her friend, Shug Avery:

> She say, My first step from the old white man [i.e. God] was trees. Then air. Then birds. Then other people. But one day when I was sitting quiet and feeling like a motherless child, which I was, it came to me: that feeling of being part of everything, not separate at all. I knew that if I cut a tree, my arm would bleed. And I laughed and I cried and I run all around the house. I knew just what it was. In fact, when it happen, you can't miss it. (178)

The passage narrates the transition from a conception of God as a transcendent, raced, and gendered being ("old white man") to an ecospiritual conception of the divine in nature. A few lines earlier, Celie learns from Shug that "God is everything . . . And when you can feel that . . . you've found It" [i.e. the genderless God] (178). Indeed, Celie progresses toward a redeeming pantheistic sensibility. Thus, the form of address of her concluding letter—"Dear God. Dear stars, dear trees, dear sky, dear peoples. Dear Everything. Dear God" (249)— signals her ability to perceive divine cosmic interconnectedness. This perception marks the completion of a process of spiritual healing, after a degrading life of sexual, physical, and mental abuse.

The foregoing excerpts belong to a long tradition of mystical writing in which the experience of cosmic union is seen as the condition for salvation. Suffice here to recall the Neoplatonist narrative of the soul, which returns from its diaspora in the inferior "emanation" of matter, to perfect unity with the "One," or the Upanishadic concept of Brahma (or Atman), the World Soul from which all individual souls originate and to which, by virtue of yogic practices, they will return. There are those New Age syncretic mysticisms that claim the experience of "cosmic consciousness."[7] And within academia itself, credibility is accorded to notions of cosmic interconnectedness. For example, the State University of New York Press has recently published a series of books, several under the expert and meticulous editorship of David Ray Griffin, on the subjects of postmodern theology and postmodern spirituality. In one of these volumes, *Sacred Interconnections: Postmodern Spirituality, Political Economy, and Art* (1990), Griffin introduces the concerns of the contributors (all but one or two of whom are academics):

> Catherine Keller says that "interconnection is the cosmic case," and that "no one and no thing is really separate from anything else". . . . Joanna Macy speaks of "interexistence," of "a vision of radical and sustaining interdependence," of an "experience of profound interconnectedness with all life," and of ourselves as "inseparable from the Web of life in which we are as intricately interconnected as cells in a larger body." Steve Odin speaks of an "aesthetic continuum of harmonious interpenetration between the many and the one". . . . John Cobb speaks of "God as interconnected with the whole interconnected creation." (1–2)

Whence Griffin's summary statement: "That this universal connectedness is a fact can be said to be the first thesis of this book" (3).[8]

Ecospirituality is a specific instance of a currently flourishing field of thought that confers a measure of scholarly respectability on the notion of universal spiritual community. Here the general claim is that all forms of life on the planet are linked by virtue of a sacred ecological communion. This may amount to an emphasis on the divine in nature, as in Matthew Fox's concept of "panentheism" ("God is in everything and everything is in God" [qtd. in Teasdale 229]) but more representative of the ecospiritual movement is Thomas Berry's "Pax Gaia" (220), a spiritual variant of James Lovelock's Gaia hypothesis. Thus, in *The Dream of the Earth* (1988), Berry, for whom, "the natural world is the larger sacred community to which we belong" (81), defines a functional ecospirituality as "grounded in the basic characteristics of the universe as manifested from the beginning: the unique and irreplaceable qualities of the individual and the inseparable bonding with every other being in the universe" (120).

Of course, ideas of universal spiritual community were vulnerable to critique long before the emergence of postmodern thinking. I shall briefly discuss ideology critique later, but psychoanalytic critique also merits a few words. In 1927, in an exchange of letters between Freud and Romain Rolland, the latter coined the phrase "oceanic feeling." He described the feeling as a "spontaneous religious sensation of the 'eternal'" (qtd. in Fisher 9). This experience has much in common with the sublime as understood by Kant; an experience that defies representation insofar as it amounts to an intuitive and primeval feeling of "contact" with forces that are so vast as to transcend all empirical limits and categories of understanding. And a crucial element of this experience is the sense of universal spiritual community and cosmic union. As David Fisher explains:

> The oceanic feeling was an intimate sensation of identity with one's surroundings, of sublime connection to other people, to one's entire self, to nature, and to the universe as an indivisible whole. It ended the separation of the self from the outside world and from others. (10)

For Freud, however, oceanic feeling was a comforting adult fantasy, a regression to the prelinguistic stage of ego development, when the boundaries of the infant's ego were blurred so that he/she experienced an indissoluble and intimate bond with the surrounding world. In this ecstatic condition, the self cannot be differentiated from others; in a "limitless narcissism," it encompasses all humanity and the universe.[9]

In addition to ideas of spiritual community at the cosmic level, we can also find ideas of it at the exclusively human level, that is, a spiritual community that links all humankind. By way of illustration, here are two more accounts of literary visionary moments.

In Saul Bellow's *Seize the Day,* the people of New York City are afflicted by an acute sense of alienation and atomization. Hence, "every other man spoke a language entirely his own" (83). Nevertheless, the protagonist, Tommy Wilhelm, finds hope in the belief that "There is a larger body, and from this you cannot be separated" (84), and he recalls the visionary moment of a few days earlier that occasioned this belief. As he walked through a subway (for convenience I repeat the quotation):

> all of a sudden, unsought, a general love for all these imperfect and lurid-looking people burst out in [his] breast. He loved them. One and all, he passionately loved them. They were his brothers and sisters. He was imperfect and disfigured himself, but what difference did that make if he was united with them by this blaze of love? (84–85)

And in Paule Marshall's *Praisesong for the Widow,* Avey Johnson, a black widow, is suffering from a diminished sense of self after assimilating to white bourgeois culture and divesting herself of her "heritage." However, while on vacation in Grenada, her spiritual healing begins with a recollection of her early days with Jay, her husband, when "something in [their] small rites, an ethos they held in common, had reached back beyond her life and beyond Jay's to join them to the vast unknown lineage that had made their being possible. And this link, these connections . . . had both protected them and put them in possession of a kind of power"

(137). It is an experience of spiritual communion with African ancestry (see also 255). Later, Avey recalls a more expansive sense of communion she had as a child: visionary moments, experienced during day trips to the Hudson, when she suddenly felt linked to *all* the blacks around her:

> [S]he would feel what seemed to be hundreds of slender threads streaming out from her navel and from the place where her heart was to enter those around her. And the threads went out not only to people she recognized from the neighborhood but to those she didn't know well, such as the roomers just up from the South and the small group of West Indians. . . .
>
> Then it would seem to her that she had it all wrong and the threads didn't come from her, but from them, from everyone on the pier, including the rowdies, issuing out of their navels and hearts to stream into her as she stood there. . . .
>
> . . . [F]or those moments, she became part of, indeed the center of, a huge wide confraternity. (190–91. See also 249, where a spiritually transformed Avey reexperiences the same visionary moment.)

We should note that the threads, issuing from such fundamental sources as "navels and hearts," connect Avey with the most unlikely and diverse people. The implication is that spiritual connection transcends class status and cultural type. Indeed, Marshall works to identify interconnections between Africa and the black diaspora, between ancestors, the present generation, and future generations. In short, she envisions a vast transhistorical lineage that links all blacks in spiritual unity. But, judged from the standpoint of postmodern thought, her idea of "confraternity" or Bellow's idea of universal brother/sisterhood masks over relations of difference at two levels. First, recall the familiar postmodern insistence on the self as an aggregate of discursively constituted and contradictory subject-positions. Hence, the idea of a spiritual community of all humankind appears to be premised on the assumption of a human essence or soul, an ontological or "primordial self" (Bellow) that precedes, and thus survives, this fragmentation of the subject into competing and shifting identities. Second, postmodernism emphasizes incommensurable differences not only within the subject but between *groups* of subjects, an "irreducible plurality" (Laclau and Mouffe 139) of sociopolitical identities organized around gender, racial, class, and other relations and giving rise to multiple sites of antagonism. Accordingly, Marshall and Bellow suggest what, by the standards of postmodern theory and postmodern political experience, appears as a miraculous homogenization that overcomes sociopolitical difference: a seamless integration of radical Otherness, of heteroglot voices. For postmodern consciousness makes it difficult to think of a world beyond the politics of difference and exclusion. This hyperpoliticization of social relations (partly a consequence of the Foucauldian perception of the horizontal diffusion of power) makes the condition of *unmediated connectedness*—which is implicit in the idea of a spiritual community of humankind—look quite implausible, not to say naïvely utopian. All this is not to deny the existence of postmodern forms of spiritual community. This type of community exists and may be defined as an *invented*, even ad hoc, entity, often conscious of its historical contingency and distinguished by the local, sectarian nature of its membership. Its members see themselves as connected not by some primordial or universal identity but by a spiritual lifestyle to which they adhere by deliberate choice, albeit in a temporary and provisional way. Such communities are numerous within what George McKay and other cultural theorists call "DIY [do-it-yourself] culture": the Ecstasy/rave subculture, the traveler movement, the groups organized around Green radicalism, and so on. (See McKay 1–53.) Essays by DIY activists emphasize the spiritual bonding among members of these movements, chiefly young working-class people disenfranchised by, or alienated from, the corporate-capitalist system. For example, Mary Anna Wright acclaims the "spiritual revelation and metanoia" (228) experienced by those in the rave scene, thanks to the psychoactive drug Ecstasy. On the dance floor, the drug "can induce feelings of empathy" and a profound sense of "unity" among youth from diverse subcultures (233). Wright observes that "large numbers of people taking Ecstasy together share in what is essentially an ineffable experience communicating nonverbally in ways often related afterward as telepathic or intuitive" (233).

The inherently unstable, fissiparous, and disjunctive structure of the postmodern social field has, quite independently of postmodern theory, put into crisis grand narratives of communal identity. In particular, this applies to identity as predicated on the nation-state and economic class. Thus, the sovereignty and autonomy of the nation-state have been partially eroded by the formidable expansion of transnational forces, notably, globalization, hegemonic power blocs, international organizations, and international law (see Held). Moreover, this erosion from "above" has been matched by an erosion from "below" with the rise of regional nationalisms and ethnic constituencies. In the late-capitalist period we have what Arjun Appadurai labels shifting "ethnoscapes," which comprise "tourists, immigrants, refugees, exiles, guestworkers and other moving groups" (297), and which have extensively pluralized the composition of the nation-state. Collectively, these developments largely qualify the use of the "imagined community" of the nation-state as a basis for identity formation.

The "collapse" of the grand narrative of class has been a defining issue of the postmodernism debates. Laclau and Mouffe, for example, have critiqued the "essentialist discourse" (88, 97) and "monist aspiration" (4) of Marxism for representing the working class as the universal subject of history. However, it is Fredric Jameson's account of a cognitively unmappable late-capitalist conjuncture that will be more relevant here. He has noted "the incapacity of our minds, at least at present, to map the great global multinational and decentered communicational network in which we find ourselves caught as individual subjects" (*Postmodernism* 44). At issue here is the disorientation and weakening of class consciousness in (a) a (putatively) nonfigurable hyperspace where capital is decentered (multina-tionalized and deregulated) and (b) a media-generated hyperreality where history becomes a commodified spectacle and the real is consumed in the form of pseudo-events, factoids, and PR advertising. Moreover, the diminished capacity to identify ourselves in terms of class position is compounded by the fragmentation of the postmodern subject into a multiplicity of nonclassist subject positions.[10]

The foregoing examples indicate how postmodern social experience has produced a sensibility that no longer accommodates grand narratives of commu-nal identity. Instead, we have an epistemology that is sensitive to the logic of disjuncture: fragmentation, decentering, difference, dispersion. Indeed, the post-modern subject might well repeat the words of the narrator of a story by Donald Barthelme: "Fragments are the only forms I trust" ("See the Moon?" 98).

Against the "worldly" concept of solidarity, which is often invoked in the practical context of uniting around an oppositional cause, appeals to the concept of a universal spiritual community—at least, as formulated in literary texts—tend to lack practical content; a progressive, transformative agenda cannot be derived from them. Moreover, while the concept of solidarity can accommodate the stubborn fact of irreconcilable social division, mystical appeals to an all-inclusive spiritual family must understate or ignore such division. Here, it should also be observed that appeals to forms of mystical union may be read as one type of nostalgia critique of modernization, where the dislocations and migrations conse-quent upon capitalist development have produced a yearning for enduring forms of community.

We also need to consider how appeals to a spiritual community of human-kind may amount to one constituency seeking to represent its interests as univer-sal. For example, Steinbeck's invocations of "the People" (*Grapes* 360, 542, etc.) as the essence of authentic spiritual community look suspect when we note signifi-cant exclusions—the interests of Native and Mexican Americans. Ironically, his white farmers of the Southwest, who are victims of land expropriation by corpo-rate interests, had themselves, barely two generations earlier, been land expropria-tors, driving Indians and Mexicans from their settlements. Nowhere in Steinbeck's narrative does the figure of "the People" accommodate nonwhites. Indeed, to raise this issue is to reflect how the postmodern awareness of a radical pluralism within populations leads to the distrust of appeals to a common humanity. Sharon Welch advocates the replacement of a "communal ethics" with a "communicative ethics." The latter calls for "conversation" among different communities as the basis for a genuinely progressive transformative politics, a dialogue that avoids the danger of a single community assuming the sole prerogative of moral decision-making. Hence, "the aims of equality and respect are met by *highlighting differences,* not by transcending them or looking beneath them for a common foundation" (Welch 83). Welch's "ethic of solidarity and difference" is characteristically postmodern in its rejection of the undifferentiated appeals to the transcendent or foundational, which are implicit in the idea of a spiritual community of humankind.

We need to acknowledge the conjunctural limits of mystical experiences of total community. For example, while Steinbeck's "big soul" vision of community acquires meaning primarily vis-à-vis the open class warfare in the United States in the thirties, the ecospiritualist view of all the Earth's creatures linked in an "entire planetary community" (Berry 82) acquires meaning in response to the enhanced awareness of the degradation of the environment fifty or so years later.

The context of Paule Marshall's conception of total community merits more detailed attention. In *Praisesong,* Avey Johnson attends a fête on the "out-island" of Carriacou. (In terms of the novel's geopolitics, the island is an auspicious site for spiritual experience: a purely indigenous space, untouched by the colonial forces that have degraded other Caribbean cultures.) The fête, dedicated to the "remembrance" of "the Long-time People" (165), proves a crucial event in Avey's growing identification with a spiritual community. The "fragments" of old songs and "shadowy forms of long-ago dances" (240) are rituals that connect her and other Afro-Caribbeans to their African ancestors: acts of "Saluting their nations. Summoning the Old Parents" (238). At a key moment, a note struck on a keg drum invokes feelings of "separation and loss" and ancestral "memories." The note, moreover, has "its source . . . [in] the bruised still-bleeding innermost chamber of *the collective heart*" (244–45, emphasis added). This mobilization of cultural memory is perceived as essential to diasporic black communities if their members are to achieve a positive sense of identity (see below 143, n.4). All this resolves into a question of heritage, a question that has long haunted Afro-American literature. But with the programmatic and militant raising of black consciousness in the sixties and the corollary interest in Africa (the sentiment of "Back to Africa," Rastafarianism, and so on), the question of heritage became a pressing and orthodox concern of Afro-American fiction. To give just three eminent examples, recall Alex Haley's *Roots* (1976), Toni Morrison's *Song of Solomon* (1977), and Alice Walker's "Everyday Use" (1973) (the last being a critical response to the Afro-American obsession with "roots" at that time [see Chapter 7]). This is the current of popular feeling from which *Praisesong* (1983), with its focus on mystical connectedness, emerges. However, for Marshall, mystical connectedness is not only historical; it also extends across space: "[T]he coming together . . . of the entire black community throughout the world—the possibility, the necessity of that union sustains me" ("Interview" 4).[11] Her global "confraternity" of blacks (*Praisesong* 191, 249) and black "collective heart" (245) constitute a vision of spiritual community and (in consequence of which) cultural regeneration. The vision implies a mode of existence that is radically alternative to the competitive, individualistic, hierarchically organized Euro-American social structure. And, to be sure, this notion of a spiritually revitalized black people embodies both an inspiring image of the possibilities of life beyond the diaspora—that is, beyond the disabling effects of deracination, dispossession, and dispersion—and a cogent criticism of the spiritually enervating effects of institutionalized racism. However, in the book, any political initiative or program of action that might bring about the desired unity exists only tenuously as an abstraction. (For example, at the end of the novel, a spiritually transfigured Avey merely *plans* to educate a new generation of Afro-Americans in the ways to redemption [254–56].) This attenuation of "the political" is partly a consequence of the economic status of Marshall's protagonist: as an upper-middle-class black, she, unlike most blacks, is privileged with an unusually high measure of security and self-determination. But, more important, this attenuation is a consequence of the conjuncture at which Marshall writes. *Praisesong* was written in the late seventies and/or early eighties when, compared to the years of the Civil Rights movement, Afro-Americans—the principal victims of Reagan's free-market economics—were hampered by political disorganization (see e.g., Davis *Prisoners* 224, 311). (Such disorganization was, and still is, evident in the disproportionately high levels of voter abstentionism and unemployment among blacks.) The point here is that one can read in this vision of mystical unity a displaced expression of the exigent need for the solidarity and political organization of blacks in the here and now.

Marshall's perception of a "confraternity" of all blacks or Steinbeck's belief in "one big soul ever'body's a part of" are vulnerable to the postmodern charge of totalization. First, there is the problematic assumption of a transcendent or panoptic vantage point from which to totalize. From where does one speak when one employs such totalizing concepts as "confraternity" and "one big soul"? Whence comes this privileged knowledge of universal human connectedness? On what basis does one assume that spirituality is definable or knowable in terms of such totalizing categories? Second, given the antitotalizing impulse of postmodernism, universalist appeals to an undifferentiated humankind appear suspect.[12] Under postmodernism's valorization of difference, its elevation of the particular, the Transcendental Subject of universal spiritual community must be replaced by a complex of specific subjectivities: gendered, racial, ethnic, classed, sexual, generational, national, religious, and so on. Third, the postmodern critique of totalization has given rise to a micropolitics, in the light of which ideas of mystical union seem far too abstract and devoid of practical content. After all, there is a characteristically postmodern preference for pursuing single issues and short-term goals (a localization of political struggle in response to the perception of a diffusion of power across a multiplicity of sites). Micropolitics has a pragmatic orientation toward the concrete, toward tangible results; its objectives are legitimized by micronarratives and it refuses to recognize "grand narratives" of *global* salvation— precisely the type of narrative in which the notion of universal spiritual community is deeply imbricated.

Membership of a universal spiritual community is not a primordial given but an imaginary identification produced by mystical discourses like the visionary moment. The sense of belonging to such a community no doubt helps redeem one from the desolating knowledge of the sheer contingency of one's being, from the dislocating and atomizing effects of capitalism (as in the pressures for an increasingly mobile workforce or consumerism's need of transmutable and unsettled identities). Yet, from a postmodern perspective, the idea of a universal spiritual community now appears untenable. The postulated subject of this community—disencumbered of worldly subject positions, unconstrained by power relations, transcending the limits of historicity and culture—lacks credibility. In short, postmodernism's focus on the disjunctive—where difference displaces unity, where dispersion displaces integration, where disparateness displaces commensurability, where the particular displaces totality—radically contests and weakens claims for the truth of universal forms of mystical union.

4

The Romantic Metaphysics of Don DeLillo

Don DeLillo has been widely hailed as an exemplar of postmodernist writing. Typically, this assessment rests on readings that focus on his accounts of the postmodern experience of living in a hyperreality.[1] But to postmodernize DeLillo is to risk losing sight of the (conspicuously unpostmodern) metaphysical impulse that animates his work. Indeed, the terms in which he identifies visionary experience in his fiction will be seen to align him so closely with a Romantic sensibility that they must radically qualify any reading of him as a postmodern writer.

The Primal Language of Vision

In Part II of *White Noise,* the Gladney family shelters at a local barracks from the toxic cloud of a chemical spill. As Jack Gladney observes his children sleeping, he recounts a visionary moment. It begins as follows:

> Steffie . . . muttered something in her sleep. It seemed important that I know what it was. In my current state, bearing the death impression of the Nyodene cloud, I was ready to search anywhere for signs and hints, intimations of odd comfort. . . . Moments later she spoke again . . . but a language not quite of this world. I struggled to understand. I was convinced she was saying something, fitting together units of stable meaning. I watched her face, waited. . . . She uttered two clearly audible words, familiar and elusive at the same time, words that seemed to have a ritual meaning, part of a verbal spell or ecstatic chant.
> *Toyota Celica.* (154–55)

Before I continue the quotation, consider the following issues. Up to this point, DeLillo has manipulated his readers' expectations: what we expect from Gladney's daughter, Steffie, is a profound, revelatory utterance. Instead, we are surprised by (what appears to be) a banality: "Toyota Celica." Here it looks as if DeLillo is mocking the traditional faith in visionary moments or, more precisely, ironically questioning the very possibility of such moments in a postmodern culture. After all, a prominent feature of that culture is the prodigious, media-powered expansion of marketing and public relations campaigns to the point where their catchwords and sound bites colonize not just the public sphere but also, it seems, the individual unconscious. Henceforth, even the most personal visionary experience appears to be constituted by the promotional discourses of a consumer society. However, the irony of this apparently postmodern account of a visionary moment proves to be short-lived as Gladney immediately recounts his response to Steffie's words:

> A long moment passed before I realized this was the name of an automobile. The truth only amazed me more. The utterance was beautiful and mysterious, gold-shot with looming wonder. It was like the name of an ancient power in the sky, tablet-carved in cuneiform. It made me feel that something hovered. But how could this be? A simple brand name, an ordinary car. How could these near-nonsense words, murmured in a child's restless sleep, make me sense a meaning, a presence? She was only repeating some TV voice. . . . Whatever its source, the utterance struck me with the impact of a moment of splendid transcendence. (155)

The tenor of this passage is not parodic; the reader is prompted by the analytical cast and searching tone of Gladney's narration to listen in earnest. Gladney's words are not to be dismissed as delusional, nor are they to be depreciated as those of "a modernist displaced in a postmodern world" (Wilcox 348). The passage is typical of DeLillo's tendency to seek out transcendent moments in our postmodern lives that hint at possibilities for cultural regeneration. Clearly, the principal point of the passage is not that "Toyota Celica" is the signifier of a commodity (and as such has only illusory significance as a visionary utterance), but that *as a name* it has a mystical resonance and potency: "It was like the name of an ancient power in the sky," a name that is felt to be "part of a verbal spell or ecstatic chant." For what is revealed to Gladney in this visionary moment is that names embody a formidable power. And this idea is itself the expansive theme, explored in its metaphysical implications, of *The Names,* the novel that immediately preceded *White Noise.* Indeed, when read in conjunction with *The Names,* the metaphysical issues of *White Noise* can be brought into sharper relief.

The Names addresses the question of the mystical power of names: secret names (210, 294), place names (102–103, 239–40), divine names (92, 272).[2] For DeLillo wants to remind us that names are often invested with a significance that exceeds their immediate, practical function. Names are enchanted: they enable insight and revelation. As one character explains: "'We approach nameforms warily. Such secret power. When the name is itself secret, the power and influence are magnified. A secret name is a way of escaping the world. It is an opening into the self'" (210).

Consider the remarkable ending of *The Names*—an extract from the manuscript of a novel by Tap, the narrator's (James Axton's) nine-year-old son, replete with misspellings. In Tap's novel, a boy, unable to participate in the speaking in tongues at a Pentecostal service, panics and flees the church: "Tongue tied! His fait was signed. He ran into the rainy distance, smaller and smaller. This was worse than a retched nightmare. It was the nightmare of real things, the fallen wonder of the world" (339). These lines conclude both Tap's novel and *The Names* itself. "The *fallen* wonder of the world" connotes the failure of language, in its (assumed) postlapsarian state, to invest the world with some order of deep and abiding meaning, to *illuminate* existence. More specifically, the language that has "fallen" is the language of name, the kind of pure nomenclature implied in Genesis where words stand in a necessary, rather than arbitrary, relationship to their referents.[3] The novel follows the lives of characters who seek to recover this utopian condition of language. For example, people calling themselves "abecedarians" (210) form a murder cult whose strategy is to match the initials of their victims' names to those of the place names where the murders occur—all in a (misguided) effort to restore a sense of the intrinsic or self-revealing significance of names. And note Axton's response to the misspellings in his son's manuscript:

> I found these mangled words exhilarating. He'd made them new again, made me see how they worked, what they really were. They were ancient things, secret, reshapable.
> . . . [T]he spoken poetry in those words. . . . His . . . misrenderings . . . seemed to contain curious perceptions about the words themselves, second and deeper meanings, original meanings. (313)

The novel suggests that the visionary power of language will only be restored when we "tap" into its primal or pristine forms, the forms that can regenerate perception, that can *reveal* human existence in significant ways. Hence the novel's inquiry into "original meanings," the concern with remembering "the prototype" (112–13); hence "[i]t was necessary to remember, to dream the pristine earth" (307). The "gift of tongues" is also understood as a primal and therefore visionary language: "talk as from the womb, as from the sweet soul before birth" (306)— and, as such, it is revered as "the whole language of the spirit" (338), the language by which "[n]ormal understanding is surpassed" (307). (And far from DeLillo keeping an ironic distance from such mystical views of glossolalia, he has endorsed them in interviews.[4]) Moreover, one can hardly miss the novel's overall insistence on the spoken word—especially on talk at the familiar, everyday, pre-abstract level of communication—as the purest expression of primal, visionary language:

> We talked awhile about her nephews and nieces, other family matters, commonplaces, a cousin taking trumpet lessons, a death in Winnipeg. . . . The subject of family makes conversation almost tactile. I think of hands, food, hoisted children. There's a close-up contact warmth in the names and images. Everydayness . . .
> This talk we were having about familiar things was itself ordinary and

familiar. It seemed to yield up the mystery that is part of such things, the
nameless way in which we sometimes feel our connections to the physical
world. *Being here....*Our senses are collecting at the primal edge. . . . I felt I
was in an early stage of teenage drunkenness, lightheaded, brilliantly happy
and stupid, knowing the real meaning of every word. (31–32)[5]

The affirmation of a primal, visionary level of language which, moreover,
finds its purest expression in "talk" (glossolalia, conversation), is vulnerable to
postmodern critique on the grounds that it is premised on a belief in original and
pure meanings. Such meanings are assumed to exist (as in some transcendent
realm) outside the space of intertextuality, or beyond the "logic of supplementarity" whereby, according to Derrida, "the origin . . . was never constituted
except reciprocally by a nonorigin" (*Grammatology* 61).

The idea that language has "fallen" or grown remote from some pure and
semantically rich primal state is characteristically (though not exclusively) Romantic, and most reminiscent of views held by, among others, Rousseau and Wordsworth. In his "Essay on the Origin of Languages" and *Confessions,* Rousseau
identified speech, as opposed to writing, as the natural condition of language
because it "owes its form to natural causes alone" ("Essay" 5). In the face of a
culture that conferred greater authority on writing than on speech, he affirmed the
priority of the latter on the grounds that "Languages are made to be spoken,
writing serves only as a supplement to speech" (qtd. in Derrida 144). While
writing "substitut[es] exactitude for expressiveness" ("Essay" 21), the bias of
speech is toward passionate and figurative expression that can "penetrate to the
very depths of the heart" (9). Indeed, "As man's first motives for speaking were of
the passions, his first expressions were tropes. . . . [Hence] [a]t first only poetry
was spoken; there was no hint of reasoning until much later" (12). Moreover, it
was "primitive," face-to-face speech—as opposed to the sophistications of writing,
and especially the tyranny made possible by the codification of laws—that, according to Rousseau's anthropology, once bound humans together naturally in an
organic, egalitarian community. And recall that in his "Preface" to the *Lyrical
Ballads,* Wordsworth deplored the "arbitrary and capricious habits of expression"
of poets who, following urbane conventions of writing, had lost touch with the
elemental language of rustics. The latter, by virtue of their "rural occupations"
(that is, their regular intercourse with nature) are "such men [who] hourly communicate with the best objects from which the best part of language is *originally*
derived" (emphasis added). Furthermore, this is a "far more philosophical language" than that used by poets (735). Of course, all this is not to suggest that
DeLillo would necessarily endorse Rousseau's or Wordsworth's specific claims. But
what all three share is that familiar Romantic myth of some primal, preabstract
level of language that is naturally endowed with greater insight, a pristine order of
meaning that enables unmediated understanding, community, and spiritual communion with the world around.

If we return to Jack Gladney's visionary moment, we should note that while "Toyota Celica" may be a brand name, Gladney perceives it as having an elemental, incantatory power that conveys, at a deeper level, another order of meaning. He invokes a range of terms in an effort to communicate this alternative meaning: "ritual," "spell," "ecstatic," "mysterious," "wonder," "ancient" (155). Similarly, for Murray Siskind, Gladney's friend and media theorist, the recurring jingle "'*Coke is it, Coke is it*'" evokes comparisons with "mantras." Siskind elaborates: "'The medium [that is, television] practically overflows with sacred formulas if we can remember how to respond innocently'" (51). DeLillo highlights the paradox that while so much language, in the media society, has degenerated into mere prattle and clichés, brand names not only flourish but convey a magic and mystical significance. Hence they are often chanted like incantations: "Toyota Corolla, Toyota Celica, Toyota Cressida" (155); "Tegrin, Denorex, Selsun Blue" (289); "Dacron, Orlon, Lycra Spandex" (52).

Earlier passages in *White Noise* derive their meaning from the same Romantic metaphysics of language as Gladney's "moment of splendid transcendence." First, consider Gladney's response to the crying of his baby, Wilder (and note, by the way, the typically Romantic impression of the mystique of desolate spaces, and the appeal to "the mingled reverence and wonder" of the Romantic sublime):

> He was crying out, saying nameless things in a way that touched me with its depth and richness. This was an ancient dirge. . . . I began to think he had disappeared inside this wailing noise and if I could join him in his lost and suspended place we might together perform some reckless wonder of intelligibility. . . .
> . . . Nearly seven straight hours of serious crying. It was as though he'd just returned from a period of wandering in some remote and holy place, in sand barrens or snowy ranges—a place where things are said, sights are seen, distances reached which we in our ordinary toil can only regard with the mingled reverence and wonder we hold in reserve for feats of the most sublime and difficult dimensions. (78–79)

And, for Siskind, "'Supermarkets this large and clean and modern are a revelation to me'"; after all, "'Everything is concealed in symbolism, hidden by veils of mystery and layers of cultural material. But it is psychic data, absolutely. . . . All the letters and numbers are here, . . . all the code words and ceremonial phrases'" (38, 37–38). Evidently, for DeLillo, language operates on two levels: a practical, denotative level, that is, a mode of language oriented toward business, information, and technology; and a "deeper," primal level that is the ground of visionary experience—the "second, deeper meanings, original meanings" that Axton finds in Tap's childishly misspelled words; the "ancient dirge" that Gladney hears in Wilder's wailing; the "language not quite of this world" that he hears in Steffie's sleep-talk; the "psychic data" that Siskind finds beneath white noise.

In communications theory, "white noise" describes a random mix of frequencies over a wide spectrum that renders signals unintelligible. DeLillo applies the metaphor of a circumambient white noise to suggest, on the one hand, the entropic state of postmodern culture where in general communications are degraded by triviality and irrelevance—the culture of "infotainment," factoids, and junk mail, where the commodity logic of late capitalism has extended to the point where cognition is mediated by its profane and quotidian forms. Yet, on the other hand, DeLillo suggests that within that incoherent mix of frequencies there is, as it were, a low wavelength that carries a flow of spiritually charged meaning. This flow of meaning is barely discernible, but, in the novel, it is figured in the recurring phrase "waves and radiation" (1, 38, 51, 104, 326)—an undercurrent of invisible forces or "nameless energies" (12) that have regenerative powers. And how do we "tune in" to this wavelength? Siskind says of his students, who feel alienated from the dreck of popular television, "'they have to learn to look as children again'" (50), that is to say, to perceive like Gladney's daughter, Steffie, or Axton's son, Tap, are said to perceive. In an interview, DeLillo has observed, "I think we feel, perhaps superstitiously, that children have a direct route to, have direct contact to the kind of natural truth that eludes us as adults" ("Outsider" 302). The boy protagonist of *Ratner's Star* (1976) is considered, by virtue of his minority, more likely than adults to gain access to the "primal dream" experience of "racial history," of "pure fable, myth, archetype": as one character tells him, "'you haven't had time to drift away from your psychic origins'" (264–65). And here it must be remarked that this faith in the insightfulness of childhood perception is a defining feature of (but, of course, not exclusive to) that current of Romantic writing that runs from Rousseau's *Émile* (1762), through the writings of Blake and Wordsworth, to De Quincey's *Suspiria de Profundis* (1845). For Coleridge, "To carry on the feelings of childhood into the powers of manhood; to combine the child's sense of wonder and novelty with the appearances which every day for perhaps forty years had rendered familiar . . . this is the character and privilege of genius" (49). And recall, especially, the familiar lines from Wordsworth's "Intimations of Immortality" that lament the (adult's) loss of the child's "visionary gleam," that "master-light of all our seeing"; that celebrate the child as a "Seer blest! / On whom those truths do rest, / Which we [adults] are toiling all our lives to find, / In darkness lost" (460–61). In *The Prelude,* Wordsworth also argued that adult visionary experience is derived from childhood consciousness, the "seed-time [of] my soul," a consciousness that persists into adulthood as a source of "creative sensibility," illuminating the world with its "auxiliar light" (1:301; 2:360, 368).

The Romantic notion of infant insight, of the child as gifted with an intuitive perception of truth, sets DeLillo's writing apart from postmodern trends. For, of all modes of fiction, it is postmodernism that is least hospitable to concepts like insight and intuition. Its metafictional and anti-metaphysical polemic has collapsed the "depth model" of the subject (implied by the concept of *inner seeing*) and audaciously substituted a model of subjectivity as the construct of chains of signifiers. In such fiction as Robert Coover's *Pricksongs & Descants,* Walter Abish's *In the Future Perfect,* and Donald Barthelme's *Snow White,* for example, we find subjectivity reconceived as the conflux of fragments of texts—mythical narratives, dictionaries and catalogues, media clichés and stereotypes.

The Sublime and the Transhistorical

In an interview, DeLillo has said of *White Noise* that "Perhaps the supermarket tabloids are . . . closest to the spirit of the book" ("I Never Set Out" 31). What one might expect from any critique of postmodern culture is a satirical assault on the tabloids as a debased and commodified form of communication. Yet the frequency with which DeLillo cites tabloid news stories—their accounts of UFOs, reincarnation, and supernatural occurrences (see, for example, *White Noise* 142–46)—suggests that there is more at issue than simply mocking their absurd, fabricated claims. For he recognizes our need for a "weekly dose of cult mysteries" (5), and that by means of tabloid discourse "we [keep] inventing hope" (147). In *White Noise,* the tabloids are seen to function as a concealed form of religious expression, where extraterrestrials are substituted for messiahs and freakish happenings for miracles. In short, on a wavelength of which we are virtually unconscious, the tabloids gratify our impulses toward the transcendental: "They ask profoundly important questions about death, the afterlife, God, worlds and space, yet they exist in an almost Pop Art atmosphere" ("I Never Set Out" 31).

White Noise abounds with extensive discussions about death and the afterlife (38, 99, 196–200, 282–92, etc.), a concern of the book that is surely symptomatic of a nostalgia for a mode of experience that lies *beyond* the stereotyping and banalizing powers of the media, a mode of experience not subject to simulation. In a culture marked by an implosive de-differentiation of the image and its referent, where "'Once you've seen the signs about the barn, it becomes impossible to see the barn'" (12), the nonfigurability of death seems like a guarantee of a domain of human experience that can transcend hyperreality.

In another visionary experience, Gladney has mystical insight into the force—a huge, floating cloud of toxic chemicals—that threatens his life:

> It was a terrible thing to see, so close, so low. . . . But it was also spectacular, part of the grandness of a sweeping event. . . . Our fear was accompanied by a sense of awe that bordered on the religious. It is surely possible to be awed by the thing that threatens your life, to see it as a cosmic force, so much larger than yourself, more powerful, created by elemental and willful rhythms. (127)

This "awed," "religious" perception of a powerful force, which seems in its immensity capable of overwhelming the onlooker, is characteristic of that order of experience explored by the Romantics under the term "the Sublime." The concept of the sublime has had a long and complex evolution since Longinus's famous treatise on the subject, and here it must suffice to note just one key statement that has served as a foundation for the notion of the Romantic sublime. In his *Philosophical Enquiry into the Origin of Our Ideas of the Sublime and the Beautiful* (1757), Edmund Burke advanced the following definition:

> Whatever is fitted in any sort to excite the ideas of pain, and danger, that is to say, whatever is in any sort terrible, or is conversant about terrible objects, or operates in a manner analogous to terror, is a source of the *sublime;* that is, it is productive of the strongest emotion which the mind is capable of feeling. (39)

Burke identified the *sources* of "terrifying" sublimity in such attributes as "power," "vastness," "infinity," and "magnificence," and among the effects of the *experience* of the sublime, he identified "terror," "awe," "reverence," and "admiration." It is remarkable that Gladney's experience of the sublime yields almost identical terms: "terrible," "grandness," "awed," "religious," "cosmic," "powerful." Moreover, such terms are familiar to us from descriptions of sublime experience in Romantic literature. For example, in *The Prelude,* in such accounts as his epiphanies at the Simplon Pass or during the ascent of Mount Snowdon (6:624–40; 14:28–62), Wordsworth frequently invokes impressions of the "awful," the "majestic," "infinity," and "transcendent power" to convey his sense of the terrifying grandeur of nature. In the violent, turbulent landscape of the Lepontine Alps, he perceived "Characters of the great Apocalypse, / The types and symbols of Eternity, / Of first, and last, and midst, and without end" (6:638–40). Wordsworth's invocation of "Apocalypse," like the sense in *White Noise* of a life-threatening "cosmic force," reveals a defining property of the experience of the sublime: the subject's anxious intimation of a dissolution of the self, of extinction, in the face of such overwhelming power. "[T]he emotion you feel," says Burke of such "prodigious" power, is that it might be "employed to the purposes of . . . destruction. That power derives all its sublimity from the terror with which it is generally accompanied" (65). And here it should be added that the experience is all the more disturbing because such immense power defies representation or rational comprehension (hence the recourse of Wordsworth, DeLillo, and others to hyperbole—"cosmic," "infinite," "eternal," and so on).[6]

The Romantic-metaphysical character of DeLillo's rendering of sublime experience is evident in the pivotal place he gives to the feeling of "awe." Not only is the term repeated in Gladney's description of his feelings toward the toxic cloud, but it is used three times, along with the kindred terms "dread" and "wonder," in a later account of that characteristically Romantic experience of the sublime, namely, gazing at a sunset:[7]

> The sky takes on content, feeling, an exalted narrative life. . . . There are turreted skies, light storms. . . . Certainly there is awe, it is all awe, it transcends previous categories of awe, but we don't know whether we are watching in wonder or dread. . . . (324)

Given the Romantics' valorization of "I-centered" experience (in respect of which, *The Prelude* stands as a preeminent example), the feeling of awe has received special attention in their literature. After all, that overwhelming feeling of spell-bound reverence would seem like cogent testimony to the innermost life of the psyche, an expression of what Wordsworth, in "Tintern Abbey" and *The Prelude,* called the "purer mind" (164; 2.314). However, that deep-rooted, plenitudinous I-centered subject of awe is a far cry from postmodern conceptions of the self as, typically, the tenuous construct of intersecting cultural codes. As noted earlier, this is the model of the self we find in the quintessentially postmodern fiction of Abish, Barthelme, and Coover, among others. This model accords with Roland Barthes's view of the "I" that "is already itself a plurality of other texts, of codes which are infinite. . . ." (*S/Z* 10). Evidently, DeLillo's awestruck subjects contradict the postmodern norm.[8] Finally, why create such subjects at all? Perhaps they may be regarded as an instance of DeLillo's endeavor to affirm the integrity and spiritual energy of the psyche in the face of (what the novel suggests is) late capitalism's disposition to disperse or thin out the self into so many consumer subject-positions (48, 50, 83–84). In short, we might say that sublimity is invoked to recuperate psychic wholeness.

Studies of *Libra,* which identify it as a postmodernist text, typically stress its rendering of Lee Harvey Oswald as the construct of media discourses and its focus on the loss of the (historical) referent and the constraints of textuality.[9] And yet for all its evident postmodern concerns, a current of thinking in the novel proves highly resistant to any postmodernizing account of it. Consider, for example, this observation by David Ferrie, one of the book's anti-Castro militants:

> "Think of two parallel lines. . . . One is the life of Lee H. Oswald. One is the conspiracy to kill the President. What bridges the space between them? What makes a connection inevitable? There is a third line. It comes out of dreams, visions, intuitions, prayers, out of the deepest levels of the self. It's not generated by cause and effect like the other two lines. It's a line that cuts across causality, cuts across time. It has no history that we can recognize or understand. But it forces a connection. It puts a man on the path of his destiny." (339)

Observations of this type abound in *Libra:* elsewhere we read of "patterns [that] emerge outside the bounds of cause and effect" (44); "secret symmetries" (78); "a world inside the world" (13, 47, 277); "A pattern outside experience. Something that *jerks* you out of the spin of history" (384). Clearly, repeated invocations of invisible, transhistorical forces that shape human affairs do not amount to a *postmodern* rejection of empiricist historiography. Rather, this is the stuff of metaphysics, not to say the occult. Indeed, in a discussion of *Libra,* published in *South Atlantic Quarterly,* DeLillo seriously speculates on supernatural interventions in human history:

> But Oswald's attempt on Kennedy was more complicated. I think it was based on elements outside politics and, *as someone in the novel says, outside history*—things like dreams and coincidences and even the movement or the configuration of the stars, which is one reason the book is called *Libra.* . . .
>   . . . When I hit upon this notion of coincidence and dream and intuition and the possible impact of astrology on the way men act, I thought that Libra, being Oswald's sign, would be the one title that summarized what's inside the book. ("Outsider" 289, 293–94, emphasis added.)

I also cite this interview as evidence that DeLillo is more likely to endorse his characters' beliefs in transcendent realities than to dismiss them as, in the words of one commentator, a "fantasy of secret knowledge, of a world beyond marginalization that would provide a center that would be immune to the play of signification" (Carmichael 209).

Libra appeals to the truth and sovereignty of "the deepest levels of the self," that is, the levels of "dreams, visions, intuitions" (339). Indeed, alongside those readings of the novel that point to its postmodern rendering of the subject without psychic density—"an effect of the codes out of which he is articulated" (Carmichael 206); "a contemporary *production*" (Lentricchia, "*Libra*" 441)—we must reckon with the book's insistent focus on "another level, . . . a deeper kind of truth" (260), on that which "[w]e know . . . on some deeper plane" (330), on that which "speaks to something deep inside [one]. . . . the life-insight" (28). Such appeals to insight or intuition are common in Romantic literature and conform with Romanticism's depth model of subjectivity. That model is premised on the belief that truth lies "furthest-in," that is, in the domain of the "heart" or "purer mind"; the belief that truth can only be accessed by the "inner faculties" (Wordsworth), by "inward sight" (Shelley), or, recalling the American Romantics, by "intuition." "[W]here," Emerson rhetorically inquired, "but in the intuitions which are vouchsafed us from within, shall we learn the Truth?" (*Collected Works* 182).[10] The comparisons may be schematic but still are close enough to indicate that the mindset of *Libra* is neither consistently nor unequivocally postmodern. No less emphatic than the book's evidence for a model of mind as an unstable "effect" of media codes is the evidence for a model of it as self-sufficient and self-authenticating, as an interior source of insight or vision.

What are the ideological implications of DeLillo's Romantic metaphysics? A common reading of Romanticism understands its introspective orientation in terms of a "politics of vision."[11] This is to say first, that Romantic introspection may be seen as an attempt to claim the "inner faculties" as an inviolable, sacrosanct space beyond the domain of industrialization and the expanding marketplace. Second, the persistent appeal to the visionary "faculty" of "insight" or "intuition" or "Imagination" supplied Wordsworth, Blake, and others with a vantage point from which to critique the utilitarian and positivist ethos of capitalist development. But the crucial component of the "politics of vision" is the concept of what M. H. Abrams has called "the redemptive imagination" (117–22). Abrams notes how Blake repeatedly asserts that the "'Imagination . . . is the Divine Body of the Lord Jesus'" and quotes from *The Prelude* to emphasize that Wordsworth also substituted Imagination for the Redeemer:

> Here must thou be, O Man!
> Strength to thyself; no Helper hast thou here;
>   . . .
> The prime and vital principle is thine
> In the recesses of thy nature, far
> From any reach of outward fellowship[.] (Qtd. in Abrams 120–21)

What needs to be added here is that this faith in the "redemptive imagination" is premised on an idealist assumption that personal salvation can be achieved primarily, if not exclusively, at the level of the individual psyche. Indeed, this focus on salvation as chiefly a private, spiritual affair tends to obscure or diminish the role of change at the institutional level of economic and political practice as a *precondition* for the regeneration of the subject.[12] And it is a similar "politics of vision" that informs DeLillo's writing and that invites the same conclusion. DeLillo's appeals to the visionary serve to affirm an autonomous realm of experience and to provide a standard by which to judge the spiritually atrophied culture of late capitalism. Thus against the impoverishments and distortions of communication in a culture colonized by factoids, sound bites, PR hype, and propaganda, DeLillo endeavors to preserve the credibility of visionary experience and, in particular, to validate the visionary moment as the sign of a redemptive order of meaning. He has remarked, "the novelist can try to leap across the barrier of fact, and the reader is willing to take that leap with him as long as there's a kind of redemptive truth waiting on the other side. . . ." ("Outsider" 294). Yet, as we have already seen, that "leap" is into the realm of the transhistorical, where "redemptive truth" is chiefly a spiritual, visionary matter. And it is in this respect that his fiction betrays a conservative tendency; his response to the adverse cultural effects of late capitalism reproduces a Romantic politics of vision, that is, it is a response that obscures, if not undervalues, the need for radical change at the level of the material infrastructure.

The fact that DeLillo writes so incisively of the textures of postmodern experience, of daily life in the midst of images, commodities, and conspiracies, does not make him a postmodern writer. His Romantic appeals to a primal language of vision, to the child's psyche as a medium of precious insight, and to the sublime contravene the antimetaphysical norms of postmodern theory. Moreover, while there is, to be sure, a significant strain of irony that runs through his fiction, it does not finally undercut his metaphysics. As Tom LeClair has noted in a discussion of *White Noise,* "DeLillo presses beyond the ironic, extracting from his initially satiric materials a sense of wonderment or mystery" (214). "Wonder" and "mystery," to say nothing of "extrasensory flashes" (*White Noise* 34), are frequently invoked in DeLillo's writing as signifiers of a mystical order of cognition, an affirmation that the near-global culture of late capitalism cannot exhaust the possibilities of human experience. But it is precisely this metaphysical cast of thinking that separates DeLillo's fiction from the thoroughgoing postmodernism of, say, Walter Abish or Robert Coover, and that should prompt us to qualify radically our tendency to read him as an exemplary postmodern writer.

5

Saul Bellow's Transfigurable Subjects

In this chapter, I want to switch tactics and move from a head-on critique of the visionary moment to probe one of its foundational assumptions, namely, the assumption of human transfigurability. The literary visionary moment rests on the premise of the human capacity for *transfiguration,* a term I invoke in its New Testament sense of a specifically *spiritual* transformation (e.g., Matthew 17:1–2, Mark 9:2–3).[1] The visionary moment usually signals the proximity, if not the occurrence, of a transfiguration. Yet the very notion of transfigurability is extraordinary. Implicit here is the belief in the possibility of a radical mutation of being whereby a redemptive spiritual self is born and, by virtue of its inherent power, displaces or annuls a debased worldly self. It is almost like being asked to believe in the literal truth of those redeeming metamorphoses of mortals recounted in myth or fairy tale.[2] Here I want to focus a postmodern reading on Saul Bellow's model of the transfigurable subject, both as it is revealed in his regular use of visionary moments and as it informs his fiction in general. The aim is to expose some theoretical problems that inhere in his conception of human transfigurability and that, by extension, inhere in the visionary moment itself.

Typically, Bellow's leading characters are haunted by the potential for their own transfiguration. Hence, Eugene Henderson, striving to "burst the spirit's sleep" (*HRK* 77, *passim*)[3], declares, "I believed I could change: I was willing to overcome my old self" (HRK 297; see also 236, 272, 276). His royal friend, Dhafu, maintains, "What Homo sapiens imagines, he may slowly convert himself to" (271). For Kirby Allbee, "'There's no limit to what I can be . . . . It makes sense to me that a man can be born again'" (*V* 185–86). Herzog exclaims: "*Each to change his life. To Change!* Thus I want you to see how I, Moses E. Herzog, am changing. I ask you to witness the miracle of his altered heart" (*H* 173; see also 57, 209). And one hears the same conviction voiced by many other protagonists in Bellow's fiction, including Tommy Wilhelm, Charlie Citrine, and Artur Sammler. However, Bellow's conception of the transfigurable subject raises a number of epistemological and political issues that in the light of postmodern theory appear highly problematic. I shall address these issues under three rubrics: (a) metaphysics of the heart; (b) paradigm of the conversion narrative; (c) politics of transfiguration.

Metaphysics of the Heart

> The more I retreat into myself . . . the more plainly do I read these
> words written in my soul: be just and you will be happy. . . . I do not
> derive these rules from the principles of higher philosophy, I find them
> in the depths of my heart written by nature in characters which nothing
> can efface. (Rousseau, *Émile* Book IV; qtd. in Derrida, *Grammatology*
> 17)

Given the compelling force and long history of the prejudice that truth lies
"furthest in," it must have been a short step from invoking the heart as a metonym
for inner being (e.g., I Peter 3:3–4) to its invocation as a repository of truth. The
idea that we should turn "inward" in search of truth, that truth is indelibly
inscribed in "the depths of the heart," acquired a powerful and popular institutional base when it became incorporated into the Puritan dogma. The doctrine of
preparationism had taught, in opposition to the predestinarianism of Reformed
Theology, that through an arduous process of spiritual cleansing, one could pre-
pare the "heart" for saving grace (though ultimately without guarantee of God's
mercy). The prestige of this doctrine reflected the transition from the authority of
revelation (i.e., the visually revealed truths recounted in the Old Testament, as in
Ezekiel or Daniel) to the authority of inner experience, in which the "heart"
becomes the medium for the perception of spiritual truth. In his study of the
Puritan idea of grace, Norman Pettit emphasizes this privileging of inner experience as a source of spiritual cognition:

> If men followed the workings of the Spirit in their hearts and looked to the
> inner self for signs of grace, perhaps this was the beginning of the Christian
> life. . . .
>   By preparation [the Puritan divines] meant a period of prolonged in-
> trospective meditation and self-analysis in the light of God's revealed
> Word. . . . From conviction of conscience, the soul moved through a series
> of interior stages, always centered on self-examination, which in turn were
> intended to arouse a longing desire for grace. (17)

By "metaphysics of the heart," then, I mean a model of cognition that
assumes that *transfigurative* truth is encountered "furthest in"; that this truth is
known, independently of inference and sense observation, through the "heart."
This (primarily) Christian metaphysics is deeply inscribed in Bellow's work.[4]
Hence for Sammler, it is the "inmost heart [that] knows" (MSP 286) and he refers
to "the deepest layers of the soul . . . where undiscovered knowledge is" (*MSP*70).
For Eugene Henderson, the spiritual quester who seeks to quell a "disturbance in
[his] heart" (*HRK*24; see also 18, 82), the trip to Africa is a metaphorical journey
into his own "interior" (331). Having "penetrate[d] beyond geography" (55), he

hears the "voice of inward communication" (252), "the silent speech of the world to which [his] most secret soul listened continually" (187). In the novel appropriately titled *Herzog,* the eponymous hero declares, "Let each man now examine his heart" (*H* 57) and, accordingly, he reflects on "the inner experience of the heart" (*H* 113).

In this metaphysics, the heart is understood as the medium of a nonrational and preintellectual mode of knowledge. Thus, in his capacity as an academic, Herzog fears he has "committed a sin of some kind against his own heart, while in pursuit of a grand synthesis" (215), a synthesis defined earlier as "the dream of intellect, the delusion of total *explanations*" (173, Bellow's emphasis). Indeed, the novel is largely organized around the trite and nebulous premise that the "Heart" and "Reason" are to be understood as competing modes of knowledge. (Much of the thinking behind *Mr. Sammler's Planet* [e.g., 7, 216] and *Humboldt's Gift* [e.g., 306, 364] is also premised on this stark dualism.) At the end of *Herzog,* the heart prevails, hence:

> And inside—something, something, happiness . . . 'Thou movest me'. . . . Something produces intensity, a holy feeling. . . . There are those who say this product of hearts is knowledge, 'Je sens mon coeur et je connais les hommes.' . . . [T]his intensity, doesn't it mean anything? . . . And he has it in his breast? But I have no arguments to make about it. 'Thou movest me.'
> (347)

These lines are remarkable for their emotive and emphatically nonrational appeal to the heart as a medium of spiritual knowledge. Aptly, Bellow quotes Rousseau (*Confessions* Book 1, 17; repeated *H* 135), Romanticism's principal adversary of classical rationalism, although the sentiments could have been penned by Pascal, for whom, famously, "le coeur a ses raisons que la raison ne connait pas" (Pascal 154).[5] Moreover, refusing the contaminating influence of reason to argue his case, Bellow falls back on poetic resonance and blunt insistence ("'Thou movest me'")—maneuvers also used in the concluding lines of *Mr. Sammler's Planet:* "The terms which, in his inmost heart, each man knows. As I know mine. As all know. For that is the truth of it—that we all know, God, that we know, that we know, we know, we know" (*MSP* 286; see also 239, *V* 184).

Some of the thinking behind this metaphysics can be found in Bellow's nonfictional statements. In an interview with Matthew Roudane, he has remarked: "In almost everything I write there appears a primordial person. He is not made by his education, nor by cultural or historical circumstances. He precedes culture and history. . . . This means that there is something invariable, ultimately unteachable, native to the soul" ("Interview" 276. See also "World" 6 and "Paris Review" 184). And in his foreword to Allan Bloom's *The Closing of the American Mind,* Bellow observes: "In the greatest confusion there is still an open channel to the soul . . . and it is our business to keep it open, to have access to the deepest part of ourselves—to that part of us which is conscious of a higher consciousness, by means of which we make final judgments and put everything together" ("Fore-word" 16).

One characteristic of Bellow's metaphysics of the heart that suggests itself to the postmodern reader is the extent to which it depends on a number of rhetorical strategies. Let us hastily recall Nietzsche's genealogical critique of the rhetorical foundations of all thinking: his recognition that arguments are sustained by figures and tropes and other techniques of persuasion. Hence, for example, his oft-quoted definition of truth as "a mobile marching army of metaphors, metonymics, anthropomorphisms" (Nietzsche 46–47). Indeed, the army metaphor seems calculated to remind us that rhetoric is always engaged in a battle for one "truth" over another; rhetoric is language deployed in the service of truth claims. Thus, while Bellow claims the insightfulness of the heart over that of reason (e.g., Citrine's demotion of "*ratio*" vis-à-vis "the listening soul that can hear the essence of things" [*HG* 306]), a number of rhetorical moves work to advance this claim. But whereas postmodern writers, like Pynchon or Barth, will often expose narrative dependence on rhetorical maneuvers, Bellow does not reflect on the rhetoricity of his own narratives; were he to do so, he would see how it is crucial to his effort to persuade a sceptical, rationalistic culture of the heart's "knowledge."

In Bellow's metaphysics of the heart, each rhetorical strategy works the same effect, that is, to suggest the purity and power of spiritual knowledge by disengaging it from the contaminating and corrosive forces of culture and history. The first strategy is to "interiorize" the knowledge, whereby it becomes knowledge experienced through the "inmost heart" (*MSP* 286), through "the deepest part of ourselves" ("Foreword" 16); knowledge that is "the silent speech of the world to which [Henderson's] most secret soul listened. . . . [Thus] within—within [he] heard" (*HRK* 187; see also 193). Here, the rhetorical effect is to suggest that if spiritual truth is located furthest in, then it will be safely insulated from the pollution of rationalistic "head-culture" (*HG* 349, "World" 6). However, we should remember that the depth in this context is purely metaphorical; there is no literal topography of the mind's knowledge. Rather, the metaphor encodes a preference for prerationalist thinking. Moreover, the contrived context of deep interiority conveniently places the postulated knowledge beyond empirical investigation and, therefore, enables the suggestion that an occult or supernatural force (the "heart") has gained access to it.

A second rhetorical strategy is to "prehistoricize" the knowledge; hence it is that which issues from the "primordial person" ("Interview" 276) or "primordial feelings" (*HG* 314) or "primitive prompter" ("Paris Review" 184); it "precedes culture and history."[6] This context guarantees the truth of this knowledge on the grounds that it is "invariable"; a pristine truth, unspoiled by and surviving the disruptive forces of change, especially the influence of faddish philosophies (a theme central to *Herzog;* see "Paris Review" 195). Here the rhetorical effect of Bellow's emphasis on primacy (the "primordial" and "primitive") is to appeal to the popular prejudice that accords an inviolable identity to that which exists at the point of (a putative) origin; a pure and immutable knowledge immune to the profanations and contingencies of history. And, as we shall see, his use of visionary moments serves this strategy very well since, by force of literary convention, the knowledge they convey will be read as transcending the temporal limits of understanding.

A third rhetorical strategy is to "immediatize" spiritual knowledge. That is to say, the knowledge is not derived from the processual means of induction, deduction, or argumentation; after all, such means would render it susceptible to error or ideological distortion. Rather, the knowledge is understood to be unmediated, hence, says Asa Leventhal, "the truth must be something we understand *at once,* without an introduction or explanation" (*V* 140, emphasis added); hence Charlie Citrine observes, "matters of the spirit are widely and *instantly* grasped" (*HG* 91, emphasis added). Of course, the visionary moment, with its instantaneous delivery of "higher" knowledge, is an especially expedient form of this strategy.

The rhetorical force of such strategies lies in their appeal to the dream of a kind of primal attunement: the instantaneous and noise-free reception of pristine truths through an innate and occult faculty; a "pure receptive contemplation," which Bellow defines as "listening to the essence of things" ("World" 8). In short, then, rhetoricity is deeply inscribed in the mystical discourse within which Bellow speaks. It serves as a powerful resource in his effort to validate a spiritual order of knowledge in the face of a culture ruled by "modern rationality and calculation" (*HG* 221), by "rationalistic practices" (*MSP* 206).

Bellow's account of the transfigurative truth of the heart is formulated in terms that occlude any explanation of the institutional and ideological processes involved in its construction and legitimation; his is a self-sufficient, self-evident, and self-validating truth. Thus Herzog insists, "I have no arguments to make about it" (*H* 347). That one, like Herzog, is simply "moved" by this truth is legitimation enough. Sammler says of the "spirit" (or heart), "it knows what it knows, and the knowledge cannot be gotten rid of" (*MSP* 215). For Henderson, there is no question about it: "truth is truth" (*HRK* 191). Moreover, this conception of truth is premised on the assumption of a monadic subject; that is to say, a subject whose "deepest" insights owe nothing to the dialogical interactions of his/her social existence. Bellow is proposing a type of truth that transcends the dynamics of worldly textuality: a species of truth unsullied or unconstrained by the ideologies, paradigm dependence, and historical contingencies that invariably characterize the production of knowledge. In short, the truth of the heart amounts to an impossibly transperspectival discourse or metalanguage. Finally, Bellow's conception of the (precultural, prediscursive, prerational) "truths" of the heart implies a phantom, entropy-free channel for their reception. That is to say, exactly *what* the "inmost heart knows" or exactly *what* we hear when we listen to the "voice of inward communication" escapes all the contexts and constraints of interpretation. Wondrously, this type of truth can be "read" in its own light; its meaning is never delimited by the socio-historical situation of the "reader."

Paradigm of the Conversion Narrative

"It's a Christian idea . . . . Change yourself . . . and be another man."
(Bellow, *The Victim* 185)

Narratives of human transfigurability are historically persistent and culturally pervasive. However, a principal claim here is that the Christian conversion narrative—arguably, the chief precursor of the literary visionary moment (see 32–33)—serves as Bellow's paradigm both for understanding, and validating his literary accounts of, transfigurability. I should add that to make this claim is *not* to suggest that Bellow has modeled the transfigurations of his characters under the immediate inspiration of Christian conversion narratives. Rather, it is a matter (as we shall see) of the pervasive intertextual pressure of such narratives on writing about spiritual change. When, for example, we recall that such conversion narratives as Thomas Merton's *The Seven Storey Mountain* (1948) and Billy Graham's *Peace with God* (1953) easily count among the best-sellers of their (and Bellow's) time; when we recall that "televangelist" broadcasts are received in tens of millions of American homes, we get a sense of the extraordinary diffusiveness of this paradigm of change. The point is that the Christian conversion—in its capacity as the paradigmatic and culturally privileged form of sudden and profound spiritual change—informs the everyday metaphysics of American popular culture.

  It needs to be said at once that the term "Christian conversion narrative" is in many respects an ahistorical generalization, for this type of narrative has, over the centuries, evolved in many divergent ways. For example, the preoccupation with sin and damnation that characterizes the seventeenth-century Puritan accounts of conversion is significantly muted in the narratives of nineteenth-century African-American women, for whom conversion is essentially a "sacralization of identity" (Connor 4). A typology of Christian conversion narratives would have to identify distinctions arising from the narrator's historical situatedness, his or her church denomination, gender, race, class, ethnicity, and region (see Brereton 10). Nevertheless, a popular stereotype of this narrative has come to serve the modern writer as its representative form. The key elements of this stereotype amount to a familiar formula: (a) the narrator suffers a prolonged and acute crisis from a sense of being "convicted" by his or her sinful state; (b) his or her surrender to God's will is achieved by a sudden conversion that either signifies redemption or at least points the way there; (c) backsliding may occur but confidence in God's grace finally prevails. In short, this stereotype represents the conversion experience as a success story, which chronicles the transition from sin to salvation. And we shall see how Bellow's model of the transfigurable subject amounts to a quasi-religious variant of this stereotype (with the proviso that the context of sin is replaced by that of eroded spirituality[7]).

If readers find the transfigurability of Bellow's protagonists convincing, it is in large part because this defining feature of his fiction is underwritten by the authority of the Christian conversion narrative. The validating power of the latter lies, in part, in the abiding canonical status of many of its texts (e.g. Augustine's *Confessions* and Bunyan's *Grace Abounding to the Chief of Sinners*). Suffice it here to list some classic and popular American conversion narratives, key excerpts from which are frequently anthologized for general education courses: Jonathan Edwards's "Personal Narrative" (c.1740); *The Narrative of Sojourner Truth* (1850); *Narrative of the Life of Frederick Douglass* (1845); Billy Graham's *How to Be Born Again* (1977). This validating power also lies in the conversion narrative's institutionalization, under Puritan theology, as a prestigious form of Christian discourse, and in its wide dissemination through literature, autobiography, and sermons.

The author of a conversion narrative, perceiving him- or herself to be purged of sin, will speak in the redemptive language of "the newborn soul" or "feel[ing] clean, fully clean, inside and out" (Brereton 21,54) or "born again." Indeed, accounts of conversion typically demand the narrative construction of a depraved self, which is conceived in diametrical opposition to the redeemed self in order, one suspects, to dramatize the epic scale of the regenerative experience. For example, prior to their conversions, John Bunyan characterized himself as "the chief of sinners," while Jonathan Edwards observed, "[I]f God should mark iniquity against me, I should appear the very worst of all mankind" ("Personal" 70). For many converts to Christianity, it is grace that redeems humankind from beasthood (cf. Pascal 66; Brereton 19, 130n.14).

Turning to Bellow, we find he employs the same strategy, which works to enhance the contrast between the pretransfigured and transfigured states of his characters. Thus, the profane, self-confessedly "too gross" (*HRK* 214) pig farmer, Eugene Henderson, is represented almost as a pig himself in his own "pig kingdom" (20, 33): "I kept going . . . in pigskin gloves and pigskin shoes, a pigskin wallet in my pocket, seething with lust and seething with trouble" (12; see also 21).[8] And the spiritually impoverished, cadaverous Artur Sammler is described as "Someone between the human and not-human states" (*MSP* 264). These are the debased, mythic identities from which Bellow's protagonists, like prospective converts who believe in their own capacity for spiritual transformation, seek redemption.[9]

Bellow's literary accounts of human transfigurability acquire still stronger validation from the Christian conversion narrative through his use of the convention of the visionary moment. Typically, conversion narrators will speak of "the blinding power of grace as a lightning flash," of "grace as an instantaneous illumination" (Pettit 6, 13). The redeeming insight or vision occurs, they say, "in an instant" or "suddenly." Hence, Saint Augustine recollects that, after reading a passage from Paul's Epistles, "*in an instant,* as I came to the end of the sentence, it was as though the light of confidence flooded into my heart" (Augustine 178). And recall Bunyan's account of how, in the midst of a game of cat, "a voice did *suddenly* dart from heaven into my soul" (section 22). Bellow's fiction abounds with similar instances of sudden redemptive insight or what I am calling transfigurative visionary moments. For example, there is Sammler's redemptive insight: "Then it *struck* him that what united everybody was a beatitude of presence" (*MSP* 263). Henderson, who recounts several visionary moments in his narrative (*HRK* 101, 187–88, 192–93, 283), observes that "truth comes in blows" (23, 67, 213; see also 244) and that "the sleep of the spirit" ends not with a gradual awakening but, instead, is "*burst*" (67, 77, *passim*). There is Joseph, the hero of *Dangling Man*, whose penultimate journal entry reads, "It was *suddenly* given to me to experience one of those consummating glimpses that come to all of us periodically" (*DM* 190; see also 46).[10]

It is noteworthy that Bellow's dependence on the convention of the visionary moment has gone unquestioned, not to say unremarked, by his commentators. At the very least, given its mystical notion of transfigurability and an embedded metaphysics of the heart, this convention stands in need of interrogation. This gap in Bellow criticism may itself be a symptom of the general acceptance of the visionary moment as a credible mode of cognition, thanks in large part to the validating force of the Christian conversion narrative.

It may be argued that it is with good reason that the Christian conversion narrative serves to validate the notion of transfigurability and belief in visionary moments; after all, religious conversion is a fact of life. But while conversions undeniably occur, can they be said to amount to transfiguration as it is understood here? Consider the following points.

First, empirical data indicate that the number of converts who backslide within a year or two of religious conversion exceeds 85 to 90 percent (Ullman 92–93; James 252–53). These findings suggest that this type of conversion generally constitutes but an inconclusive, tenuous change rather than a radical mutation of being.[11] Of course, there are (however few) long-term, if not lifelong, conversions, but whether they can be taken as proof of a pure transfiguration remains highly questionable, as the following points would suggest.

Second, sociological research points to a complex and intense group dynamics at work in the conversion experience. Typically, evangelizing and other conversionist groups institutionalize practices, which are often manipulative, to support the conversion (e.g., pressure to regularly attend church meetings or study groups). As Roger Straus puts it, "these practices keep evangelical reality real" for the convert (163). The conversion has to be strategically maintained by, as far as possible, isolating the convert from those outside the conversionist group. This level of intervention suggests that a sustainable conversion says more about the effectivity of ritual and administrative practices than the intrinsically transformative powers of a pure and redeeming spirituality. Moreover, in her examination of the role of "group process" in the conversion experience, Chana Ullman observes how the prospective convert tends "to interpret inexplicable arousal experiences in terms of the immediate context [i.e., the religious group] in which they occur" (91).

Third, recent studies informed by narratology sharply distinguish between the conversion narrative and the actual conversion experience, in ways that discredit the former as a reliable source of information (see Stromberg; C. Griffin). Virginia Brereton, for example, has revealed the significant extent to which the narration of conversion experiences is mediated by the "highly formulaic" conventions of popular literature. She observes that "conversion narratives themselves can hardly provide a full picture of the experience since ipso facto they all end happily—they are invariably success stories" (xiii).

Finally, while the convert will very likely explain his or her experience in terms of supernatural agency (e.g., the Grace of God), the explanation may be recoded in the more feasible terms of psychodynamics. In "A Religious Experience," Freud discussed the conversion experience as a regressive defense against Oedipal hostility by way of "complete submission to the will of God the [surrogate] Father" (246). In his analysis of conversion accounts given by evangelical Christians in interviews, Peter Stromberg has identified a highly ritualized language "performance" (14) (a complex interplay of "canonical" and "metaphorical" language) by means of which the convert redefines, and thus alleviates, deep-rooted psychic conflicts. It is a strategic use of discourse in the service of an "unacknowledged aim," that is, the ongoing effort to resolve psychodynamic tensions (98). Ullman compares prospective converts entering the group process to "hopeful psychotherapy patients" who often have a long history of "emotional distress" (94).

The conversion experience, therefore, may be evidence of human convertibility, but whether the latter may be taken as an instance of authentic and sustainable transfiguration, and whether it may be taken as evidence of the "Truth of the Heart," seems highly questionable. Furthermore, I would submit that *any* claim of spiritual self-transformation—and Bellow's transfigurative visionary moments clearly constitute such a claim—is, in its key respects, vulnerable to the same criticisms and radical qualifications as advanced here vis-à-vis the Christian conversion narrative. That is to say, any such claim must contend with the contradictory implications of backsliding, dependence on a support group, narrativity, and psychodynamics.

The Politics of Transfiguration

In general, visionary moments in Bellow's fiction do not signify a conclusive transfiguration; rather, they are more an intimation of the proximity or, at least, the possibility of redemption. Indeed, the very tentativeness of these transfigurations may be read as symptomatic of a model of human change that is politically defective. To elucidate this issue, first consider Jurgis Rudkus's conversion to socialism at the end of *The Jungle* (1906) and Mikey's conversion to communism at the end of *Jews Without Money* (1930). Both conversions are "slow," the gradual result of painful social experience and systematically acquired (political) education. They may be figured in quasi-religious language, insofar as they have the impact of a religious conversion (Sinclair 308, Gold 309) but, unlike the transfigurations in Bellow's fiction, which are only intimated or fleetingly felt, they are conclusive, solidly affirmed, and enduring. Sinclair and Gold need not rely on the convention of the (tenuously experienced) visionary moment because the transformations they describe can be sustained by the social and political circumstances of their characters. The point here is that Bellow's understanding of human transfigurability is not linked to historical conjunctures or any notion of social praxis. The road to redemption for his (monological) subjects is an intensely private, individualized one. To make this comparison is not to forget that as both (literary) naturalists and members of the Socialist/Communist Parties, Sinclair and Gold confidently assumed a knowable world of class relations and a teleological model of history—assumptions less readily shared in Bellow's time. Nevertheless, as the phenomenon of backsliding indicates, transfigurative changes that occur exclusively at the level of a private or "monadic" consciousness cannot be lasting and efficacious without a supporting infrastructure, without long-term changes at the institutional level of social and political relationships. This amounts to a significant limitation in Bellow's thinking about human change. (Yet, on a more sympathetic note, we might value Bellow's focus on human transfigurability as, in part, a redeeming counterstatement to what he sees as the pessimistic modernist obsession with "crisis, alienation, apocalypse and desperation" [*H* 324; see also *H* 81, "Paris Review" 195].)

Sinclair, Gold, and other "proletarian novelists," writing at conjunctures that enabled the Socialist and Communist Parties to flourish, were able to conceive of redemption as, first and foremost, a political matter. However, Bellow's recourse to the "Heart" or soul as a source of redemption may be seen as a sign of his own time's diminished sense of political agency. Irving Howe, Bellow's contemporary, has diagnosed this diminished sense of agency as a defining symptom of the post-1945 "mass society":

> By the mass society we mean a relatively comfortable, half-welfare and half-garrison society in which the population grows passive, indifferent, and atomized; in which traditional loyalties, ties, and associations become lax or dissolve entirely; in which coherent publics based on definite interests and opinions gradually fall apart; and in which man becomes a consumer, himself mass-produced like the products, diversions, and values that he absorbs. (196)

Bellow's oeuvre is distinguished by a sustained assault on "rational orthodoxy" (*HG* 363; see Pifer *passim*). Sammler laments that "Intellectual man [has] become an explaining creature" (*MSP* 7; see also 21). Citrine deplores the limitations of what qualifies as knowledge in a rationalist "head-culture" (*HG* 350; see also 227–28); indeed, *Humboldt's Gift* is preoccupied with the triumph of "*ratio*" over "intellectus" (306). Hostility to rationality leads Herzog not only to recoil from "abstract intellectual work" (*H* 272) but to welcome the condition of being "out of [one's] mind" (*H* 7; repeated 322; cf. HRK 235). In Bellow's view, "modern rationality and calculation" (*HG* 221) interdict spiritual forms of knowledge. He has written of a culture that "has developed a tedious sort of rationality by ruling that certain kinds of knowledge are illegitimate" ("World" 6); that "true knowledge is supposed to be a monopoly of the scientific worldview. But human beings have all sorts of knowledge" (*HG* 364). First, however, note that Bellow works with an undifferentiated concept of rationality,[12] which leads, if not quite to its wholesale rejection, then at least to its wholesale demotion. Second, note that for Bellow spiritual recuperation is an individualized and "inward" matter of attunement to the heart's "knowledge"; it is not a matter of collective action to effect a transformation of the institutions and discourses that produce and legitimate rationality in its spiritually damaging forms. And yet the problem *is* radically social; after all, systemic or functionalist rationality becomes hegemonic chiefly because it constructs the technocratic consciousness essential to a social formation organized under the imperative to maximize productivity. Moreover, rationality has acquired the authority of a master narrative (e.g., the assumption of the technocratic "solution" to social problems) that is all too often invoked to repress those modes of knowledge that fail to conform to its "scientific" criteria of truth. (Cf. Foucault: "What types of knowledge do you want to disqualify in the very instant of your demand: 'Is it a science'?" [*Power/Knowledge* 85].) The point here is that the precondition for a viable and more-than-intermittent spirituality is a *political* one of struggling against those practices that marginalize or repress "alternative" knowledges. (Of course, whether spirituality, as Bellow understands it, counts as a form of knowledge remains a moot point.) Yet Bellow's heart-centered model of transfigurability is impervious to the political dimension of the problem.

We can say that a Bellovian protagonist is transfigured when he or she recovers the "primordial" self, that is, the prerational "root simplicities of being" ("Foreword" 17). Transfiguration occurs because, Bellow assumes, the "primordial" self, disencumbered of intellectual abstractions, can occupy the present, the here-and-now. This, for Bellow, is the domain in which the spirit flourishes and may be roughly equated with the divinely blessed portion of the Creation into which the redeemed soul of the Christian convert enters. Thus, in *Seize the Day*, Dr. Tamkin tells Wilhelm,

> Nature only knows one thing, and that's the present. Present, present, eternal present, like a big, huge, giant wave—colossal, bright and beautiful, full of life and death, climbing into the sky, standing in the seas. You must go along with the actual, the Here-and-Now, the glory (89; see also 66, 90).

Sammler learns in a visionary moment that "what united everybody was a beatitude of presence. As if it were—yes—blessed are the present" (*MSP* 263; see also
84). Henderson declares, "'I've just got to stop Becoming. Jesus Christ, when am I
going to Be?'" (*HRK* 191). And Herzog concludes his tortured reflections with a
joyful affirmation: "I am pretty well satisfied to be, to be just as it is willed, and for
as long as I remain in occupancy" (*H* 347). Here we are to understand that he has
recovered his "primordial," preintellectual self, hence he can say, "If I am out of my
mind, it's all right with me" (7; repeated 322). Once again, we can see that for
Bellow, redemption is an individualized and ahistorical affair. Rather than engagement in a collective struggle to overturn or reconstitute those practices and re-
gimes of knowledge that are thought to impede redemptive spiritual growth, the
transfiguration of the subject is understood to depend on connecting with the
"primordial" self, which, moreover, lives in the "eternal present." This carpe diem
philosophy is of a piece with those Romantic and antirationalist tendencies in
literature that celebrate the experience of the immediate and the spontaneous.[13]
However, quite apart from raising the familiar postmodern objection that experience (other than that at the level of animal sentience) is discursively structured and
thus never available in some pristine, unmediated form, we must ask: just how
viable could a preintellectual or primordial consciousness possibly be as a basis for
redemption? But no answer is forthcoming; typically, Bellow's narratives terminate
just at the point of the protagonist's transfiguration.

Bellow's idea of transfiguration, his idea of what it means for a human being
to be redeemed, is so abstract on account of his ahistorical and universalist stance
that, inevitably, either at the point of transfiguration or with the promise of it, his
stories simply fade out. Perhaps this is what prompted John Updike to speak of
"the soft focus of Bellow's endings" (qtd. in T. Tanner 304). Recall, for example,
the hazy last lines of *Seize the Day*, where we learn that Wilhelm, weeping in a
funeral home, "sank deeper than sorrow . . . toward the consummation of his
heart's ultimate need" (*SD* 118). Or recall the ending of *Henderson the Rain King*,
where Henderson leaps for joy around a parked airplane in—of all symbolically
named places—Newfoundland (*HRK* 340–41). Thus, awkward questions about
what happens to Wilhelm, Henderson, and other transfigured characters *the next
day* are forestalled. If Bellow *were* to extend the narrative into the next day, he
would risk enmeshing his redeemed subjects in the local and temporal, risk
exposing them to the spiritually corrosive forces of history at street level. In short,
he must avoid the quotidian circumstances that challenge the viability of the
transfigured condition. And here, on a comparative note, it is worth remarking
that conversion is rarely a once-and-for-all phenomenon; relapses to the precon-
version state are very common. To remain a convert, one has to network regularly
with conversionist support groups to avoid "backsliding" (see Straus). However,
we must assume that Bellow's protagonists—many of whom are isolated or semi-
reclusive beings—are able to sustain *their* transfiguration by purely private, *intra-
psychic* means.

A postmodern account of Bellow's model of the transfigurable subject also reveals that he must conceive of it as, at least *potentially,* a unitary self rather than an aggregate of competing subject positions. It is as if we are invited to assume that multiple subject positions will melt away at the emergence of a transfigured core identity. (And here we might note that Bellow's depth model of "the Heart" conveniently substitutes for the Unconscious and, accordingly, exempts him from the notion of an eternally split subject.) Furthermore, we have to make the fanciful assumption that power relations, and in particular ideology, will no longer play a part in the constitution of subjectivity after transfiguration. Indeed, insofar as Bellow's novels often end at the very moment of transfiguration or on the verge of it, any questions concerning the operation of ideology or the survival of refractory subjectivities *after* transfiguration are occluded.

The very idea of human transfigurability depends on a larger, overarching discourse, a "metanarrative" (Lyotard 31–37), about the ultimate redeemability of humankind. As a metanarrative, this discourse does not recognize its own social "constructedness" and historical limits, thus to think within its parameters is to risk universalizing and homogenizing prescriptions for salvation. For example, when Artur Sammler speaks of "the terms which, in his inmost heart, each man knows" (*MSP* 286), we are reminded that Bellow's redeemable subject is implicitly conceived as a universal one. That is to say, the conditions for transfigurability, as they are seen to apply to Sammler and other white, bourgeois, Eurocentric, male characters, are assumed to apply to everyone else. Indeed, Bellow's model of the transfigurable subject is generalized to the point that it occludes attention to the multiplicity of subject types and historically variable conjunctures, both of which require the accommodation of alternative models of what may count as trans-figuration and the conditions under which it might be achieved.

The notion of transfigurability—a crucial component in our reading of the literary visionary moment—does not bear close scrutiny; it rests on a model of knowledge whose metaphysical implications are inadmissible to postmodern the-ory: the assumption of a "primordial" (i.e., prehistorical, precultural) order of knowledge; an order of knowledge whose locus is exclusively individual, which resides in the "inmost heart"; knowledge that can be apprehended in an unmedi-ated, instantaneous form; a knowledge whose truth is self-legitimizing; a knowl-edge impervious to ideology or power relations; a knowledge that is assumed to be universally and eternally valid. It is one thing to recognize that individuals have profound spiritual experiences, which they may call "visionary moments," and which may, indeed, reform their thinking and behavior in significant ways; it is quite another to explain those experiences in terms of the operation of some primal knowledge or Truth that, moreover, has the power to transfigure the subject. And as we have seen the metaphysical implications are compounded by a model of the knowing subject as a monological and universal being who, further-more, it is assumed, can be exempted—miraculously lifted free—from the forces and constraints of his or her social conjuncture.

6

Jack Kerouac's Rhetoric of Time

> Each society has its regime of truth, its 'general politics' of truth: that is, the types of discourse which it accepts and makes function as true. . . . [I]t's not a matter of a battle "on behalf" of the truth, but of a battle about the status of truth and the economic and political role it plays.
>
> —Foucault, *Power/Knowledge*

As a writer and self-proclaimed "solitary Catholic mystic" (qtd. in Sorrell 189), Kerouac readily incorporated visionary moments into his fiction. Indeed, his novels abound with occasions when a flash of insight brings spiritual enlightenment and intimations of redemption to a protagonist. Nevertheless, while such moments may be represented as sacred and unsullied by worldly powers, their *use* is far from innocent and disinterested. The proposition here is that Kerouac deploys a *rhetoric of time* to validate the truth claims he makes in the form of visionary moments.[1] Specifically, his moments—in their *formal* capacity as narrative constructions—encode temporal concepts (such as suddenness, momentariness, and timelessness) that he mobilizes to promote the truth of his visionary insights.[2] It is a mode of rhetoric engaged in the struggle for the status of a marginalized order of knowledge. This knowledge is valued for its (supposed) transcendence and redemptive potential while, at the same time, being disqualified by a technocratic regime of truth in the service of commodity production.

Rhetoric of Instantaneousness

Consider the following visionary moments, as recounted by Kerouac, alias Ray Smith, in *The Dharma Bums:*

> [*I*]*nstantly* the tender bliss of enlightenment was like milk in my eyelids and I was warm. And I realized that this was the truth Rosie [a suicide] knew now, and all the dead, . . . the truth that is realizable in a dead man's bones and is beyond the Tree of Buddha as well as the Cross of Jesus. Believe that the world is an ethereal flower, and ye live. I knew this! (*DB* 137)

> But then *suddenly* under the tree at night, I had the astonishing idea: "Everything is empty but awake! Things are empty in time and space and mind." (*DB* 144)[3]

I have stressed Kerouac's use of the words *instantly* and *suddenly,* for implicit in these and other accounts of visionary moments is the common assumption that the *instantaneous acquisition* of knowledge is a hallmark of its transcendence and purity. Thus, if delivery of the knowledge had been negotiated or prearranged, or if its production had followed from arduous, intellectual struggle, then that knowledge would seem to have been profaned by the mediation of mundane processes.

The popular belief that instantaneously acquired knowledge is likely to be of a transcendent and immaculate kind appears largely to be derived from those prestigious discourses that are premised on the idea of a nonmaterial (or phantom) channel of communication. For example, Christian conversion narratives typically claim that God speaks directly to the soul and that divine truth, as a rule, reveals itself suddenly. Thus, in *The Narrative of Sojourner Truth, a Northern Slave* (1850), the author recalls how "God revealed himself to her, with all the suddenness of a flash of lightning, showing her, 'in the twinkling of an eye, that he was all over' . . . and that there was no place where God was not" (qtd. in Connor 80). And in *The Healing Gifts of the Spirit* (1966), Agnes Sanford writes, "The spirit of God entered in a way so defying understanding that I never tried to explain it. Nor could I explain it now. I can only say that for a split second I lived consciously and awarely in the bliss of eternity" (qtd. in Brereton 70). "A Divine and Supernatural Light Immediately Imparted to the Soul by the Spirit of God" was the title of a sermon by Jonathan Edwards (102), who famously recounted his own conversion in his "Personal Narrative." In these examples, the worldly channels of understanding, namely reason and the senses, are bypassed so that a "higher" knowledge may be directly received and its significance immediately grasped.[4] On the other hand, in his discussion of "phonocentrism," Derrida implicitly contests this assumption of a nonmaterial channel for the direct, unmediated communication of truth. In what is by now a familiar argument, he maintains that this assumption is ingrained in philosophical discourse from Plato to Rousseau and beyond. It takes the form of a privileging of speech in tandem with a debasement of writing on the grounds that "the voice, producer of *the first symbols,* has a relationship of essential and *immediate proximity* with the mind," while material inscriptions are mediated through and through insofar as they are "on the side of culture, technique, and artifice" (Derrida, *Grammatology* 11, 15, second emphasis added). In other words, the age-old prejudice is that the "natural" living voice gives instantaneous expression to the primal and self-authorizing "truths" of the soul (as if those truths, in their passage from the soul to the voice, required no translation or transcription), while "artificial" writing is purely derivative, "a fall into the exteriority of meaning" (13). Thus, we are seduced by the "simulated immediacy" of voice (15).

Other categories of discourse that reinforce the belief that instantaneously acquired knowledge is likely to be of a transcendent nature are those Romantic and high-modernist epistemologies that are premised on the concept of the illuminating moment. *The Prelude* is usually read as a meditation on those revelatory instants that Wordsworth calls "spots of time": moments that bring "profoundest knowledge" and are "scattered everywhere" (12:208, 221, 224); moments that "with a flash" reveal "[t]he invisible world" and are understood as "gleams / Of soul-illumination" (6:601–602, 513–14). And for Emerson, "Our faith comes in moments . . . Yet there is a depth in those brief moments which constrains us to ascribe more reality to them than to all other experiences" (Emerson 261). In respect of modernist discourse, it is sufficient to note the typicality of such pivotal expressions as Wallace Stevens's "moments of awakening," (qtd. in Beja 46), Woolf's "exquisite moments" (*Mrs Dalloway* 34), Pound's "'magic moment' or moment of metamorphosis" defined as a "bust thru from quotidien into 'divine or permanent world'" (qtd. in Langbaum 38). The list goes on: Joyce, Faulkner, Eliot, Wolfe. It looks as if, given the global disruptions and dislocations of accelerated and self-sustaining economic development, the high modernists sought redemptive knowledge in a zone they imagined could not be penetrated by the forces of modernization, that is, the quasi-mythical timescape of the elusive and evanescent moment.

In the mid-fifties, while under the influence of Gary Snyder, Kerouac embraced Buddhist thought. And while, to be sure, biographers and critics cannot agree on the strength of his commitment to Buddhism,[5] the doctrine of satori has a crucial place in his writing, notably in *The Dharma Bums, Desolation Angels,* and *The Scripture of the Golden Eternity.* Here I want to emphasize that *satori* signifies not just enlightenment; rather, the term has a temporal inflection that connotes a *sudden burst* of enlightenment. As Ninian Smart observes, an "important feature of Ch'an [Zen] Buddhism . . . which gives it its own characteristic flavour is the notion that illumination is sudden or instantaneous. This awakening (*tun wu*—known better through its Japanese name of *satori*) is likened to the way a mirror instantaneously reflects whatever appears in front of it. It is like a sudden conversion" (240). Consider the following parable in *The Dharma Bums* when Kerouac (alias Ray Smith) goes mountain climbing with Gary Snyder (alias Japhy Ryder):

> Then *suddenly* everything was just like jazz: *it happened in one insane second or so:* I looked up and saw Japhy running down the mountain in huge twenty-foot leaps . . . and *in that flash* I realized it's impossible to fall off mountains. . . .
> . . . "Ah Japhy you taught me the final lesson of them all, you can't fall off a mountain."
> "And that's what they mean by the saying, When you get to the top of a mountain keep climbing, Smith."

> . . . "[W]hen I looked up and saw you running down that mountain I *suddenly* understood everything."
>
> "Ah a little *satori* for Smith today." (*DB* 85–86, emphases added)[6]

The temporal coordinates of this visionary moment, like others, work to imply an alternative time zone for the truth of the moment's propositional content. Constructions such as "in one insane second" and "in that flash" signify the suspension of mundane clock time and thus suggest the transcendent nature of the insight.

To affirm the value of the knowledge conveyed by the visionary moment, Kerouac deploys his rhetoric in the face of a technocratic regime of truth that threatens to devalue that knowledge. This point can be understood in the context of the emergence of technology and science as governing ideologies, an issue examined by Jürgen Habermas. Developing under the fierce logic of its inherent tendency to self-expansion, capitalism has institutionalized and eulogized the scientific and technical forces on which, first and foremost, its model of economic growth depends. This has led to the gradual delegitimization of the "traditional" ideologies, that is to say, "the older mythic, religious, and metaphysical worldviews" (96). In the era of "advanced" (or late) capitalism, "technocratic consciousness" has become the ruling ideology. Accordingly, "practical" questions (i.e., ethical and existential questions that focus on the welfare of the social "lifeworld" and that had traditionally been addressed by the older ideologies) have been eliminated by the "technical" concern with "system maintenance" (112). Under the rule of technocratic criteria, we can say that Kerouac's visionary moments are automatically disqualified because they are a "traditional" form of knowledge. Kerouac, therefore, must draw on the resources of rhetoric to assert and promote his visionary knowledge.

Given the increasing professionalization and specialization of knowledge, where its validation is the privilege and preserve of academics and technicians, one can also appreciate Kerouac's foregrounding of the instantaneousness of visionary insights as a dramatic attempt to claim an order of knowledge for the nonprofessional. That is to say, insofar as the knowledge in question is conspicuously produced outside of the academy or laboratory, insofar as it is neither researched nor argued, this knowledge, if not exactly of demotic status, is nevertheless beyond the province of experts and therefore accessible to the (appropriately attuned) ordinary American. And here we should recall Kerouac's contempt for intellectuals. In *On the Road,* he complains of "tedious intellectualness" and berates his "New York friends" for "giving their tired bookish or political or psychoanalytic reasons" (OR 10). Moreover, as if to signal his disdain for the academic, the erudite, the technical, he writes in a distinctively colloquial register[7] and gladly describes himself as "a man of the earth" (97), a man who "sees with innocent road-eyes" (108).

Instantaneousness implies that the knowledge conveyed through the visionary moment is *not* the product of alienated intellectual labor; it implies that the alienating effects of such labor have been bypassed. At issue here is the systematic incorporation of intellectual labor into the process of capitalist production. This occurred conspicuously in the two decades after 1945, that is, precisely the period in which Kerouac was actively writing. In a discussion of the acceleration of technological innovation that largely focuses on these decades, Ernest Mandel begins by quoting from the *Grundrisse,* where Marx had anticipated a time when " 'all the sciences have been pressed into the service of capital' " (Mandel 249). He then cites statistics that confirm this prediction in the context of the development of organized corporate research in the United States. For example, in 1914, there were less than 100 industrial research laboratories but by 1920 (i.e., around the time Kerouac was born), the number had increased to 220. By 1960, there were 5,400 "company-dominated laboratories." In the meantime, the number of scientists engaged in research increased more than fourfold from 87,000 in 1941 to 387,000 in 1961 (252). Within Kerouac's own lifetime (1922–1969), expenditure on research and development in the United States rose from under $100 million in 1928 to $20.7 billion in 1970 (257). This exponential growth in R&D vastly increased the demand for "highly skilled intellectual labour-power [hence] the 'university explosion'" (259). Thus, the number of students of the 20 to 24 age group enrolled in U.S. higher education more than doubled in just fifteen years from 20 percent (2,297,000) in 1950 to 41 percent (5,570,000) in 1965 (260). At the same time, technocratic reforms of the education system served to "subordinate the production of intellectual skills to the needs of the valorization of capital" (261). These and similar observations lead Mandel to argue:

> The more higher education becomes a qualification for specific labour processes, the more intellectual labour becomes proletarianized, in other words transformed into a commodity, and the more the commodity of intellectual labour-power is sold on a specific "labour market for intellectual and scientific qualifications" . . . The more fragmented intellectual qualification and labour become, the more alienating university education merges into alienated intellectual labour subsumed under capital, within the total production process of late capitalism. (263)

Of course, this is not to suggest that Kerouac would have made sense of the social condition of knowledge in the terms of an economist like Mandel. Nevertheless, the cogency of the visionary moment lies in experiencing its knowledge as if it were transcendent and immaculate, but whether consciously understood or not, these putative qualities acquire meaning chiefly vis-à-vis the pervasive condition of a *worldly* knowledge that is tainted by its alienated relation to the production process.

We can say, then, that the temporal characteristics of Kerouac's visionary moments (i.e., the suddenness of their occurrence, the momentariness of their duration) inherit much of their rhetorical force from the authority of discourses that are based on the assumption that knowledge instantaneously acquired is of a transcendent type. The rhetoric of instantaneousness constructs a safe, hermetic time zone by virtue of which Kerouac's "insights"—e.g., "Believe that the world is an ethereal flower, and ye live" or "everything is empty but awake!"—are assumed to be preserved from ideological contamination and free of the vagaries and contingencies of worldly signification. (Moreover, given that these insights range anywhere between the nebulous and the vacuous, they may, at least, persuade some readers with the aid of rhetorical manipulation.) In short, Kerouac deploys a rhetoric of instantaneousness whereby the reader is prompted to see in the un-mediated reception of the visionary insight a condition of its untainted and transcendent Truth. Thus, the rhetoric resonates a truth effect.

Rhetoric of Eternity

The rhetoric of the visionary moment often promotes the transhistorical status of the revealed truth by representing the moment as the point where eternity inter-sects with clock time. That eternity might be compressed within a moment is an idea especially familiar to Kerouac's Romantic predecessors, notably Blake (*Milton* 28:62–63, 29:1–3) and De Quincey (104). The idea also finds expression in Kerouac's visionary moments:

> *And for just a moment* I had reached the point of ecstasy that I always wanted to reach, which was the complete step across chronological time into time-less shadows. . . . I realized that I had died and been reborn numberless times. . . . (*OR* 173, emphasis added)

> I went outside and *suddenly* my shadow was ringed by the rainbow as I walked on the hilltop, a lovely-haloed mystery making me want to pray: "O Ray, the career of your life is like a raindrop in the illimitable ocean which is eternal awakenerhood."
> . . . The vision of the freedom of eternity was mine forever. (*DB* 241, 243, emphasis added)

Invocations of the eternal not only seek to validate the "truth" of the visionary moment by suggesting its timelessness or immortality, but also seek to validate it in their antagonistic relation to the limited horizons of a culture of short-termism. Surveying the fifties and sixties (Kerouac's decades as an active writer), Mandel observes that "the reduction of the turnover-time of fixed capital is one of the fundamental characteristics of late capitalism" (223). And from here we may infer that in a timescape characterized by ever-diminishing cycles of investment, by the increasing rate of product obsolescence, and by the ongoing reduction in the service life of capital equipment (225–27), temporal experience is biased toward the short term: the quick return, the instant of fashion, the accelerated rate of innovation, instant consumability, the production schedule, the deadline, time-and-motion economies. Accordingly, in the *hegemonic* context of this limited temporal experience (beyond which ideas of an extended temporal horizon begin to look extravagant, deviant, or suspect), a social dissident like Kerouac comes to assign value to appeals to knowing the world sub specie aeternitatis.

However, the use of invocations of the eternal to endorse the "truths" intuited in visionary moments prompts several postmodern rejoinders. First, in recognition of a nontotalizing model of history as a complex of discontinuous and disparate processes (see Foucault, *Archaeology* 14), in recognition of "histories" as the partisan constructs of competing historiographies, we should observe the local and temporal limits of truth claims and their factional nature. Thus, I have suggested that Kerouac's visions are best understood as if they were in rival dialogue with a conjuncture defined by technocratic values and economic short-termism. Second, truth finds its legitimation not in some transhistorical metalanguage but in historically specific language games that reduce it to the status of a paradigm or temporal narrative (cf. Lyotard 1984). In this respect, I have argued that Kerouac's visions find a measure of validation in such historically circumscribed forms as the discourse of conversion, the Romantic/high-modernist epistemology of the illuminating moment, and the Zen doctrine of satori. Third, Kerouac may claim eternal truth for his visionary moments only if the "infinite play" of the signs that constitute the meaning of those moments is frozen (cf. Derrida, *Writing* 278–93). This would amount (impossibly) to the once-and-for-all end to the ever-shifting, intertextual relations between signs that continually invest words with new meanings—meanings that must overflow *any* formulation of a permanent order of knowledge.

Finally, one might well hypothesize that it is the often incommunicable nature of the "knowledge" gained in mystical moments (in William James's pithy terms, "noetic" but "ineffable" experience [371]) that sways the individual toward the hyperbolic language of "the eternal," "the infinite," "the cosmic." In particular, given the frequency with which "eternity" (or "the eternal") is invoked in mystical narratives, at least from Augustine and the Neoplatonists onward,[8] the term seems to have acquired the power of a cue word, one almost ritually employed to persuade the reader that the reported mystical experience has gained access to the ultimate truth. "Eternity," "the eternal," and cognate terms ("everlasting," "forever," "timeless") are clearly among the most frequently used words in Kerouac's spiritual lexicon. Moreover, the (largely self-created) legend of Kerouac as a mystic can only add to the rhetorical force of his invocations of eternity.

Rhetoric of Spontaneity

One need look no further than the titles of monographs, articles, and chapters to see that "spontaneity" is the most salient concept in Kerouac criticism.[9] Invariably the term is understood in the context of Kerouac's compositional technique: the poetics of an "unrevised" automatic writing that flatly contravenes the protocols of "crafted" literature. (Whether or not his writing is genuinely spontaneous is a question that has no bearing on this discussion. My own impression is, on the whole, that his sentences have enough coherence to suggest partially revised speed writing rather than "writing whatever comes into your head as it comes" [Kerouac, *GBO* 74].[10]) However, spontaneity is also a defining property of Kerouac's vision-ary moments where as *temporal concept* it acquires a subversive charge of meaning vis-à-vis the managed and hegemonic time of capitalist production. The claim here is that his recurrent invocations of spontaneous experience can be read as a strategy that aims to persuade the reader of the value of visionary knowledge by locating it in a countertime, that is, a time zone antithetical to the organized (technocratic) time of production.

I am concerned, then, with spontaneity not as method but as rhetoric. This difference can be illustrated with reference to the role that jazz plays in Kerouac's writing. It is a commonplace in Kerouac criticism that jazz improvisation served as a paradigm for his approach to composition (see Tytell, Hipkiss, Weinreich). In his epigrammatic essays on writing, Kerouac frequently invokes jazz as the central analogy for his prose experiments. Thus, in "Essentials of Spontaneous Prose," under the rubric "Procedure," he writes: "Time being of the essence in the purity of speech, sketching language is undisturbed flow from the mind of personal secret idea-words, *blowing* (as per jazz musician) on subject of image" (*GBO* 69). In jazzspeak, "blowing" means improvisation, that is, spontaneous (unpremeditated, impulsive) performance. Through blowing, the musician is said to achieve a trancelike ecstatic state, the very state Kerouac pursued through his writing (*GBO* 72–73: #6, #7, #12, #28, #30). His "spontaneous bop prosody" (Ginsberg) is a form of literary blowing in which the writer (ideally) composes on impulse, uninhibited by grammar and syntax, rejecting the procedures of "craft" and "revision" (72).[11] But what needs to be emphasized is that, in Kerouac's writing, almost every reference to jazz as spontaneous performance is made in tandem with a reference to time. When, for example, in *On the Road*, Sal Paradise (Kerouac) and Dean Moriarty (Neal Cassady) listen to the live jazz of Slim Gaillard, Sal notes his spontaneity: "He does and says anything that comes into his head," and Dean adds, "Slim knows time, he knows time" (176; see also *VC* 296; *GBO* 69–70; *OR* 206, 208; *DB* 85–86). Of particular relevance here is Sal's report of a jazz perfor-mance where blowing induces a mystical state in both musician and audience. In fact, he narrates a jazz-inspired visionary moment—and note the attention to the temporal elements of the experience:

"Now, man, that alto man last night had IT—he held it once he found it. . . ." I wanted to know what "IT" meant. "Ah well"—Dean laughed— "now you're asking me impon-de-rables—ahem! . . . Up to [the alto man] to put down what's on everybody's mind. He starts the first chorus, then lines up his ideas, people, yeah, yeah, but get it, and then he rises to his fate and has to blow equal to it. All of a sudden somewhere in the middle of the chorus he *gets it*—everybody looks up and knows; they listen; he picks it up and carries. Time stops. He's filling empty space with the substance of our lives, confessions of his bellybottom strain, remembrance of ideas, rehashes of old blowing. He has to blow across bridges and come back and do it with such infinite feeling soul-exploratory for the tune of the moment that everybody knows it's not the tune that counts but IT—" Dean could go no further; he was sweating telling about it. (*OR* 206)

The car was swaying as Dean and I both swayed to the rhythm and the IT of our final excited joy in talking and living to the blank tranced end of all innumerable riotous angelic particulars that had been lurking in our souls all our lives. . . .

    . . . "[W]e know what IT is and we know TIME and we know that everything is really FINE." (*OR* 208)

Clearly, in conjunction with, inter alia, "infinite feeling soul-exploratory" and "angelic particulars," "IT" connotes, in Robert Hipkiss's words, "a mystical kind of knowing" (35). But to persuade the reader of the spiritual value of the knowledge gained, to affirm the truth of this visionary moment, Kerouac has to do more than exploit the method of "spontaneous prose." Accordingly, he also makes a rhetorical appeal to the timescape of the visionary knowledge. He conspicuously locates the knowledge in a (nonworldly) countertime: "All of a sudden," "Time stops," "we know TIME," and so on. (And here we might recall how the black narrator, in Ellison's *Invisible Man*, alienated from the white world, describes inhabiting an alternative—nonwhite?—temporality when listening to Louis Armstrong's music.[12]) But why countertime? The spontaneity of the visionary moment—the way the moment bursts upon the subject, unwilled, unpremeditated—suggests an interruption of normal temporal experience. Thus the reader is prompted to feel that the knowledge gained has its origin outside of standard, chronological time, in some autonomous time zone. And this other time of the visionary knowledge seems to serve as a guarantee of its truth and value when the dominant time code—i.e., the managed time of capitalist production—is perceived as antipathetic to visionary experience.

    The organization of time into the schedules and routines of the workplace is, of course, driven by the need to appropriate, as efficiently and intensively as possible, the time of workers. Consider a manual published by The Systems and

Procedures Association of America in 1960 (i.e., at the very time Kerouac is writing). The manual, entitled *A Guide to Office Clerical Time Standards,* comprised data contributed by, among others, the General Electric Company and the General Tire and Rubber Company. The data took the form of analyses of the unit time values of the elemental motions of office tasks. The following chart is, in its obsessively detailed tabulation, typical of many others found in the manual:

Punch time clock	*Minutes*
Identify card	.0156
Get [card] from rack	.0246
Insert in clock	.0222
Remove from clock	.0138
Identify position [in rack]	.0126
[Return] card to rack	.0270
Total:	.1158

(qtd. in Braverman 323; see also 321–22, 324)

Evidently, when time is perceived as an exploitable resource, time management becomes a crucial aspect of the production process. Moreover, insofar as more and more time is absorbed by the constant imperative to raise the level of productivity, the time spent outside of work increasingly takes *its* meaning in opposition to work time (e.g., "leisure time" or "quality time"). And this common experience of rotating our lives between work time and nonwork time supplies the context for these prescient remarks by Gary Snyder, alias Japhy Ryder, speaking in the late fifties:

> "[S]ee the whole thing is a world full of rucksack wanderers, *Dharma Bums* refusing to subscribe to the general demand that they consume production and therefore have to work for the privilege of consuming, all that crap they didn't really want anyway such as refrigerators, TV sets, cars . . . all of them imprisoned in a system of work, produce, consume, work, produce, consume, I see a vision of a great rucksack revolution thousands or even millions of young Americans wandering around with rucksacks, going up to mountains to pray . . . all of 'em Zen Lunatics who go about writing poems that happen to appear in their heads for no reason . . . and also by strange unexpected acts keep giving visions of eternal freedom to everybody." (*DB* 97–98, emphases added)

The passage is evidently planned around a binary opposition: on the one hand, we are "imprisoned in a system" or time cycle of "work, produce, consume, work, produce, consume"; on the other hand, we have those impromptu writings, "unexpected acts," and unscheduled movements ("wandering") that embody the countertime of the spontaneous and sporadic: the "Zen Lunatic" time that cannot be assimilated to, or exploited by, the "system."

In general, the spontaneous occurrence of Kerouac's visionary moments—which is to say, they happen suddenly and at irregular intervals—highlights the unexpected and unpremeditated expression of the visionary insight. In this respect, the visionary moments resemble the spontaneous "Zen Lunatic" poems "that happen to appear in . . . heads for no reason." Here, then, is a form of experience whose timing cannot be managed. Where the purpose of time management is to regulate production by the clock and increase the efficiency with which labor is exploited, that which occurs outside the zone of manageable time acquires value by virtue of belonging to an alternative, unexploitable mode of time. Accordingly, the spontaneity of Kerouac's visionary moment may be said to enhance the status of the moment's insight by purging it of any association with the managed time of capitalist production.

Spontaneity is a deeply coded term, one that, among other things, condenses the Romantic and modernist privileging of the immediate and the primal (cf. Ginsberg: "first thought, best thought" [*Collected Poems* xx]). Immediacy and primalcy are commonly understood as preconditions for short-circuiting the inhibiting and censorious effects of reason and the superego. Thus spontaneity has come to connote a time zone in which, as Kerouac would have it, "the unspeakable visions of the individual" and "the true story of the world" (*GBO* 72) find unrestricted and therefore *pure* expression. (Kerouac's faith in spontaneous prose as "*purity* of speech" looks naïve vis-à-vis the "phonocentric" fallacy or the semantic subversions of intertextual "play.") In fact, for almost any writer to invoke the spontaneous is to appeal to the popular and culturally ingrained belief in what is colloquially known as "the truth of the moment." However, that truth is not self-sustaining: as with invocations of instantaneousness and eternity, the invocation of the spontaneous amounts to yet another rhetorical prop for visionary truth claims.

7

Ideology of the Visionary Moment

There is no univocal politics of the visionary moment. Depending on the conjuncture of a literary text's production and reception, its visionary moment may be read as performing either a critical or ideological function. In the first section of this chapter, I shall discuss a context in which a visionary moment may be seen to perform a critical function on behalf of a radical democratic politics. In the second and third sections, I shall identify contexts in which the visionary moment may be seen to perform ideological functions. As indicated earlier (see the introduction), the focus of this critique is on the ideological character of this convention; hence the uneven "weighting" of this chapter.

The critical potential of the visionary moment may not be immediately apparent. After all, to the extent that we think of the moment as a mystical convention—premised as it is on metaphysical assumptions about the nature of truth—we tend to focus on how it mystifies and obscures the conditions of our social existence. Nevertheless, we should keep in mind that there are conjunctures when currents of mystical thinking may acquire a positive, adversarial force. Thus Engels could write: "The revolutionary opposition to feudalism was alive all down the Middle Ages. It took the shape of mysticism, open heresy, or armed insurrection, all depending on the conditions of the time" (454). E. P. Thompson has remarked the "anti-hegemonic" essence of the Christian doctrine of justification by faith in its seventeenth-century antinomian form: "It displaced the authority of institutions and of received worldly wisdom with that of the individual's inner light—faith, conscience, personal understanding of the scriptures" (5). The oppositional force of mysticism was also a staple resource of the Sixties Counterculture, where mystical discourse served as a radical critique of bourgeois consciousness (see Roszak). One must simply recall the renewed interest across American campuses of the time in William Blake's "Prophetic Books" as a source of critique (see Ginsberg, "Interview" 302–317).[1] Accordingly first, the moment may be invoked in the name of a counterhegemonic discourse. That is to say, it often gives voice to and affirms precisely those values and orders of knowledge that have been disqualified by a technological-rationalist culture organized under the imperative to maximize productivity. (See p. 102). Second, insofar as the visionary moment often suggests the acme of a character's spiritual development, we have a model of the subject—an assumed radical purity and psychic wholeness—that implicitly critiques the alienating and atomizing effects of capitalist development. Third, the visionary moment may be embraced as an affirmation of the self in the face of social forces that marginalize the identities of those perceived as Other. And it is precisely in respect of this issue of marginality that it is instructive to examine Alice Walker's best-known story, "Everyday Use" (1973), as an example of how a visionary moment may acquire a progressive political meaning.

Empowerments of Vision

For the socially marginalized, the visionary moment may be valued as an endorsement of self-worth. Thus, in a monographic study of the spiritual narratives of African-American women, Kimberly Rae Connor examines the role of visionary experience in the "sacralization of identity" (5). Walker's "Everyday Use" also can be productively read in these terms.

The story centers on a poor black family in the rural South, which comprises the mother-narrator and her daughters: the college-educated and attractive Dee and the untutored and homely Maggie. When Dee, on leave from college, pays the family a visit, the mother observes how she has fabricated a new identity. In honor of her "heritage," Dee has assumed the African name of Wangero (53) and donned ostentatiously African clothes, hairstyle, and jewelery (52). Tension develops when Dee, in the name of her heritage, lays claim to quilts, hand-pieced by her grandmother, which have been promised to her elder sister:

> "Maggie can't appreciate these quilts!" [Dee] said. "She'd probably be backward enough to put them to everyday use."
> "I reckon she would," [the mother] said. "God knows I been saving 'em for long enough with nobody using 'em. I hope she will!" I didn't want to bring up how I had offered Dee (Wangero) a quilt when she went away to college. Then she had told me they were old-fashioned, out of style.
> "But they're *priceless!*" she was saying now, furiously. . . .
> "She can have them, Mama," [Maggie] said. . . . "I can 'member Grandma Dee without the quilts." (57–58)

This exchange illustrates how each daughter serves as a locus for the values of radically opposed cultures: in Dee/Wangero's case, values we shall identify with postmodern culture and, in Maggie's case, values that Walker wants us to associate with the marginalized Black culture of the rural South. We can begin to see this opposition when we consider the contrasting attitudes to ancestral history introduced in the passage just quoted. We are by now familiar with the notion of postmodernity's "crisis of historicity." Given the universal power of the commodity-form—as Guy Debord would have it, "the moment when the commodity has attained the *total occupation* of social life" (section 42)—our sense of history cannot escape the logic of commodity fetishism. Henceforth, we encounter the past through the reifying and abstract forms of exchange-value and, thus, history is transformed into inert spectacle. Fredric Jameson has observed "the waning of our historicity, of our lived possibility of experiencing history in some active way" (*Postmodernism* 21). Accordingly, "we are condemned to seek History by way of our own pop images and simulacra of that history" (25). One symptom of this situation is the rise of what Robert Hewison has called "the heritage industry," that is, history consciously produced as an object for consumption. This is the history of commercially oriented tourist boards, the themed entertainments of the Disney Imagineers, the "heritage" of the patriotic conservationists, and the retrochic artists of fashion and the nostalgia film.[2] As Hewison puts it: "We have no understanding of history in depth, but instead are offered a contemporary creation, more costume drama and reenactment than critical discourse" (135).

When Dee protests the quilts are "priceless," we can see that the logic of the commodity has contaminated her sense of heritage. The family heirlooms are valued as trendy folk art, as collectibles for a connoisseur. Thus along with the quilts, which she intends to "hang" (58), Dee sets about stripping the family home of other heritage items for display in her own home: "I can use the churn top as a centerpiece for the alcove table . . . and I'll think of something artistic to do with the dasher" (56). In contrast, heritage for Maggie is not something that can be publicly exhibited as a badge of identity. Rather, it is a relation of spiritual kinship with the (deceased) relatives who made the heirlooms—a kinship that counts for more than the heirlooms themselves. Hence her remark, "I can 'member Grandma Dee without the quilts" (58); hence her recollection of the names given to the uncle who whittled the dasher—the uncle her sister has forgotten (55–56). While for Dee heritage is largely an abstract matter of genealogy, for Maggie it is a matter of putting to "everyday use" those objects made by her ancestors. In this respect, she *lives* the experience of heritage.[3] In short, where Dee grasps her heritage in terms that embody the reifying logic of exchange-value (see Marx, *Capital* 163–67), we can say that Maggie's sense of heritage—with its appreciation of everyday use-value—preserves a felt human connection.

The college-educated Dee invokes her heritage while scornfully distancing herself from the "backward" (57) rural community she has left behind. On the other hand, Maggie's conception of heritage is derived from direct emotional proximity to relatives within living memory. After all, "It was Grandma Dee and Big Dee who taught [Maggie] how to quilt herself" (58). Hence, the story's dedication: "for your grandmama" (47). Writing in the seventies, Walker critiques the current African-American fashion for constructing identity in terms of "roots."[4] The mother-narrator refuses to identify herself in relation to ancestors other than those she knew directly: " 'There I was not . . . before 'Dicie' cropped up in our family, so why should I try to trace it that far back?' " (54). In opposition to some vague Afrocentric genealogy, the mother and Maggie derive their sense of identity from a historically and geographically *familiar* lineage.[5]

Hitherto, the mother has invested her hopes in the worldly success of Dee

(47–48), while overlooking the quiet virtues of the obtuse and plain Maggie. But as the sense of estrangement from her pretentious younger daughter peaks, there is a dramatic reversal of focus, when the mother suddenly intuits the spiritual worth of Maggie:

> When I looked at her like that something hit me in the top of my head and ran down to the soles of my feet. Just like when I'm in church and the spirit of God touches me and I get happy and shout. I did something I never had done before: hugged Maggie to me. . . . (58)

This visionary moment marks the climax of the story. It serves as an affirmation of a value system marginalized by late-capitalist development. For it is not just Maggie's character that the moment reveals in a redeeming light, but the continuity and worth of a disappearing way of life, of which Maggie is seen to be the embodiment. Hers is a way of life in which the spiritual is grounded in simple daily chores by virtue of an ancestral history that survives in everyday use-values. These are the shared values of a community organized around self-sufficient domestic production, production for immediate, personal needs rather than for the market. The moment enhances the mother's sense of heritage as an expression of spiritual kinship with this (precapitalist) community. Accordingly, Dee's parting words—"You just don't understand . . . your heritage" (59)—now lack credibility. While the mother, who lacks formal education (50), is endowed with visionary insight, the limits of Dee's vision are suggested by reference to her snapshooting Polaroid and the sunglasses she wears (53, 59).

We should also note that the mother's visionary moment is invested with a sacred significance: an experience that, for her, is "like when I'm in church and the spirit of God touches me." Walker consciously situates herself in that tradition of African-American women mystics famously represented by Rebecca Jackson and Sojourner Truth. She counts these women among her "spiritual ancestors" ("A Name" 98). In an essay on Jackson, Walker (albeit credulously) writes: "For the most part, Jackson's spiritual insights came from direct, frequently ecstatic, revelation in either a dreaming or a waking state. She was also literally instructed in matters both spiritual and temporal by a spirit who arrived almost daily to give her lessons" ("Gifts" 74).[6] Insight, for Walker, is communion with divine spiritual presence. Hence Nettie, in *The Color Purple,* observes: "God is different to us now, after all these years in Africa. More spirit than ever before, and more internal" (227). And Shug Avery maintains: "God is inside you and inside everybody else. . . . But only them that search for it inside find it. *And sometimes it just manifest itself even if you not looking*" (177, emphasis added). A sudden connection with this interior power is what emboldens the mother in "Everyday Use" to confront the assertive Dee, recover the quilts from her and bequeath them to the deserving Maggie (58). But, more important, her visionary moment must be read as an affirmation of that same power, that sacred spirit, in the face of a ruthless and expanding postmodernity that will not recognize or accommodate it. Dee/ Wangero is intimately associated with that postmodernity, in such of its forms as TV celebrity culture (47–48), the heritage industry, the instantaneous image (her Polaroid camera), and her embrace of the "new day" (59). And, finally, the moment is the *self*-affirmation of a poor, uneducated woman. Spiritual insight is the resource by which she expresses her self-worth in opposition to a culture that has marginalized her and the values of her community.

Ideology of a Temporal Construct

Any attempt to read Faulkner's thematics of time in political terms should acknowledge the inevitability of readings that construct conflicting political positions. For example, an oppositional stance can be identified in his subjectivization of time where, typically, memories affectively interpenetrate present experience. In the context of, say, *The Sound and the Fury,* this technique can be read as an implicit critique of the routinizing clock time of capitalist production. Recall the emotionally rich timescape inhabited by Benjy Compson—where past moments poetically animate present ones—as opposed to the deadening schedules that constrain the thinking of the entrepreneurial Jason Compson. Consider also Faulkner's obsessive invocations of lineage and heritage, which can be read in contexts that reveal them as a critique of the dislocations and disintegration suffered by Southern communities under the disruptive forces of modernization. Recall, for instance, those recurring appeals in *Go Down, Moses* to ancient bloodlines, which are valued as links to an ancestral history remote from the corrosive effects of economic development. Yet while subjective and ancestral countertime may be read as having critical potential, both may also be read as constituting mythical time zones, which amount to an evasion or occultation of social history as it unfolds at the time Faulkner is writing. And it is this type of conservative position that I want to explore from the standpoint of Faulkner's dependence on visionary moments. Specifically, I shall argue that, quite apart from any meaning assigned to the *content* of the visionary moment, this narrative convention encodes a conservative ideology of time *in its very structure and presuppositions.* Commentary on just two visionary moments, both from *Go Down, Moses,* will suffice to make the case.

In "The Old People," Ike McCaslin is a boy of twelve who, at dawn, has shot his first deer and then, at dusk, seen its spirit. This vision marks a rite of passage, that is, his initiation into a spirit-community of hunting fathers that haunts a mythical (i.e., primal, undeveloped) wilderness:

> *So the instant came.* He pulled trigger. . . . The buck still and forever leaped, the shaking gun-barrels coming constantly and forever steady at last, crashing, and still out of his *instant of immortality* the buck sprang, forever

immortal; . . . *the moment of the buck,* the shot, Sam Fathers and himself
and the blood with which Sam had marked him forever one with the
wilderness. . . . (171, emphases added).

The second visionary moment is taken from "Delta Autumn," where McCaslin,
now a man of eighty, drifts off to sleep during his last hunting excursion into a
wilderness which is disappearing with the invasion of loggers and developers:

> *Then suddenly he knew* why he had never wanted to own any of [the
> land]. . . . It was because there was just exactly enough of it. He seemed to
> see the two of them—himself and the wilderness—as coevals, his own span
> as a hunter, a woodsman, not contemporary with his first breath but trans-
> mitted to him . . . from that old Major de Spain and that old Sam Fathers
> who had taught him to hunt, the two spans running out together, not
> toward oblivion, nothingness, but into *a dimension free of both time and
> space* where once more the untreed land warped and wrung to mathematical
> squares of rank cotton . . . would find ample room for both—the names,
> the faces of the old men he had known and loved, . . . moving again among
> the shades of tall unaxed trees and sightless brakes where the wild strong
> immortal game ran forever before the tireless belling immortal hounds,
> falling and rising phoenix-like to the soundless guns. (337–38, emphases
> added)

Faulkner's visionary moments clearly present a nondialectical temporality,
that is, one from which the contradictions of the South's social history have been
eliminated. At the heart of each moment is a kind of frozen tableau depicting the
time of a mythical eternal present, where "immortal game runs forever," is killed
by hunters and then resurrected—all in an unbreakable cycle. Here, cyclical time
is, of course, to be understood as the antithesis of the linear time of capitalist
development. In precisely this time zone, McCaslin fulfills his desire to "arrest at
least that much of what people called progress" (337), the "progress" that has
"deswamped and denuded and derivered" the land in two generations (347).

The agrarian nostalgia for a sacrosanct and precapitalist relationship with
the natural world is crystallized in these momentary visions of an eternal, unspoiled, and inexhaustible wilderness. Indeed, in a typically conservative reaction,
Faulkner invokes the ideal of a primordial nature that can serve as a repository of
value against the anomic and alienating effects of modernization. (And here we
might add that emblematic of the general loss of norms and morals, which
Faulkner sees as characteristic of an emergent New South, is the decline of the
hunting code—"the ancient and immitigable rules" [184]—as seen in Roth
Edmonds' disregard of the prohibition against doe hunting [347–48] and Boon
Hoggenback's presumptuous claim to all the squirrels in a tree [315].)

Another ideological implication of Faulkner's mythical vision of the wilderness is that it neatly occludes the contemporaneous question of class struggle. Recall the near-destitution of eight million sharecroppers and tenant farmers on Southern cotton plantations during the Depression and their fight against the disruptive effects of the New Deal's rationalization of agriculture. Resistance was embodied in mass-action movements, in particular, that of the Southern Tenant Farmers' Union, whose membership agitated for a takeover of the plantations.[7] The STFU was especially active in the Delta region (see Fekete 238–39). Yet, in the face of deep and extensive social conflict, Faulkner responds with visionary moments that invoke the mythic harmony of ancestral hunting communities.[8] Thus, in an inversion of history, he divests the future of redemptive potential— the very future toward which radical organizations like the STFU struggled—and instead relocates that potential in the past, in a precapitalist relation to nature.

However, in addition to their ideological content, Faulkner's visionary moments are ideologically significant by virtue of their form. That is to say, the narrative form of the visionary moment incorporates temporal properties that serve to reinforce and dramatize Faulkner's conservative thematics of time. One of these temporal properties is suddenness. Typically, a literary visionary moment is introduced with words like: "Suddenly, he realized" or "in an instant, she understood." In the moment excerpted from "Delta Autumn," we have "Then suddenly he knew". This kind of phrasing signals to the reader that the visionary moment does not slowly evolve into being but rather bursts upon the subject unannounced. It suggests both the irruption of an idea into consciousness and that this moment cannot be prepared for or summoned at will. Its occurrence is unpredictable and sporadic. The implication is that the visionary moment has its source in another temporal order from which it has intruded into the present of calendar time. And, as already noted, in the context of Faulkner's work, that temporal order can be identified as a mythical, eternal present. This temporality, insofar as it is privileged over the profane time of capitalist modernization, threatens to ephemeralize and attenuate the reality of the latter.

Another temporal property is precisely the momentary duration of the vision: the insight or vision is always a fleeting experience. Hence, in the account of McCaslin's vision of the phantom deer, we are told, "the instant came"; we are referred to "his instant of immortality" and to "the moment of the buck." A little later we read, "*in less than a second* he had ceased forever to be the child he was yesterday" (175, emphases added). This momentary duration suggests that the vision cannot be accommodated within the prevailing mindset of the subject. The evanescent, fragile nature of the vision seems symptomatic of the transfigured consciousness, idealized by Faulkner, that cannot be secured at that stage of social evolution as defined by capitalist modernization. Thus, once again, the implication is that the visionary moment has its source in another temporality. It is as if the moment is a fragment from a mythical timescape, which cannot endure in the modernized chronological time of the New South. Indeed, we can think of the visionary moment in Faulkner's work as the point at which myth intersects with history—but just for an instant and tenuously, for there it can find no foothold.

A third temporal property of the visionary moment should, by now, be apparent: its transhistoricality. That is to say, by abstracting the vision from the mundane clock time of the New South, by erasing its historical coordinates, Faulkner can suggest the eternal nature of the truth revealed to McCaslin. For, it goes without saying, the knowledge gained from a visionary moment cannot be of a profane and temporal kind; rather, the moment has intensity precisely because of the "ageless" and "imperishable" knowledge it brings.

We can identify a fourth temporal property in the way that the visionary moment typically reveals the subject's place in the universe sub specie aeternitatis rather than in relation to a specific historical conjuncture. For example, in his last visionary moment, McCaslin sees himself as "coeval" with the wilderness, which, we are told, runs into "a dimension free of both time and space" (337). In other words, the primacy accorded to the moment obscures the role of historical forces (e.g., political movements or changes in the balance of power between classes, races, or the sexes) in producing a sense of how one is located in the world.

A fifth temporal property is evident in that the visionary moment is represented as a primordial form of cognition. Early in "The Old People," McCaslin's cousin, Cass, says of Sam Fathers (the son of a Chickasaw chief and quadroon slave woman) that "'When he was born, all his blood on both sides, except the little white part, knew things that had been tamed out of our blood so long ago that we have . . . forgotten them'" (161). What Sam knows "in his blood" is the existence of the occult spirit world of the wilderness, that primal space still haunted by his hunting forbears. And under the tutelage (or spiritual "Fathering") of Sam, Mc-Caslin, in the form of a visionary moment, first glimpses the spirit-deer and, in this way, intuits the whole spirit world of "the old people." But the point implied is that *only* by virtue of a visionary moment can this archaic knowledge *now* be acquired, for the visionary moment is all that remains of that ancestral endowment of prerational, precultural cognition. Indeed, we learn that even Sam's Chickasaw blood has been tainted ("betrayed" 161–62), thus suggesting that the links, by way of bloodlines, to a still-living ancestral past, have become tenuous. Now that past can only be sporadically experienced through the mediation of visionary moments. In short, the moment is constituted as an innate, essentially *prehistorical* mode of knowledge.

In summary, Faulkner's visionary moment is a dehistoricizing move that recoils from the conflictual time zone of social change so as to preserve the image of a stable mythic social order. And it is in the service of this endeavor that the very form of the visionary moment—by virtue of its ideologically charged temporal properties—proves itself so useful.

Following the postmodern impulse to pluralize, we must note the politically and culturally diverse contexts in which the visionary moment may be employed or received. And it is in just this respect that a comparison of texts by Faulkner and Walker proves so instructive. Both writers are from the rural South. Both write about the rural South. Both are concerned with the continuing relevance of ancestry and heritage. And both deploy visionary moments to invoke a premodernized world, whose image serves as an implicit critique of the disruptive effects of capitalist development. Yet, today, insofar as we locate these authors through the categories of modernity and postmodernity, we arrive at radically divergent political readings of their use of visionary moments. Thus, Faulkner's moment, invoked in the context of the South's modernization, makes sense primarily as an agrarian reaction—a mythifying nostalgia—for a precapitalist relationship with the natural world. And Walker's moment, invoked in the context of an invasive postmodern culture (as figured by Dee's intrusion into the family home), makes sense primarily as a source of empowerment for a subaltern voice: that of the poor black woman who speaks up for the threatened values of a socially and economically disadvantaged community. In short, the former moment is read as encoding a conservative ideology, while the latter is read as an instance of postmodern radical pluralism, where a discursive space is opened for a marginalized form of cultural difference to flourish.

Ideological Inflections

While a comparison of texts by Faulkner and Walker can show that the politics of the literary visionary moment is context-dependent, nevertheless, I have tended to read this convention as biased toward a conservative ideology. I want to conclude this chapter with a few brief generalizations about this ideological bias. These generalizations chiefly apply to the redemptive visionary moment, but not necessarily to every redemptive moment discussed in the previous chapters.

The visionary moment is always conceived as belonging to an interior or private timescape, a temporality implicitly opposed to the public timescape of social history. For the timing of the moment's occurrence locates it at a transitional stage or turning point in the *personal* development of the self. Hence, the redemptive experience of the insight is understood as an exclusively individual affair, thus occluding any sense of a historical conjuncture where collectivist or class action is the precondition for individual salvation. We should also note the ideological implications of a literary convention that inflates the significance of but one singular moment (as Virginia Woolf would have it, "The moment was all; the moment was enough" [*Waves* 239]). This amounts to a dehistoricizing practice that demotes or obscures the transformative effects of the deeper, socially rooted changes that transpire over years or decades. The significance of momentary experience is elevated above that of historical process; the material history generated by social contradictions is displaced by the inward, existential temporality of the moment.

As a conspicuously individualized form of knowledge, the visionary moment articulates a key component of the ideology of individualism; that is to say, the moment is premised on the assumption that redemption *begins* with the individual. Moreover, writers who represent the visionary moment as an intensely private and self-centered experience not only privilege the individual as the primary source of redemptive knowledge but implicitly downgrade the redemptive potential of collectively produced forms of knowledge—a point I shall return to later.

Insofar as the visionary moment is unsought, that is to say, it *happens to* the subject, and insofar as it is understood to *deliver* the knowledge in quasi-oracular fashion, the moment may be said to promote the "virtue" of passivity as the precondition for enlightenment: higher truth is that order of truth that, like Grace, is *received*. But whether or not this assumed role of passivity in the acquisition of knowledge is correct,[9] one might argue that it amounts to an epistemology that lacks emancipatory potential. The issue here is that agency—in the forms of organized political struggle and practical critical activity—is needed to *produce* emancipatory forms of knowledge and to combat the authority of those institutions that produce knowledge in the ideological forms that mystify the conditions of social existence and sustain relations of domination.

We must also reckon with the effects of an ideology of gender when examining the convention of the visionary moment. Martin Bidney, for example, notes the possibility of feminist criticism's interest in how Elizabeth Barrett Browning adheres to or departs from the "male-influenced" norms of epiphanic writing in the composition of her own literary epiphanies (199). However, he does not specify the nature of these norms. Here, I shall suggest the presence of one such norm. Given its frequent deployment at the climax of the story's rising action, and given that the illumination is usually defined as a peak (even, ecstatic) experience, the visionary moment will often appear as the critical element in a narrative trajectory that privileges, and is analogous to, masculine orgasmic experience.

We must be alert to the universalizing disposition of many visionary moments; that is to say, the moment is frequently used with the implicit claim that it speaks the truth for humankind. This claim rests on the visionary-moment conception of truth as always already existing in some dimensionless and transhistorical realm, waiting, like an unknown planet, to be discovered by the intuitive or graced mind. The truths revealed to Jack Kerouac's itinerants or Flannery O'Connor's conceited protagonists are offered as truths for us all. The ideological implication is clear enough: the rhetoric of the visionary moment is used to assign universal validity to a culturally and historically specific voice (e.g., Kerouac and O'Connor speaking as alienated Catholics, writing in the United States in the 1950s and 1960s). And if we are to contest the universal pretensions of knowledge delivered through the literary medium of the moment, we must locate the conjuncture from which the knowledge arises, trace the knowledge back to the worldly authority (ecclesiastical, literary, academic) that produces or legitimizes it.

Finally, in the convention of the moment we encounter the fanciful notion of an escape from history. All too often, from the Romantics through to the high modernists and beyond, we can read in the literary use of private visionary experience a flight from the alienating and anomic effects of capitalist modernization. By way of illustration, consider Wordsworth's "Tintern Abbey." In his panoramic view of the Wye River landscape, "wreaths of smoke" remind him of "vagrant dwellers in the houseless woods" (20). The date is 1798, one of the most active decades of enclosure, and the vagrants are those commoners displaced by the capitalist rationalization of agriculture. But their incongruous presence must be ignored if the poet's "purer mind" is to achieve its "elevated thoughts; a sense sublime" (29; 95); this disquieting hint of social discord must be erased so that "with an eye made quiet by the power / Of harmony . . . / We see into the life of things" (47–49).[10] Thus the poem makes an abrupt shift (22–23) from its picture of the landscape to a "picture of the mind" (61). The following year, Wordsworth began *The Prelude,* the autobiographical poem distinguished by its numerous visionary "spots of time" (12:208) and by its author's persistent monitoring, analysis, and celebration of his exalted mental states. (Recall the poem's subtitle: "Growth of a Poet's Mind.") Indeed, the poem may be read as a testament to the "Profoundest knowledge to what point, and how, / The mind is lord and master" (12:221–22). *The Prelude* and "Tintern Abbey" are deeply inscribed with the ideological illusion of the redemptive power of pure consciousness: each suggests that salvation lies beyond the arena of socio-historical contradictions in the "purer mind" ("Tintern Abbey" 29; *Prelude* 2:314). Subsequently, high modernism would advance this ideology through its explorations of the limits of consciousness; in particular, recall the preoccupation with the subjective experience of time (e.g., Woolf's "exquisite moments" or Faulkner's scrambled chronologies) in the endeavor to register the impressionistic flux and heightened intensities of mental life. The modernist sense of pure consciousness as a transcendent, transhistorical condition is especially evident in the later epiphanies of *A Portrait,* with their multiple invocations of "flight," "flying," and "soaring" (see 162–64, 218–19). And however much the pressure of socio-historical experience is registered in the high-modernist text, that experience often tends to pale against the intense light focused on "the most delicate and evanescent of moments" (Joyce, *Stephen Hero* 211).

The visionary moment enshrines a model of salvational knowledge—that is, knowledge as intuitive, instantaneous, pure, permanent, universal—that *tacitly demotes* worldly and collective forms of knowledge that have real transformative power. For example, in a point-for-point comparison between the visionary paradigm of knowledge and critical literacy or praxial knowledge, the latter appear as prosaic and uninspired—an altogether less promising channel for the Truth. Thus:

1. Visionary knowledge is (assumed to be) attained via the operation of such mythologized and occult faculties as "insight" or "intuition." This aura of

mystery and myth invests the knowledge with superior status. From the stand-points of critical literacy and the praxial model, knowledge is *produced* via the conspicuously mundane methods of critique and dialogue and planned interaction with the environment. Hence, placed beside visionary knowledge, this knowledge appears as merely worldly, as a lower degree of truth.

2. Visionary knowledge is instantaneously received, hence the "flash" of insight or "sudden" illumination. In this respect, the knowledge benefits from the drama of its delivery; the urgency of its arrival is taken as a token of its significance. On the other hand, critical literacy and praxial knowledge are acquired by relatively laborious processes: analysis, argument, research, efforts to transform the environment. The point here is that knowledge that emanates from such uninspired activities is deemed to be of an inferior order.

3. Visionary knowledge seems to have more authority by virtue of its being conceived as an interior and private experience; under this condition, the knowledge can be thought of as impacting directly on the psyche. The matrix of critique-based and praxial knowledge is necessarily social. This is knowledge that has its source in collaboration; knowledge that is collectively produced in a public domain. But, as *common* knowledge, it seems to lack the aura and compelling immediacy of privately owned and privately experienced knowledge.

4. Visionary knowledge is conceived of as a transcendent and once-and-for-all type of knowledge; it is the Voice of Truth. In contrast, critical literacy and praxial knowledge are grounded in the temporal. This is knowledge conceived of as an historically specific and ongoing process of reflection, contingent upon interactions with evolving disciplinary structures or with a changing environment. But it is precisely the temporal cast of this knowledge that seems to limit its value, which seems to profane and provincialize it.

5. Visionary knowledge is thought of as redemptive on the strength of (what is held to be) its pristine, unmediated, and transcendent nature; it is as if knowledge alone, by virtue of its spiritual purity, can transfigure an individual—without the (worldly) intervention or support of changes at the institutional or infrastructural level of society. On the other hand, critical literacy and praxial knowledge have a political rather than spiritual orientation. They are self-consciously pragmatic forms of knowledge, envisaging alternative social arrangements and conceptualizing the strategies required to realize them. And from the standpoints of critical literacy and praxial knowledge (dull, practical, and mundane as they may seem), visionary-moment knowledge—i.e., the mystical form of cognition promulgated by literature—can have no emancipatory effect; it can only leave the world as it already is.

Conclusion

Insofar as technological rationality serves to sustain and legitimize a system chiefly organized under the imperatives of production and consumption, it has acquired hegemonic status (see Habermas, ch.6). Under these circumstances, metaphysical thinking—though permeating mass culture—loses not just its relevance vis-à-vis the productive process but its intellectual legitimacy.[1] Indeed, in most spheres of academic discourse since industrialization, "metaphysical" has been a term of disparagement, denoting thinking that is unprofessional and lacking in rigor: the residue of an archaic stage of intellectual development. A relentless succession of environmentalist and materialist scholarship—Darwinism, dialectical material-ism, positivism, the physical and Earth sciences, behaviorism, Systems Theory—has, with unflagging zeal (and not a little hubris), assailed and discredited what, depending on their respective criteria, each defined as "the metaphysical." As we have seen, postmodern critique has constructed an expansive sense of "the meta-physical," targeting inter alia "metalinguistic" assumptions of Final Meaning, the transhistorical notion of "the origin," and humanism's "transcendental ego." This mode of critique is just one of our more recent and prestigious instances of a self-proclaimed anti-metaphysical discourse.[2] Thus, while the visionary moment en-codes an aspiration to locate ourselves in a transcendent relation to our worldly existence, postmodern critique locates us (and our visionary moments) resolutely and squarely in the domains of culture, the conjunctural, and the contingent.

The radically ironic nature of postmodern fiction may be seen as largely a consequence of this exile of metaphysics from the principal domains of intellectual life. Postmodern writers are, to borrow Richard Rorty's terms, "ironists" insofar as they reject the "final vocabularies" of "metaphysics" as no more than "the language games of one's time" (Rorty 73–75). No transcendental judgment can be inferred from the disjunctive, self-consciously provisional, nonclosural narratives of, for example, Walter Abish or Donald Barthelme; their prose fragments refuse to coalesce into a totalizing *grand récit* or climactic insight.

When we turn to the literary visionary moment, we can now also think of it as a symptom of the defensive posture of mystical truth claims in the face of the ascendancy of anti-metaphysical thinking. Thus, on the one hand, we have identi-fied in this convention the survival of a cluster of mystical ideas: notably, the belief in transcendent (transhistorical, transcultural) truths, salvational knowledge, mys-tical union, and occult faculties (all notions that *outside* of most intellectual life have a wide measure of credibility). On the other hand, the very *fragility* of visionary moments in literary narrative—they are invariably represented as an elusive and fleeting experience—indicates a state of (accredited) knowledge characterized by a profound loss of confidence in such metaphysical beliefs. To state the matter in broader terms, the unpredictability and sporadic nature of the moment, whose "truths," moreover, often are merely intimated, suggests a generalized social condition wherein transcendent meanings are no longer securely integrated into our rationalized way of life.

There is another sense in which the literary visionary moment reflects the marginalization of metaphysics in intellectual life: it has, with some notable exceptions, replaced the older conventions by which "higher" knowledge is communicated in fictional narratives—namely, the use of seers, oracles, omens, and ghosts.[3] Compared with this traditional reliance on supernatural media, the visionary moment is a far less obtrusive, and thus more acceptable, invocation of the metaphysical. Indeed, in the language of psychoanalysis, we might say that the visionary moment resembles a compromise formation: it satisfies a desire for the transcendent while, at the same time, escaping the "censorship" of a secular/ rationalist regime of knowledge. There is, after all, something notably evasive about the expression of truth in the form of a flash or glimpse or intimation.

Finally, I have contested a mythical paradigm of knowledge, widely promulgated through literature, whereby the subject may be transfigured or regenerated by a flash of transcendent truth. I have argued from the standpoint of a counterparadigm that, respecting the socio-historical grounds of subject formation, recognizes that human beings are not so readily transfigurable as the former paradigm suggests, and that knowledge whose transformative power is feasible, efficacious, and sustainable is, alas, not delivered in the obliging form of a private and instantaneous illumination. Transformative knowledge has to be collectively produced, struggled for, tested, and institutionalized. It must reveal to us how existing social arrangements actually impede our development—moral, intellectual, *and* spiritual. Transformative knowledge (for example, critical literacy) is not a gift of grace but an incrementally acquired practical competency. Nevertheless, the myth of the redemptive visionary moment is a popular and compelling one: an ideal paradigm of knowledge, which, by virtue of its instantaneousness, intuitability, purity, permanence, and universality, is deemed to have salvational power. It is an enchanting notion of which we should disabuse ourselves, since the point is to locate our regeneration in the realm of the possible.

Appendix
The Postmodern Sublime

Does the concept of the sublime have any relevance to a postmodern critique of the visionary moment? One might assume prima facie that a sublime experience is a type of visionary moment. For example, Robert Langbaum writes, "Epiphanies produce an effect that might be called 'the modern sublime.' . . . [T]hey produce in the reader emotions named by writers on the sublime—Longinus's 'transport,' Burke's 'terror' and 'astonishment'" (50). Moreover, one can find examples in literature where the experience of the (Romantic) sublime is represented as a visionary moment (see pp. 79–81). However, conceptions of the sublime are generally premised on assumptions radically opposed to those of the visionary moment. Essentially, the former is understood as a *failure* of cognition or imagination—"It takes place . . . when the imagination fails to present an object" (Lyotard 78; see also Tabbi 17, 25)—while the latter is understood as a *breakthrough* (achieved or impending) to a higher order of knowledge or enlightenment. Thus, assuming the mutual exclusiveness of these modes of experience, I want briefly to explore the viability of an alternative relation between them, that is, when the sublime—and specifically "the postmodern sublime"—can and cannot be enlisted as a strategy in a postmodern critique of the visionary moment.

It must be said at once that the sublime is a historically contingent concept, which has acquired distinctly variable formulations in, broadly speaking, the Classical, Enlightenment, Romantic, and postmodern periods. In the *Critique of Judgement* (1790), Kant writes, "We call *sublime* what is *absolutely large*" (qtd. in Beidler 178), with reference to those forces of nature whose terrifying immensity exceeds human powers of categorization and, in consequence, simultaneously stimulates feelings of dread and awe. For Kant, theorizing within the domain of eighteenth-century faculty psychology, the sublime object defies figuration because of the limits of the human faculties. Accordingly, faced with that which is too large to comprehend, the imagination is seen as "inadequate" and "sinks back into itself" (qtd. in Beidler 178).

A postmodernizing of the sublime has shifted the focus from the Enlightenment's and Romanticism's mingled wonder and dread before the immense forces of nature to anxious intimations of the overarching presence of massive technological power or the malign influence of worldwide conspiracies or the oppressive totality of the capitalist world system. Thus, in a brief discussion of a "postmodern or technological sublime," Fredric Jameson reads the global communicational and computer networks of cyberpunk fiction as a "faulty" or "distorted figuration," which is really an attempt "to think the impossible totality of the contemporary world system" of multinational capitalism (*Postmodernism* 37–38). And, in a remarkable analysis of the momentous presence of the sublime in postmodern writing, Joseph Tabbi selects for attention "those narrative moments when a literary figuration *fails* to match its technological object, since this is the point at which literature can begin to represent not technology itself but the tumultuous and incongruous nature of postmodern experience" (25).

An eminent example of the postmodern sublime can be found in Thomas Pynchon's *Gravity's Rainbow*. Tchitcherine, a Stalinist functionary in Central Asia, senses the existence of "A *Rocket-cartel.* A structure cutting across every agency human and paper that ever touched it. . . . [A] State that spans oceans and surface politics." This "meta-cartel" is so vast it exceeds and mocks comprehension even by means of visionary illumination. Thus, Tchitcherine must resign himself to being "held at the edges of revelations" (566). The point, here, is that the visionary mode of knowing, as traditionally promoted in literature, must fail, must appear hopelessly futile and idealistic, in the face of the non-figurable expansions of power in the postmodern period—"arrangements Tchitcherine can't see, wide as Europe, perhaps as the world" (350). Similarly, in *The Crying of Lot 49,* Pynchon appeals to the postmodern sublime in order to counter the presumptuous certainties and illusory omnipotence that characterize visionary moments. Oedipa Maas must contend with the ironic possibility of a vision devoid of enlightenment. She, a quasi-detective, tracing a plot so vast and elaborate it eludes conceptualization (179), desires an epiphany that will organize a chaotic surplus of clues into "pulsing stelliferous Meaning" (82). Yet, she fears that, instead of a revelatory vision, she will have a sublime perception of what she *cannot* know:

> [N]ever the central truth itself, which must somehow each time be too bright for her memory to hold; which must always blaze out, destroying its own message irreversibly, leaving an overexposed blank when the ordinary world came back. (95)

The passage may be read as a salutary corrective to the overweening confidence in our capacity to know. It may be read as a reminder that there are experiences that are unassimilable to human consciousness; a reminder that the literary convention of the visionary moment lacks credibility at the conjuncture of postmodernity, when the dispositions of power that define our reality are seen as cognitively unmappable.

Where, following Pynchon, one may strategically invoke the sublime to expose the limitations of the visionary moment vis-à-vis postmodern power structures that defy representation, Jean-François Lyotard invokes it in the belief that ineffable forms of experience (as conveyed by a postmodern avant-garde) are resistant to cooptation by "the system." However, as I shall presently explain, Lyotard mobilizes the sublime in terms that conflict with my agenda for mobilizing other postmodern strategies to critique the visionary moment.

Proceeding from the postmodern premise that the metanarratives that formerly sustained the (Kantian) Subject have dispersed into a multiplicity of language games, Lyotard conceptualizes the sublime as that which exceeds the limits of language (xxiii–xiv; 81). "[T]he conceivable which cannot be presented" (81) is that which cannot be narrativized. But why this renewed interest in the sublime nearly two centuries after Kant? This rehabilitation of the concept must be seen in the context of capitalism at the technocratic stage of its evolution, which Lyotard perceives as capable of incorporating all opposition. Thus, "struggles and their instruments have been transformed into regulators of the system" (13); critiques are complicit with the power relations they seek to challenge and are "used in one way or another as aids in programming the system" (13). Accordingly, Lyotard appeals to a nonnarratizable, i.e. sublime, order of experience, whose (supposed) virtue is that it eludes the incorporative pressures of "the system." And, for this reason, he places a high premium on the revolutionary aesthetics of the avant-garde.[1] The experiments of the latter are valued as transgressive insofar as they resist the rules (mimesis, communicability, etc.) of a hegemonic realism (74–75). Instead, avant-garde artists "devote themselves to making an allusion to the unpresentable by means of visible presentations" (78). In other words, because the sublime object of their art cannot be articulated, because it always exceeds symbolization, there is no standard (e.g. "the established rules of the beautiful" [75]) by which this art can be judged and, hence, coopted by "the system." Thus, Lyotard arrives at a definition of what he believes to be a truly radical postmodern art: "[T]hat which searches for new presentations, not in order to enjoy them but in order to impart a stronger sense of the unpresentable" (81).

Not only does Lyotard invoke the postmodern sublime on the grounds that it escapes cooptation; he also invokes it for its edifying effect of reminding us of the limits of discourse by alluding to the existence of a nonnarratizable excess (as in our incapacity to articulate ideas of absolute greatness or the infinitely powerful). As he sees it, the humbling awareness of these limits helps guard against the dangerous pretensions of certain political philosophies. He insists on the catastrophic consequences of an arrogant faith in, and aspiration to, "totalizing" discourses. He singles out the Enlightenment metanarratives of progress and emancipation (xxiii–xxiv) as utopian ideals, which, he argues, have served to legitimate "totalitarian" politics and their "terroristic" imposition of consensus (cf. 81; 36–37). Accordingly, he concludes his report with this exhortation: "Let us wage a war on totality; let us be witnesses to the unpresentable" (82).

Lyotard's sublime is one strategy of postmodern critique that must be rejected as incompatible with the other postmodern strategies that this study employs to counter the paradigm of knowledge embedded in the visionary moment. Insofar as I do not share Lyotard's pessimistic belief in the all-incorporative powers of "the system" (a belief that largely follows from his embrace of contemporary *systemtheorie* [11–12]), I am less susceptible to the lure of "the unpresentable" as insurance against cooptation. One need not quest after the ineffable in order to locate a domain of meaning that can effectively resist the integrative pressures of "the system." However, to the extent that Lyotard understates the condition of culture as an arena of antagonistic discourses and practices, he has no recourse to the antithetical or contestatory force of counter-hegemonies.[2] Timothy Engström has remarked that Lyotard "mislocates" the conflict: "The contest is not between presenting and unpresentability but between competing conventions of presenting, forming, and figuring. It is difficult to know how the elusiveness of 'the unpresentable' will help us to 'wage war on totality' without some good old narratives willing to run the risk of pragmatically stabilizing a few referents" (204). Contrary, therefore, to Lyotard's postmodern deployment of the sublime, which assumes the futility of narratizable forms of opposition, I have opted to use postmodern strategies explicitly in the service of a narratizable (i.e., counter-hegemonic) paradigm of knowledge. This paradigm has been introduced under the rubric of "critical literacy." A commitment to critical literacy and, by extension, to socially transformative knowledges, amounts to an endorsement of forms of human experience that are eminently "presentable." In short, I employ those forms of postmodern critique that can expose the mystifications of the visionary moment; the postmodern sublime, as formulated by Lyotard, with a reverence for the ineffable that verges on obscurantism, cannot serve my purpose.

Notes

Introduction

1. The fourth author is Sandra Humble Johnson. Her book is discussed in detail in chapter 3.

2. For additional examples of formalist approaches see: Tigges; Tinkler-Villani; Devine.

3. In a discussion of the "epiphanic moments" in the work of Wilde and Joyce, John McGowan identifies a tension between "traditional notions of the soul" and "a vision of a dispersed transient emotional life that has no unifying center." This is a postmodern reading of the early modernist epiphany as the paradoxical site where "a will to strong selfhood" competes with "an anarchistic urge to dissolve the self" ("From Pater" 418–19). And in "Epiphany and Its Discontents," a short chapter in a study of postmodern fiction, Arthur Saltzman examines the "anti-epiphanic" writing of Robert Coover, Kenneth Gangemi, and Gilbert Sorrentino. Their fiction "demands that we view art not as a formal disclosure of meaning but as an exploration of the conditions under which meaning is accomplished. . . . Revelatory impulses are either absent or confessed to be literary conventions" (27).

4. Very briefly, in a deconstructive approach to *The Mysteries of Udolpho*, Thomas Dutoit observes that Emily's epiphany occurs when she sees her father's secret papers without reading them (98). He argues that this "transgressive" epiphany—made possible by "*seeing* what ought not to be read" (97)—eloquently speaks of the "materiality" of language, when "the 'word' or 'signifier' takes over, becomes more powerful than, the 'thought' or 'signified'" (99). Jay Losey proposes that Philip Larkin and Seamus Heaney, "despite postmodern ontological uncertainty . . . creat[e] a postmodern version of [Northrop] Frye's 'demonic' epiphany" (376). That is to say, their aesthetic explores sudden visions of death while "refusing to provide closure and calling into question all rational responses to death" (388). Alison Chapman follows Kristeva in suggesting that the "uncanny" and "archaic experience of abjection [i.e. primal separation from the mother] in the pre-subject is not successfully repressed" (117) and may return to haunt the adult in the form of an epiphany. However, she argues, unlike male sonneteers, Elizabeth Barrett and Christina Rossetti design sonnets that "reject epiphany's repetition . . . of that archaic separation" (116). Lastly, Suzette Henke reads the nu-

merous "'eyeless' epiphanies" in the "Time Passes" segment of *To the Lighthouse* as a challenge to an imperious "male oculocentr[ism]." Woolf's "eyeless" or "cosmic narrator" speaks in the "lyrical" and fragmentary voice of the "semiotic *chora*," which (to baldly summarize Henke's argument) "deconstructs male master narratives" (262–64).

5. Polls conducted in the United States at the approach of the millennium have revealed an explosive spread of supernatural beliefs among the public. Thus, a poll administered by Yankelovich Partners in 1997 reported belief in a variety of occult phenomena at levels three to four times those observed in 1976: spiritualism (increasing from 12 percent to 52 percent); faith healing (from 10 percent to 45 percent); astrology (from 17 percent to 37 percent); UFOs (from 24 percent to 30 percent); reincarnation (from 9 percent to 25 percent); fortune-telling (from 4 percent to 14 percent) (Colimore). And in a survey for *Time*/CNN, also in 1997, Yankelovich Partners polled 1018 adult Americans by telephone and reported that 81 percent believed in "the existence of heaven, where people live forever with God after they die." Moreover, of the 809 respondents who believed in heaven, 93 percent believed it to be inhabited by angels and 88 percent believed that they would meet friends and family members there when they died (Van Biema).

6. It should go without saying that to read these writers from the standpoint of postmodern critique is *not* to assume that they are all postmodern writers; in fact, only DeLillo might qualify as such.

7. Fredric Jameson has discussed how the ideological force of texts can significantly depend on their "utopian" potential. See *Signatures of the Visible* (29–30) and *The Political Unconscious* (291–92).

8. Currents of such critique include postcolonial theory (see e.g. Spivak *In Other Worlds;* Bhabha), feminist theory (see e.g. Fraser and Nicholson), and critical pedagogy (see e.g. Giroux *Postmodernism*). But it is also important to note that postmodern critique is not necessarily oriented toward democratic ends. Indeed, it may be appropriated to advance, for example, a racist agenda. Thus, Joan Hawkins, who has investigated how white supremacists communicate on the Internet, observes that their "web sites seem to encourage the same kinds of reading strategies and philosophical positions that we privilege in postmodern and poststructuralist debates and in cultural studies" (53). These web sites challenge cultural hegemony, problematize race, and "are very cognizant of the way that power and identity are constructed through language and discursive formations, and, therefore, of the way that language and discursive formations are never entirely power-neutral in themselves" (55).

9. Of course, this tabulation of the strategies of postmodern critique is by no means exhaustive. I have listed only those that construct my perspective on the visionary moment. Principal among the strategies omitted here are the deconstruction of binary oppositions (see especially Derrida, *Grammatology*); "paralogy" (see Lyotard); and decanonization (see, e.g., Fiedler). Finally, the extent to which the "postmodern sublime" may be deployed as a strategy in a critique of

the visionary moment altogether depends on how the concept is formulated. For a brief account of this matter, the reader is referred to the appendix (125–128).

10. See John McGowan's discussion of how "one . . . variant of Marx's thoughts on power—the notion of ideology—has been particularly influential in postmodern thought" (McGowan, *Postmodernism* 210).

11. In addition to Marxism (albeit with a cultural materialist inflection), two other materialist paradigms currently at work in literary studies merit mention vis-à-vis postmodern theory: criticism derived from cognitive science, sometimes referred to as "cognitive poetics" (see e.g., Tsur; Spolsky), and a posthermeneutic media theory that reconceives literary studies as the study of media technologies (see e.g., Kittler; Johnston). Both critical practices may be said to converge with postmodern theory insofar as they are premised on a posthumanist conception of the subject. For example, Ellen Spolsky explains literary categorizations (e.g., genres, periods, interpretive procedures) in the light of research into how the brain creatively bridges the gaps in information caused by the limitations of its neurological equipment (2). Here, the brain is conceived as a multiplicity of discrete information-processing modules lacking full communication among themselves and thus "muddling through" (37) rather than an omnipotent "central controller" (34) (the model on which the humanist idea of the centered subject is founded). For Spolsky, this view of mental life points to "a theory of fragmented, contingent, necessarily opportunistic or pragmatic postmodern consciousness" (37). And Friedrich Kittler, who analyzes discourse as an effect of the material conditions of the medium in which it is stored, who reads literary texts as data storage systems (*Discourse/Networks* 370), argues that the limits of communications hardware set the limits of our subjectivities; after all, "technologically possible manipulations determine what in fact can become a discourse" (232). Hence, he concludes, "Media theory can dispense with the notion of 'man' left over from the human sciences" ("Technologies" kit9.htm). However, whereas key Marxist concepts have proved readily assimilable to postmodern critique, these alternative approaches extend materialist analysis beyond the radius of inquiry within which this critique typically operates. This is not to say that the business of postmodern critique—baldly stated, to challenge the authority and legitimacy of ruling discourses by contesting their universalist pretensions, their fundamentalist truth claims, their mystifications—is altogether alien to these materialisms. Nevertheless, the latter have not developed the conceptual resources and strategies (see 7 above) for pursuing precisely this kind of agenda, whereas Marxism at least operates within a problematic that specifically addresses questions of authority and legitimation.

12. I am not suggesting that postmodern critique *alone* can redeem human beings or effect democratic social transformations or even that it always works in the interest of democratic causes (see 130, n.8). Rather, as Giroux puts it, "[a]t issue here is the need to mine [postmodernisms's] contradictory and oppositional insights so that they might be appropriated in the service of a radical project of

democratic struggle" (*Postmodernism* 17). Postmodern critique can be mobilized in such ways as to play a key role in transforming subjects into critical citizens. It enables progressive, critical thinking to the extent that it has the theoretical resources to lay bare and contest the ideological and mystificatory forces at work in the ruling forms of discourse. The critical citizen is one empowered to act more effectively in the public sphere, to argue for, and to organize on behalf of, the kinds of emancipatory practices and institutions that could secure the conditions for a viable and democratic form of human regeneration.

1   Modalities of the Visionary Moment

1. In his "Preface to *The Nigger of the 'Narcissus*,'" Conrad describes his "task" as a writer, which is to isolate "a passing phase of life" in order to "reveal the substance of its truth—disclose its inspiring secret. . . . Such is the aim, difficult and evanescent . . . And when it is accomplished—behold!—all the truth of life is there: a moment of vision" (13–14). (See also *Lord Jim* 111, cited on 1 above). "Moments of Vision" is the title poem of Thomas Hardy's 1917 volume of verse. Suffice here to quote the second stanza:

> That mirror
> Whose magic penetrates like a dart,
> Who lifts that mirror
> And throws our mind back on us, and our heart,
>   Until we start? (401)

And Virginia Woolf has defined the novelist's task as the attempt "to reconstruct . . . in words" the moment when "a tree shook; an electric light danced; . . . a whole vision . . . seemed contained in that moment" (qtd. in Langbaum 39).

2. See especially Hendry Chayes 1946; J.Prescott 1949; R.Fleming 1949; Beebe 1957; Walzl 1965; Scholes and Walzl 1967.

3. I am in agreement with Zack Bowen, who writes: "[M]any of us wondered . . . what the particular purported insights in many of the epiphanies might be, for the notes consisted of jottings from conversations and of descriptive passages, brief and without illumination" (103).

4. I should acknowledge that to cite Lukács' account of commodity fetishism is, ultimately, to lean on his concept of the social totality, which is conspicuously unpostmodern in its assumption of a panoptic level of explanation. As a theorist who premised his thinking on "the primacy of the category of totality" (27), he has written, "the commodity can only be understood in its undistorted essence when it becomes the universal category of society as a whole" (86).

5. Some commentators think it an error to take the account of the grandmother's redemption at face value. For Stephen Bandy, the old woman is essen-

tially "a calculating opportunist who is capable of embracing her family's murderer, to save her own skin" (110). And an anonymous referee of an earlier version of this chapter maintains I have missed the point of the story which, he/she insists, concludes with a "savagely *ironic misapprehension*" of redemption. Yet, the case for reading "A Good Man . . . " as a narrative of actual redemption remains a strong one. First, consider O'Connor's own view of the matter: she speaks of "the action of grace in the Grandmother's soul" (*Mystery* 113); of "the fact that the old lady's gesture is the result of grace" (*Collected Works* 1150). Second, the account of redemption given in this story is absolutely consistent with the account of it given in so many others by O'Connor: an agent of divine grace violently intrudes into the life of a smug and sanctimonious woman (as in, for example, "Revelation," "Greenleaf," "A Circle in the Fire," and "Everything That Rises Must Converge") and creates the conditions for the latter's redemption. Third, if we read the account of the grandmother's redemption as essentially ironic, then many elements in the story will appear extraneous. For example, why should O'Connor tell the reader that, after the woman has been killed, "her legs [were] crossed under her like a child's" (132) unless to allude to Jesus's words in Mark 10:15: "'. . . whoever does not receive the kingdom of God like a child shall not enter it'"? Or why conclude the story with the Misfit's words, "'It's no real pleasure in life'" (133), unless to suggest that "real pleasure" is a condition of the *afterlife* of the redeemed woman?

6. Other examples of auratic moments can be found in Bellow's *Henderson the Rain King* (100–101), Don DeLillo's *The Names* (32), and Kerouac's *The Subterraneans* (34–35).

7. See chapter 3 of Jonathan Freedman's *Professions of Taste* for a perceptive discussion of the mode of aestheticism that links James and Pater.

8. See e.g., "The Windhover" and "That Nature is a Heraclitean Fire and of the Comfort of the Resurrection" (Hopkins 30, 65–66).

9. Other examples of catastrophic visionary moments can be found in Katherine Mansfield's "Miss Brill" (190–91) and Eudora Welty's "A Still Moment" (198).

10. As opposed to popular notions of insight, which mystify it as a type of supernatural faculty, we should recall that, since at least as far back as the learning experiments of the first Gestalt theorists (e.g. Wolfgang Köhler's experiments with chimpanzees in Tenerife during World War I), it has been argued that (a) trial-and-error behavior ("behavioral hypotheses" that are tested and discarded) is a necessary prelude to insight; there is no act of pure insight; and (b) insightful learning is essentially a sudden reorganization of the problem situation or perceptual field (Chaplin and Krawiec 242–43, 387). More recently (1988), Pat Langley and Randolph Jones have argued that insight may occur through the recall process of "spreading activation": one remembered idea may activate related memories, which in turn activate more related memories, thus proceeding in a ramifying pattern until a particular memory supplies or cues the required insight (Sternberg

344). Robert Weisberg (1988) takes the "nothing-special" view of insight, hence he argues that it is just an extension of ordinary cognitive processes: the "insightful" thinker is one who selects the problem he/she contemplates on the basis of accumulated expertise and extraordinary commitment (Sternberg 325, 344).

11. For a detailed study of the antihegemonic value of Blake's writing, see E. P. Thompson's *Witness Against the Beast,* especially Ch.7.

12. William James quotes an account of "cosmic consciousness," in which are described feelings of "elevation, elation, and joyousness . . . enhanced intellectual power . . . and a sense of immortality" (389–90).

13. Put another way, it would appear that this disruptive psychical energy was, in a defensive reaction, largely absorbed by the idea-complex (and by Ginsberg's hypersexuality, the latter frequently alluded to throughout the interview), while that which could not be absorbed is that which leaves Ginsberg feeling in a near-psychotic (ego-disintegrating) state at the time of the experience (see e.g., 306, 311).

14. Consider the following anecdotal evidence. Twelve undergraduates, enrolled in my seminar, "The Visionary Moment" (West Chester University, PA, Fall 1994), were each required to read to the class a prepared account of a personal visionary moment. Eight of the students recounted experiences that simply failed to meet the criteria by which we had earlier defined visionary moments. The remaining four recounted experiences in terms that, I felt, had a suspiciously literary cast, as if their conception of what counted as a visionary moment had been inherited from reading fiction. Accordingly, their accounts were replete with clichéd appeals to the "infinite," the "cosmic," to "feeling at one with the universe," and so on.

15. Carver fails to convince us that his character has been radically transfigured. And to say this is not to lose sight of his typically working-class male protagonists, who are emotionally inhibited or— as the understatement of the story's last line could suggest—disadvantaged by a restricted speech code; after all, these "limitations" of character do not exhaust the (narrative) resources of his medium.

16. Similarly, the narrator of *Vineland* observes, "the knowledge won't come down all at once in any big transcendent moment" (112), while the narrator of *V* insists, "There are no epiphanies, no 'moments of truth'" (330; rpt. 337).

2   Validations of the Visionary Moment

1. I say antecedent rather than prototype, for we must observe the distinction between the conversion premise of truth as revealed by God and the visionary-moment premise of truth as, for the most part, intuited by the human mind (the visionary moments of Flannery O'Connor and Gerard Manley Hopkins being notable exceptions).

2. Cf. Bunyan, section 229: "But one day, as I was passing in the field, and that too with some dashes on my conscience, fearing lest yet all was not right, *suddenly this sentence fell upon my soul,* Thy righteousness is in heaven; and methought withal, *I saw with the eyes of my soul* Jesus Christ at God's right hand. . . ." (emphases added).

3. Cf. *Paradise Regained,* where Milton's Christ, in dialogue with Satan, speaks the following lines:

"God hath now sent his living Oracle
Into the world, to teach his final will,
And sends his Spirit of Truth henceforth to dwell
In pious hearts, an inward oracle
To all truth requisite for men to know." (1.460–464)

And, in his sermon, "A Divine and Supernatural Light . . . ," Jonathan Edwards writes, "This evidence that they that are spiritually enlightened have of the truth of the things of religion, is a kind of intuitive and immediate evidence" (109).

4. Keats averred, "I am certain of nothing but . . . the truth of Imagination. What the Imagination seizes as beauty must be truth. . . . I am the more zealous in this affair, because I have never yet been able to perceive how anything can be known for truth by consequitive reasoning" ("Letter" qtd. in J.S. Hill 70). And recall Shelley's pronouncement in *A Defence of Poetry:* "Reason is the enumeration of quantities already known; imagination is the perception of the value of those quantities. . . . Reason is to imagination as the instrument to the agent, as the body to the spirit, as the shadow to the substance" (qtd. in J.S. Hill 80). I would add that, even though the Reason/Imagination opposition has long since become a tired cliché, questions remain about the extent to which the Romantics used such monolithic terms with consistency among themselves and over time. To keep within the confines of this project, generalizations about how these concepts were understood must suffice.

3 Metaphysics of the Visionary Moment

1. In *Ghosts,* the second novel of Auster's *New York Trilogy,* we read of a detective whose "method is to stick to outward facts, describing events as though each word tallied exactly with the thing described, and to question the matter no further. Words are transparent for him, great windows that stand between him and the world, and until now they have never impeded his view, have never even seemed to be there" (174).

2. In 1971, Mobutu renamed the Democratic Republic of the Congo as Zaire but, since Laurent Kabila's coup in 1997, the country is, once more, officially known as the Democratic Republic of the Congo.

3. Possibly near Kisangani, on the Zaire River. (See L. Prescott 550.)

4. Heavy dependence on income from mineral exports (notably copper, diamonds, and cobalt) leaves the Congo's economy vulnerable to international speculation on the commodity markets.

5. Naipaul has definite views about how servants should know their place, about the disadvantages they can expect to experience if they break free of their subordinate position. See e.g., *A Bend in the River* (115) and the story of Santosh ("One out of Many") in *In a Free State,* especially 57–58.

6. In a meditative passage in *The Log from the Sea of Cortez* (an autobiographical account of a fishing trip with Ed Ricketts), Steinbeck observes: "The whole is necessarily everything, the whole world of fact and fancy, body and psyche, physical fact and spiritual truth, individual and collective. . . . Quality of sunlight, blueness and smoothness of water, boat-engines, and ourselves were all parts of a larger whole and we could begin to feel its nature but not its size" (208).

7. For a classic account of "cosmic consciousness," see William James 389–91.

8. To be fair, the essays collected in *Sacred Interconnections* succeed on their own terms but the discussions owe nothing to postmodern thought as the term is understood in literary and cultural studies. The contributors (with the occasional exceptions of Suzi Gablik and William Beardslee) appear oblivious to the key theorists who have staked out the terrain of the postmodernism debates (their names and concepts are, but for a few minor instances, absent from the text). Instead, centering on the concept of "prehension," it is the metaphysics of Alfred North Whitehead (!) that pervades most of the discussions, while Descartes emerges as the principal villain on the grounds that his definition of substance—as that which requires nothing but itself to exist—amounts to a denial of interconnectedness. One would have thought, however, that today the real quarrel should be with (secular) postmodern theory, whose overwhelming focus on disjunctiveness (i.e., difference, dispersion, discontinuity, dissensus, of which more later) threatens the coherence of Griffin's and his contributors' thesis of "the cosmic web of interconnections" (2).

9. In Lacanian terms, oceanic feeling looks like a hyperinflated case of the Imaginary, where the self is "misrecognized" not merely as a unified, centered whole, but as an encompassment of all that exists: the "ideal ego's" dream of completeness and omnipotence.

10. This is not to say that Jameson has rejected the explanatory power of the "grand narrative" of class, but only that he sees serious difficulties in maintaining or developing a class identity in the postmodern period.

11. Marshall has had intimate experience of disunity among blacks. Growing up in Brooklyn, in the thirties and forties, she was acutely aware of "conflicts" between her Afro-Caribbean community and Afro-Americans. As she recalls, "This was very painful for me because I saw myself belonging to both [groups]" (*Melus* Interview 118)

12. For an illustrative statement of the Enlightenment's assumption of a

common humanity, consider the following excerpt from David Hume's *Inquiry Concerning Human Understanding* (1748):

> It is universally acknowledged that there is a great uniformity among the acts of men, in all nations and ages, and that human nature remains still the same in its principles and operations. . . . Would you know the sentiments, inclinations, and course of life of the Greeks and Romans? Study well the temper and actions of the French and English: you cannot be much mistaken in transferring to the former *most* of the observations which you have made with regard to the latter. Mankind are so much the same, in all times and places, that history informs us of nothing new or strange in this particular. Its chief use is only to discover the constant and universal principles of human nature. (Qtd. in Hampson 109)

4   The Romantic Metaphysics of Don DeLillo

1. See, for example, Lentricchia, "Tales" and "*Libra*"; Frow; Messmer; and Wilcox.

2. Perhaps the choice of title for the novel is, among other things, calculated to evoke that long tradition of Neoplatonist and medieval mysticism that meditated on divine names. One might cite the writings of Pseudo-Dionysius, author of *The Divine Names,* or the *Merkabah* mystics, early Kabbalists who speculated on the secret names of God and the angels. For such mystics, the way to revelation is through the knowledge of secret names.

3. This is precisely the theme of an early essay by Walter Benjamin, who, reflecting on the degeneration of language into "mere signs," observed: "In the Fall, since the eternal purity of names was violated, . . . man abandoned immediacy in the communication of the concrete name, and fell into the abyss of the mediateness of all communication, of the word as means, of the empty word, into the abyss of prattle" (120).

4. "I do wonder if there is something we haven't come across. Is there another, clearer language? Will we speak it and hear it when we die? Did we know it before we were born? . . . Maybe this is why there's so much babbling in my books. Babbling can be . . . a purer form, an alternate speech. I wrote a short story that ends with two babies babbling at each other in a car. This was something I'd seen and heard, and it was a dazzling and unforgettable scene. I felt these babies *knew* something. They were talking, they were listening, they were *commenting.* . . . Glossolalia is interesting because it suggests there's another way to speak, there's a very different language lurking somewhere in the brain" ("Interview" 83–84). And "Glossolalia or speaking in tongues . . . could be viewed as a higher form of infantile babbling. It's babbling which seems to mean something" ("Outsider" 302). (Such comments help explain the significance of the crying of Baby Wilder in *White Noise* [78–79], an episode I shall discuss later.)

5. A little later we read: "People everywhere are absorbed in conversation. . . . Conversation is life, language is the deepest being" (52).

6. Kant formulated the following succinct definition: "We can describe the sublime in this way: it is an object (of nature) the representation of which determines the mind to think the unattainability of nature as a presentation of [reason's] ideas" (qtd. in Weiskel 22).

7. Recall these lines from Wordsworth's "Tintern Abbey": "a sense sublime / Of something far more deeply interfused, / Whose dwelling is the light of setting suns" (164). I am indebted to Lou Caton of Auburn University for drawing my attention to a possible Romantic context for the sunsets in *White Noise.*

8. Here, I anticipate two likely objections. First, the "airborne toxic event" may seem like an ironic postmodern version of the sublime object insofar as DeLillo substitutes a man-made source of power for a natural one. Yet Gladney's words emphasize that the power is experienced as a *natural* phenomenon: "This was a death made in the laboratory, defined and measurable, but we thought of it at the time in a simple and primitive way, as some seasonal perversity of the earth like a flood or tornado" (127). Second, I disagree with Arthur Saltzman (118–19) and others who see postmodern irony in the account of the sunset insofar as (to be sure) (a) the sunset has been artificially enhanced by pollution and (b) most observers of the spectacle "don't know . . . what it means"; after all, the passage in question clearly insists on the sense of awe irrespective of these factors.

9. See, for example, Lentricchia, "*Libra*"; Carmichael; and Cain.

10. In his lecture "The Transcendentalist," Emerson asserted, "Although . . . there is no pure Transcendentalist, yet the tendency to respect the intuitions and to give them, at least in our creed, all authority over our experience, has deeply colored the conversation and poetry of the present day" (*Selected Writings* 93).

11. M. H. Abrams, borrowing the subtitle of Mark Schorer's distinguished monograph on William Blake, has tagged Romanticism as a "politics of vision" (357). However, as Jon Klancher argues, insofar as Romanticism is an uncircumscribable, historically variable category, one whose construction alters in response to "institutional crises and consolidations," its "politics of vision" can be, and has been, read as not only radical but also conservative (77–88).

12. It is often argued that social history gets repressed in Wordsworth's "extravagant lyricizing of the recovered self" and in his "'sense sublime'" (Klancher 80).

5 Saul Bellow's Transfigurable Subjects

1. Thus, in The Gospel According to Saint Matthew, we read: "And after six days Jesus took with him Peter and James and John his brother, and led them up a high mountain apart. And he was transfigured before them, and his face shone like the sun, and his garments became white as light." (17:1–2)

2. Among the secular narratives of transfigurability, one might include the manifestos for regenerating political subjects through cultural revolution; the near-magical transformations of the consumer promised by commercial advertising; the utopian claims behind genetic engineering (e.g., the $3 billion Human Genome Project) and behind recent initiatives in psychopharmacology (e.g., Prozac acclaimed as a drug that can "remake the self"; see Kramer xiv, 267). Among the spiritual narratives of transfigurability, one might include the conversion narrative (of which more later) and its kindred Greek notion of metanoia, that is, the radical "change of heart" that characterizes certain forms of religious experience.

3. The following abbreviations are used when referring to Bellow's novels: *DM*—*Dangling Man; H*—*Herzog; HG*—*Humboldt's Gift; HRK*—*Henderson the Rain King; MSP*—*Mr. Sammler's Planet; SD*—*Seize the Day; V*—*The Victim.*

4. I am aware that Bellow sometimes seems to distance himself from mystical ideas through an ironic use of buffoonish or eccentric characters (e.g. Henderson, Wilhelm, Herzog) to voice them. Or else on occasion a character will propose a mystical idea then instantly cast doubt on its validity (e.g. *MSP* 173, *HRK* 102). Helge Nilsen goes so far as to argue that "[Bellow's] works do not present any closely defined worldviews or doctrines, but rather deal with sets of ideas as an aid to the creation of characters and situations" (Nilsen 307) and that "Bellow's emphasis is on the limitations and inadequacies of his characters, on the physical and finite rather than the infinite possibilities of spiritual values" (327). Nevertheless, while Bellow may sometimes use irony to undercut this or that spiritual certainty, he remains certain about the redemptive power of the spiritual—a point I shall argue in this chapter. Moreover, I think Stephen Tanner is closer to the mark than Nilsen when he observes, "Treating the big issues with comedy and irony and putting his own convictions in the mouths of characters who are quirky and often preposterous has allowed Bellow over the years to insinuate his ideas and values—particularly his religious values—without having to be directly accountable for them to a critical audience that would readily attack them if they were openly asserted" (S. L. Tanner 287). Ben Siegel also recognizes that Bellow runs the "risk [of] critical mockery stirred by hints of man's redemptive possibilities" (qtd. in Pifer 184).

5. Pascal also observes, "We know the truth not only through our reason but also through our heart. It is through the latter that we know first principles, and reason, which has nothing to do with it, tries in vain to refute them" (Pascal 58). As we shall see, these lines can stand as a concise summary of Bellow's own view of the matter. See also Bloomberg.

6. In the short story, "Cousins," Ijah Brodsky avers, "An original self exists or, if you prefer, an original soul" (Bellow, *Him with His Foot* 267).

7. Thus Sammler understands himself to be "poor in spirit" (*MSP* 264); Citrine perceives "a world of categories devoid of spirit" (*HG* 17); Herzog understands that he has "committed a sin of some kind against his own heart" (*H* 215); and Henderson is explicit about the rationale for the quest that takes him to

Africa: "I wouldn't agree to the death of my soul" (*HRK* 277). In a nonfictional capacity, Bellow has observed, "The soul has to find and hold its ground against hostile forces, sometimes embodied in ideas which frequently deny its very existence, and which indeed often seem to be trying to annul it altogether" ("Foreword" 17). He has also said, "A variety of powers arrive whose aim is to alter, to educate, to condition us. If a man gives himself over to total alteration I consider him to have lost his soul" ("Interview" 276).

8. Recall Flannery O'Connor's story, "Revelation" (1964), in which the smug and sanctimonious Ruby Turpin is, prior to her redeeming insight, compared to a warthog (O'Connor 500, 506).

9. In Philip Roth's *The Counterlife* (1986), Henry Zuckerman, a secular Jew, recounts a visionary moment (60–61) that led to his conversion to orthodox Judaism. He adds, "And that's when I began to realize that of all that I am, I am nothing, I have never been *anything,* the way that I am this Jew" (61). However, for Roth's narrator, a "conversion" (80, 119) like Henry's amounts to "[t]he construction of a counterlife that is one's own anti-myth . . . at its very core. It [is] a species of fabulous utopianism, a manifesto for human transformation as extreme—and, at the outset, as implausible—as any ever conceived" (147).

10. An observation by Stephen Tanner indirectly indicates one motive for Bellow's use of the visionary moment: "In Bellow's view, it is an error on the one hand to deny the existence of big truths, and on the other to think any human will ever express them purely and definitively, let alone incorporate them into daily behavior. It is best to treasure the *fragments and intimations* wherever we find them in the poignant comedy of modern life" (S. L. Tanner 288, emphasis added).

11. For the convenience of keeping this point concise, I have simplified the matter of backsliding by working with a highly generalized model of conversion. Strictly speaking, one needs to distinguish between gradual and sudden conversions and between voluntary and involuntary conversions. One also needs to distinguish between backsliding in the sense of a complete relapse from the faith and merely a loss of the initial enthusiasm for it (see W. James 253).

12. Recall, as a counterinstance, how Habermas has productively distinguished between two kinds of rationality: "purposive-rational action," oriented toward the needs of efficient systems integration, and "communicative action," oriented toward those values that, by ideology-free consensus, are defined as necessary for the health of the "social life-world" (Habermas 81–122).

13. For studies that discuss Bellow's debt to Romanticism, see Chavkin; Nilsen; Stanger.

6 *Jack Kerouac's Rhetoric of Time*

1. Given the autobiographical nature and content of Kerouac's fiction (Charters "Introduction"; Weinreich 19; *Desolation Angels* 246), the narrated

visionary moments possibly are not just fictional creations but (as with Words-worth's *Prelude*) personal experiences. However, even though Kerouac may have lived his spiritual experiences adds nothing to the validity of the truth claims that he makes in their name; after all, the experience is one thing, the terms in which it is received and recounted quite another.

2. Of course, a rhetoric of temporality is a potential resource of any writer's account of a visionary moment. However, the rhetoric acquires special relevance in the case of Kerouac, who explores and creatively exploits forms of temporal experience that deviate from normative clock time.

3. The following abbreviations are used when referring to Kerouac's works: *DA—Desolation Angels; DB—The Dharma Bums; GBO—Good Blonde & Others; OR—On the Road; VC—Visions of Cody.*

4. If one examines the full context of Kerouac's famous definition of "Beat" in *On the Road,* one finds it is intimately linked with this same mystical order of knowing. The setting is an apartment in San Francisco, where Sal Paradise (Kerouac) describes the ecstatic, visionary state of Dean Moriarty (Neal Cassady): "[H]is bony mad face covered with sweat and throbbing veins, saying, 'Yes, yes, yes,' as though tremendous revelations were pouring into him all the time now, and I am convinced they were, and the others suspected as much and were frightened. He was BEAT—the root, the soul of Beatific. What was he knowing? He tried all in his power to tell me what he was knowing. . . ." (*OR* 195). Ann Charters explains this definition of "Beat" as not just a matter of "exalted exhaustion" but, for Kerouac, "a Catholic beatific vision, the *direct* knowledge of God. . . ." ("Introduction" ix, emphasis added).

5. John Tytell (73–77), Gerald Nicosia (457–59) and William Blackburn (13) argue for the centrality of Buddhism in Kerouac's life and work. Tytell observes that "Kerouac sustained himself spiritually during his years of denial by prolonged study of Buddhism—as his thousand-page manuscript, *The Book of the Dharma,* may suggest if it is published" (73). However, Charles Jarvis writes, "But aside from the diversionary aspect of his new-found religion [Buddhism], Kerouac could never be serious about it because he was a Lowell born, Lowell reared, French-Canuck Catholic" (161). And Ann Charters (*Kerouac* 199) and Richard Sorrell (196) appear to concur with this judgment.

6. In the same year as Kerouac published *The Dharma Bums* (1958), Alan Watts published an influential essay in which he distinguished between "Beat Zen" and "Square Zen." Placing Kerouac in the former category, he wrote: "For beat Zen there must be no effort, no discipline, no artificial striving to attain *satori* or to be anything but what one is. But for square Zen there can be no true *satori* without years of meditation-practice under the stern supervision of a qualified master" (613).

7. Tytell observes that "Kerouac believed in the romantic imperative of a language fashioned from ordinary speech. His voice was representative of an endemic colloquialism in the American character" (147). Charters cites the critic,

Maurice Poteet, who argues that Kerouac's experiments with prose amount to an attempt to recover the "spontaneous" language of his childhood, that is, Joual, the French dialect of Montreal ("Introduction" xxv–xxvi).

8. In a brief four-paragraph account of one visionary experience, Augustine invokes "eternity" or kindred terms ("the eternal," "everlasting," "for ever") ten times. (Book IX, section 10; 196–99).

9. *The Spontaneous Poetics of Jack Kerouac* is the title of Regina Weinreich's book-length study of his fiction. "Eulogist of Spontanaeity" is the title of John Tytell's extensive section on Kerouac in *Naked Angels*. In *Jack Kerouac, Prophet of the New Romanticism,* Robert Hipkiss writes a long chapter under the rubric "Spontaneous Prose." George Dardess published an article in *Boundary 2* entitled "The Logic of Spontaneity: A Reconsideration of Kerouac's 'Spontaneous Prose Method.'" Allen Ginsberg is credited with originating the oft-used term "spontaneous bop prosody" to describe Kerouac's writing (Weinreich 160–61n.10). And a key influence behind this preoccupation with spontaneity was supplied by Kerouac himself in his most frequently cited essay, "Essentials of Spontaneous Prose" (*GBO* 69–71).

10. Kerouac often composed under the influence of benzedrine and marijuana (Hipkiss 82, 90) to help him write in "tranced fixation" and without "grammatical and syntactical inhibition" (*GBO* 72). However, not all critics agree that the general run of his prose is authentically spontaneous. Weinreich speaks of his "impulse to perfect a deliberate style that produces the *illusion* of spontaneity" and finds a useful analogy in a remark by Albert Murray for whom jazz improvisation is not just a matter of "on-the-spot invention" but also the "spontaneous appropriation" of stock phrases and clichés (8).

11. Kerouac has written, "What I find to be really 'stupefying in its unreadability' is this laborious and dreary lying called craft and revision by writers, and certainly recognized by the sharpest psychologists as sheer blockage of the mental spontaneous process known 2,500 years ago as 'The Seven Streams of Swiftness'" (*GBO* 145).

12. "Invisibility . . . gives one a slightly different sense of time, you're never quite on the beat. Sometimes you're ahead and sometimes behind. Instead of the swift and imperceptible flowing of time, you are aware of its nodes, those points where time stands still or from which it leaps ahead. And you slip into the breaks and look around. That's what you hear vaguely in Louis' music" (Ellison 8).

7 Ideology of the Visionary Moment

1. In a posthumously published monograph on Blake, E.P. Thompson has insightfully discussed the "consciously anti-hegemonic" impetus of Blake's "mystical and antinomian" beliefs (see especially 108–109).

2. For accounts of the Disney "imagineering" of history, see Schaffer and Rich. For a more general discussion of postmodern simulations of history, see

Hall. For an excellent monograph on patriotic conservationism, see P. Wright. For an examination of nostalgia film, see Jameson, *Postmodernism* 279–96 and *Signatures* 217–29.

3. Walker's choice of the quilt as the heritage object around which the story develops is a strategic one given the prestige and figurative power of quilting in Southern Black communities. Houston Baker and Charlotte Pierce-Baker have observed:

> [Q]uilting . . . is tantamount to providing an improvisational response to chaos . . . [and] dispersal. A patchwork quilt, laboriously and affectionately crafted from bits of worn overalls, shredded uniforms, tattered petticoats, and outgrown dresses stands as a signal instance of a patterned wholeness in the African diaspora. . . .
>
> . . . The quilts of Afro-America offer a sui generis context (a weaving together) of experiences and a storied, vernacular representation of lives conducted in the margins. . . . [T]he sorority of quiltmakers, fragment weavers, holy patchers, possesses a sacred wisdom that it hands down from generation to generation of those who refuse the center for the ludic and unconfined spaces of the margins. (706, 713)

4. In her 1978 essay, "Rootedness: The Ancestor as Foundation," Toni Morrison writes: "In *Song of Solomon* Pilate is the ancestor. The difficulty that Hagar . . . has is how far removed she is from the experience of her ancestor. . . . When you kill the ancestor you kill yourself. I want to point out the dangers, to show that nice things don't always happen to the totally self-reliant if there is no conscious historical connection" (344). And bell hooks, discussing the religious ethos of African-American communities, has observed, "ancestor acknowledgement [is] crucial to our well-being as a people" (qtd. in Connor 270). This view, as we have seen, is dramatically endorsed by Paule Marshall in *Praisesong for the Widow*.

5. In *The Counterlife*, proceeding from a questionable insight derived from a visionary moment (60–61), Philip Roth critiques the search for identity in terms of roots on the same grounds as Walker (see 109, 133).

6. In her essay, "A Name Is Sometimes an Ancestor Saying Hi, I'm with You," Walker suggests that the spirit of Sojourner Truth is incarnated in her ("Name" 97–98). Moreover, she dedicates *The Color Purple* "To the Spirit: / Without whose assistance / Neither this book / Nor I / Would have been / Written."

7. The STFU was founded in 1934, in the Arkansas cotton belt, by H. L. Mitchell and Clay East, with the help of Socialist Party leader, Norman Thomas. By the end of 1935, membership had peaked at 25,000. Of particular concern to the union was the New Deal's Agricultural Adjustment Act, whereby payments, in compensation for land taken out of production, were chiefly channeled to the landowners, leaving many tenant farmers and nearly all the sharecroppers without

means of subsistence. It was pure expediency for Roosevelt's government to refuse the claims of the STFU given that the Southern plantocracy was one of the Democratic Party's most powerful constituencies.

8. Against Faulkner's purely mythic vision of community, we should note not only the class solidarity of the STFU but also the union's interracial membership, which led to forms of assembly that violated the laws and customs of segregation.

9. In stark contrast, we might appeal to a praxial conception of truth, where it is understood that knowledge is acquired not passively (e.g., through revelation or contemplation) but actively through the labor by which a goal-oriented humankind transforms nature in order to master it. In other words, in the process of changing the world, humans develop their capacity to know it. Thus, the truth is proved *in practice* (cf. Marx, "Theses" 422).

10. Jerome McGann (to whom this account of "Tintern Abbey is partially indebted) writes: "[T]he force of lines 15–23 depends upon our knowing that the ruined abbey had been in the 1790s a favorite haunt of transients and displaced persons" (86). He concludes with the observation that "Between 1793 and 1798 Wordsworth lost the world merely to gain his own immortal soul" (88).

Conclusion

1. Cf. Lucien Goldmann, who writes:

> bourgeois thought, which like bourgeois society is tied to the existence of economic activity, is the first thought in history to be at the same time radically profane and ahistoric; the first mode of thought which tends to deny everything sacred, whether that entails the celestial sacred of transcendental religions, or the immanent sacred of the historical future. (Qtd. in Russell 10)

2. In *The Archaeology of Knowledge,* Foucault explains that his purpose is "to free the history of thought from its subjection to transcendence . . . to cleanse it of all transcendental narcissism" (203) and recall Derrida's programmatic assault on the "metaphysics of presence" (see *Writing* 279–80).

3. The exceptions I have in mind are magical realism, "neo-gothic" fiction, and those currents of fiction that explicitly draw on folklore and myth (as in the novels of Toni Morrison and Louise Erdrich). But, even in these respects, the use of the supernatural does not always imply a belief in it; the conventions of the supernatural are often exploited for political or allegorical ends.

Appendix: The Postmodern Sublime

1. For an appropriately skeptical response to Lyotard's estimate of the subversive potential of the avant-garde, see Rorty's "Habermas and Lyotard on Postmodernity" (174–75).

2. Cf. Raymond Williams: "[Hegemony] . . . has continually to be renewed, recreated, defended, and modified. It is also continually resisted, limited, altered, challenged by pressures not at all its own. We have then to add to the concept of hegemony the concepts of counter-hegemony and alternative hegemony, which are real and persistent elements of practice" (*Marxism* 112–13).

Works Cited

ABISH, Walter. *Alphabetical Africa*. New York: New Directions, 1974
———. *How German Is It*. 1980. London: Faber and Faber, 1983.
———. *In the Future Perfect*. New York: New Directions, 1975.
ABRAMS, M. H. *Natural Supernaturalism: Tradition and Revolution in Romantic Literature*. New York: Norton, 1971.
ACKER, Kathy. *Blood and Guts in High School*. 1984. New York: Grove Press, 1989.
ALTHUSSER, Louis. *Essays on Ideology*. 1970. London: Verso, 1984.
ANDERSON, Benedict. *Imagined Communities: Reflections on the Origin and Spread of Nationalism*. London: Verso, 1983.
APPADURAI, Arjun. "Disjuncture and Difference in the Global Cultural Economy." *Global Culture: Nationalism, Globalization and Modernity*. Ed. Mike Featherstone. London: Sage, 1990, 295–310.
AUGUSTINE, Saint. *Confessions*. c. 397–401. Trans. R. S. Pine-Coffin. Harmondsworth: Penguin, 1961.
AUSTER, Paul. *City of Glass*. 1985. *The New York Trilogy*. Harmondsworth: Penguin, 1990.
———. *Ghosts*. 1986. *The New York Trilogy*. Harmondsworth: Penguin, 1990.
BAKER, Houston A., Jr., and Charlotte Pierce-Baker. "Patches: Quilts and Community in Alice Walker's 'Everyday Use.'" *The Southern Review* 21:3 (1985): 706–720.
BAKHTIN, Mikhail. *Problems of Dostoevsky's Poetics*. 1929. Ann Arbor, MI: University of Michigan Press, 1973.
BANDY, Stephen C. "'One of my babies': the misfit and the grandmother." *Studies in Short Fiction* 33:1 (Winter 1996): 107–17.
BARTH, John. *Lost in the Funhouse: Fiction for Print, Tape, Live Voice*. 1968. London: Secker and Warburg, 1969.
BARTHELME, Donald. "See the Moon?" 1968. *Sixty Stories*. New York: G.P. Putnam's Sons, 1981, 97–107.
———. *Snow White*. 1967. New York: Atheneum, 1982.
BARTHES, Roland. "The Death of the Author." *Image-Music-Text*. Trans. and ed. Stephen Heath. London: Fontana, 1977, 142–48.
———. *S/Z*. Trans. Richard Miller. New York: Hill and Wang, 1974.
BAUDRILLARD, Jean. "The Ecstasy of Communication." Trans. John Johnston. *The Anti-Aesthetic*. Ed. Hal Foster. Washington: Bay Press, 1983, 126–34.
———. *Simulations*. New York: Semiotext(e), 1983.

BECKETT, Samuel. *Happy Days.* 1961. London: Faber and Faber, 1966.

————. *Krapp's Last Tape.* 1958. London: Faber and Faber, 1965.

————. *Waiting for Godot.* 1954. London: Faber and Faber, 1965.

BEEBE, Maurice. "Joyce and Aquinas: The Theory of Aesthetics." *PQ* XXXVI (January 1957): 32–34.

BEIDLER, Paul G. "The Postmodern Sublime: Kant and Tony Smith's Anecdote of the Cube." *The Journal of Aesthetics and Art Criticism* 53:2 (Spring 1995): 177–86.

BEJA, Morris. *Epiphany in the Modern Novel.* Seattle: University of Washington Press, 1971.

BELLOW, Saul. *Dangling Man.* 1944. Harmondsworth: Penguin, 1996.

————. Foreword. *The Closing of the American Mind.* Allan Bloom. New York: Simon and Schuster, 1987, 11–18.

————. *Henderson the Rain King.* 1959. Harmondsworth: Penguin, 1996.

————. *Herzog.* 1964. Harmondsworth: Penguin, 1977.

————. *Him with His Foot in His Mouth and Other Stories.* New York: Harper & Row, 1984.

————. *Humboldt's Gift.* 1975. Harmondsworth: Penguin, 1996.

————. "An Interview with Saul Bellow." With Matthew Roudane. *Contemporary Literature* 25:3 (1984): 265–80.

————. *Mr. Sammler's Planet.* 1970. Harmondsworth: Penguin, 1977.

————. "Paris Review Interview." 1965. With Gordon Lloyd Harper. *Writers at Work.* Third Series. Ed. George Plimpton. Harmondsworth: Penguin, 1979. 177–96.

————. *Seize the Day.* 1956. Harmondsworth: Penguin, 1976.

————. *The Victim.* 1947. Harmondsworth: Penguin, 1978.

————. "A World Too Much with Us." *Critical Inquiry* 2:1 (1975): 1–9.

BENJAMIN, Walter. "On Language as Such and on the Language of Man." 1916. *One-Way Street and Other Writings.* Trans. E. Jephcott and Kingsley Shorter. London: Verso, 1985. 107–23.

BERRY, Thomas. *The Dream of the Earth.* San Francisco: Sierra Club Books, 1988.

BHABHA, Homi (ed.). *Nation and Narration.* New York: Routledge, 1991.

BIDNEY, Martin. *Patterns of Epiphany: From Wordsworth to Tolstoy, Pater, and Barrett Browning.* Carbondale: Southern Illinois University Press, 1997.

BLACKBURN, William. "Han Shan Gets Drunk with the Butchers: Kerouac's Buddhism in *On the Road, The Dharma Bums,* and *Desolation Angels.*" *Literature East and West* 21:1–4 (1977): 9–22.

BLAKE, William. *Milton.* 1804. *William Blake: The Complete Poems.* Ed. Alicia Ostrika. Harmondsworth: Penguin, 1977. 513–607.

————. *The Complete Poems.* Ed. Alicia Ostriker. Harmondsworth: Penguin, 1977.

BLOOMBERG, Edward. "Pascalian Echoes in *Henderson the Rain King.*" *Saul*

Works Cited

149

Bellow: A Mosaic. Eds. L. H. Goldman, Gloria L. Cronin, and Ada Aharoni. New York: Peter Lang, 1992, 173–83.

BOWEN, Zack. "Joyce and the Epiphany Concept: A New Approach." *Journal of Modern Literature* 9:1 (1981/82): 103–114.

BORGES, Jorge Luis. "The Library of Babel." 1944. *Labyrinths.* New York: New Directions Books, 1964. 51–58.

BRAVERMAN, Harry. *Labor and Monopoly Capital.* New York: Monthly Review Press, 1974.

BRERETON, Virginia Lieson. *From Sin to Salvation: Stories of Women's Conversions, 1800 to the Present.* Bloomington: Indiana University Press, 1991.

BUNYAN, John. *Grace Abounding to the Chief of Sinners.* 1666. *The Complete Works of John Bunyan,* volume 1. New York: Johnson Reprint Corporation, 1970.

BURKE, Edmund. *A Philosophical Enquiry into the Origin of Our Ideas of the Sublime and the Beautiful.* 1757. Ed. J. T. Boulton. Notre Dame: University of Notre Dame Press, 1958.

CAIN, William E. "Making Meaningful Worlds: Self and History in *Libra.*" *Michigan Quarterly Review* 29:2 (1990): 275–87.

CARMICHAEL, Thomas. "Lee Harvey Oswald and the Postmodern Subject: History and Intertextuality in Don DeLillo's *Libra, The Names,* and *Mao II.*" *Contemporary Literature* 34:2 (1993): 204–18.

CARVER, Raymond. "Cathedral." 1983. *Where I'm Calling From.* New York: Vintage, 1989, 356–75.

CATON, Lou. "Setting Suns and Imaginative Failure in Don DeLillo's *White Noise.*" Twentieth-Century Literature Conference. University of Louisville, Louisville, KY. 1995.

CHAPLIN, James P., and T. S. Krawiec. *Systems and Theories of Psychology.* 3rd Ed. New York: Holt, Rinehart and Winston, 1974.

CHAPMAN, Alison. "Uncanny Epiphanies in the Nineteenth-Century Sonnet Tradition." *Moments of Moment: Aspects of the Literary Epiphany.* Ed. Wim Tigges. Amsterdam-Atlanta, GA: Rodopi, 1999, 115–36.

CHARTERS, Ann. "Introduction." *On the Road* by Jack Kerouac. Harmondsworth: Penguin, 1991. vii–xxx.

———. *Kerouac: A Biography.* San Francisco: Straight Arrow Books, 1973.

CHAVKIN, Allan. "Bellow and English Romanticism." *Studies in the Literary Imagination* 17:2 (1984): 7–18.

COLERIDGE, Samuel Taylor. *Biographia Literaria.* 1817. Ed. George Watson. London: Dent, 1975.

COLIMORE, Edward. "Getting into the Spirit of Millennium Change." *Philadelphia Inquirer,* 22 March 1998: A1+.

CONNOR, Kimberly Rae. *Conversions and Visions in the Writings of African-American Women.* Knoxville: University of Tennessee Press, 1994.

CONRAD, Joseph. *Lord Jim.* 1900. Harmondsworth: Penguin, 1949.

————. *The Nigger of the 'Narcissus', Typhoon and Other Stories.* 1897, 1903. Harmondsworth: Penguin, 1963.

COOVER, Robert. "The Babysitter." *Pricksongs & Descants.* New York: Plume, 1970, 206–39.

————. *Pricksongs & Descants.* 1969. New York: Plume, 1970.

DARDESS, George. "The Logic of Spontaneity: A Reconsideration of Kerouac's 'Spontaneous Prose Method.'" *Boundary 2* 3 (1975): 729–43.

DAVIS, Mike. *Prisoners of the American Dream.* London: Verso, 1986.

De QUINCEY, Thomas. *Confessions of an English Opium Eater.* 1821. Harmondsworth: Penguin, 1971.

DEBORD, Guy. *Society of the Spectacle.* 1967. Detroit: Black & Red, 1983.

DELILLO, Don. "I Never Set Out to Write an Apocalyptic Novel." Interview with Caryn James. *New York Times Book Review,* 13 Jan 1985: 31.

————. "An Interview with Don DeLillo." With Tom LeClair. *Anything Can Happen: Interviews with Contemporary American Novelists.* Ed. Tom LeClair and Larry McCaffery. Urbana: University of Illinois Press, 1983, 79–90.

————. *Libra.* 1988. Harmondsworth: Penguin, 1989.

————. *The Names.* 1982. New York: Vintage, 1989.

————. "An Outsider in This Society: An Interview with Don DeLillo." With Anthony DeCurtis. *The Fiction of Don DeLillo.* Ed. Frank Lentricchia. Special issue of *South Atlantic Quarterly* 89:2 (1990): 281–304.

————. *Ratner's Star.* 1976. New York: Vintage, 1989.

————. *White Noise.* 1985. Harmondsworth: Penguin, 1986.

DERRIDA, Jacques. *Of Grammatology.* 1967. Trans. Gayatri Chakravorty Spivak. Baltimore: Johns Hopkins University Press, 1976.

————. *Writing and Difference.* 1967. Trans. Alan Bass. London: Routledge & Kegan Paul, 1978.

DESCARTES, René. *Rules for the Direction of the Mind.* Written 1628, pub. 1701. Trans. Elizabeth S. Haldane and G. R. T. Ross. In *Descartes/Spinoza.* Chicago: University of Chicago Press, 1952, 1–40.

DEVINE, Paul. "Leitmotif and Epiphany: George Moore's *Evelyn Innes* and *The Lake.*" *Moments of Moment: Aspects of the Literary Epiphany.* Ed. Wim Tigges. Amsterdam-Atlanta, GA: Rodopi, 1999, 155–76.

DUTOIT, Thomas. "Epiphanic Reading in Ann Radcliffe's *The Mysteries of Udolpho.*" *Moments of Moment: Aspects of the Literary Epiphany.* Ed. Wim Tigges. Amsterdam-Atlanta, GA: Rodopi, 1999, 85–100.

EDWARDS, Jonathan. "Personal Narrative." c.1740. *Jonathan Edwards.* Eds. Clarence H. Faust and Thomas H. Johnson. New York: Hill and Wang, 1962. 57–72.

————. "A Divine and Supernatural Light." 1734. *Jonathan Edwards.* Eds. Clarence H. Faust and Thomas H. Johnson. New York: Hill and Wang, 1962. 102–111.

ELLISON, Ralph. *Invisible Man.* 1952. New York: Vintage Books, 1989.

ELLMANN, Richard. *James Joyce.* New York: Oxford University Press, 1959.

EMERSON, Ralph Waldo. *The Collected Works of Ralph Waldo Emerson,* vol. 1. Cambridge, MA: Belknap-Harvard University Press, 1971.

———. *The Selected Writings of Ralph Waldo Emerson.* Ed. Brooks Atkinson. New York: Modern Library, 1950.

ENGELS, Friedrich. *The Peasant War in Germany.* 1850. Excerpted in *Marx and Engels: Basic Writings in Politics and Philosophy.* Ed. Lewis S. Feuer. Glasgow: Fontana, 1969, 452–75.

ENGSTRÖM, Timothy H. "The Postmodern Sublime?: Philosophical Rehabilitations and Pragmatic Evasions." *Boundary 2* 20:2 (1993): 190–204.

FAULKNER, William. "Delta Autumn." *Go Down, Moses.* 1942. New York: Vintage, 1990, 317–48.

———. *Go Down, Moses.* 1942. New York: Vintage, 1990.

———. *Light in August.* 1932. New York: Vintage, 1990.

———. "The Old People." *Go Down, Moses.* 1942. New York: Vintage, 1990. 155–80.

———. *The Sound and the Fury.* 1929. New York: Vintage, 1990.

FEKETE, John. *The Critical Twilight.* London: Routledge & Kegan Paul, 1977.

FIEDLER, Leslie. "Cross the Border—Close that Gap: Postmodernism." 1968. *American Literature Since 1900.* Ed. M. Cunliffe. London: Barrie and Jenkins, 1975, 344–66.

FISHER, David James. *Romain Rolland and the Politics of Intellectual Engagement.* Berkeley: University of California Press, 1988.

FITZGERALD. F. Scott. *Tender Is the Night.* 1934. New York: Collier Books, 1982.

FLEMING, Bruce E. "Brothers Under the Skin: Achebe on *Heart of Darkness.*" *College Literature* Double Issue 19.3/20.1 (October 1992/February 1993): 90–99.

FLEMING, Rudd. "*Quidditas* in the Tragi-Comedy of Joyce." *UKCR* 15 (Summer 1949): 289–90.

FOUCAULT, Michel. *The Archaeology of Knowledge.* 1969. Trans. Alan Sheridan. New York: Pantheon, 1972.

———. *The History of Sexuality.* Vol.1. 1976. Harmondsworth: Penguin, 1984.

———. *Language, Counter-Memory, Practice: Selected Essays and Interviews.* Ed. Donald F. Bouchard. Ithaca: Cornell University Press, 1977.

———. *The Order of Things.* 1966. London: Tavistock Publications, 1974.

———. *Power/Knowledge: Selected Interviews and Other Writings 1972–1977.* Ed. Colin Gordon. New York: Pantheon, 1980.

FRASER, Nancy and Linda J. Nicholson. "Social Criticism without Philosophy: An Encounter between Feminism and Postmodernism." *Feminism/Postmodernism.* Ed. Linda J. Nicholson. New York: Routledge, 1990. 19–38.

FREEDMAN, Jonathan. *Professions of Taste*. Stanford: Stanford University Press, 1990.

FREUD, Sigmund. *Introductory Lectures on Psychoanalysis*. 1915–17. Harmondsworth: Penguin, 1973.

———. "A Religious Experience." 1928. *Sigmund Freud: Collected Papers*, vol. 5. Ed. James Strachey. New York: Basic Books, 1959, 243–46.

FROW, John. "The Last Things Before the Last: Notes on *White Noise*." *The Fiction of Don DeLillo*. Ed. Frank Lentricchia. Special issue of *South Atlantic Quarterly* 89:2 (1990): 413–29.

GABLER, Hans Walter. "Joyce's text in progress." *The Cambridge Companion to James Joyce*. Ed. Derek Attridge. Cambridge, UK: Cambridge Univesity Press, 1990. 213–36.

GINSBERG, Allen. "Interview with Thomas Clark." 1965. *Writers at Work: The Paris Review Interviews. Third Series*. Ed. George Plimpton. Harmondsworth: Penguin, 1977, 279–320.

———. *Collected Poems: 1947–1980*. New York: Harper & Row, 1984.

GIROUX, Henry A. "Literacy, Pedagogy, and the Politics of Difference." *College Literature* 19:1 (1992): 1–11.

———. (ed.). *Postmodernism, Feminism, and Cultural Politics*. Albany: State University of New York Press, 1991.

GOLD, Michael. *Jews Without Money*. 1930. New York: International Publishers, 1942.

GRIFFIN, Charles J.G. "The Rhetoric of Form in Conversion Narratives." *Quarterly Journal of Speech* 76 (1990): 152–63.

GRIFFIN, David Ray (ed.). *Sacred Interconnections: Postmodern Spirituality, Political Economy, and Art*. Albany: State University of New York Press, 1990.

HABERMAS, Jürgen. *Toward a Rational Society*. Trans. Jeremy J. Shapiro. London: Heinemann Educational Books, 1971.

HALL, Dennis. "Civil War Reenactors and the Postmodern Sense of History". *Journal of American Culture* 17 (1994): 7–11.

HALLEY, Janet E. "Versions of the Self and the Politics of Privacy in *Silex Scintillans*." *George Herbert Journal* 7:1–2 (1983/84): 51–71.

HAMPSON, Norman. *The Enlightenment*. Harmondsworth: Penguin, 1968.

HARDY, Thomas. "Moments of Vision." 1917. *The Works of Thomas Hardy*. Ware, Hertfordshire, UK: Wordsworth Poetry Library, 1994.

HATAB, Lawrence J. "Rejoining *Aletheia* and Truth: or Truth Is a Five-Letter Word." *International Philosophical Quarterly* 30:4, no. 120 (December 1990): 431–47.

HAWKINS, Joan. "'Click Here If You're White': The Construction of Race and Gender on White Supremacist Web Sites." *Concerns* 27:1–2 (Spring 2000): 45–58.

HEIDEGGER, Martin. *Being and Time*. 1927. Trans. J. Macquarrie and Edward Robinson. New York: Harper & Row, 1962.

————. *The Question Concerning Technology and Other Essays.* Trans. William Lovitt. New York: Harper & Row, 1977.

HELD, David. "The Decline of the Nation State." *New Times.* Eds. Stuart Hall and Martin Jacques. London: Lawrence & Wishart. 1989. 191–204.

HENDRY CHAYES, Irene. "Joyce's Epiphanies." 1946. *Joyce's Portrait: Criticisms and Critiques.* Ed. Thomas E. Connolly. Meredith Publishing Company, 1962, 204–220.

HENKE, Suzette. "Virginia Woolf's *To the Lighthouse:* (En)Gendering Epiphany." *Moments of Moment: Aspects of the Literary Epiphany.* Ed. Wim Tigges. Amsterdam-Atlanta, GA: Rodopi, 1999, 261–78.

HEWISON, Robert. *The Heritage Industry.* London: Methuen, 1987.

HILL, Christopher. *Society and Puritanism in Pre-Revolutionary England.* New York: Schocken Books, 1964.

HILL, John Spencer (ed.). *The Romantic Imagination.* London: Dent, 1975.

HIPKISS, Robert A. *Jack Kerouac: Prophet of the New Romanticism.* Lawrence: Regents Press of Kansas, 1976.

HOCHSCHILD, Adam. *King Leopold's Ghost.* Boston: Houghton Mifflin, 1998.

HOLLAND, Norman. "Re-covering 'The Purloined Letter': Reading as a Personal Transaction." *The Reader in the Text: Essays on Audience and Interpretation.* Eds. Susan R. Suleiman and Inge Crosman. Princeton, NJ: Princeton University Press, 1980.

HOPKINS, Gerard Manley. *Poems and Prose of Gerard Manley Hopkins.* Harmondsworth: Penguin, 1953.

HOWE, Irving. *Decline of the New.* New York: Harcourt, Brace & World, Inc., 1970.

HUNT, Douglas (ed.). *The Riverside Anthology of Literature.* Boston: Houghton Mifflin, 1988.

JAMES, Henry. *The Ambassadors.* 1903. Harmondsworth: Penguin, 1973.

————. "The Beast in the Jungle." 1903. *Selected Tales.* London: Dent, 1982, 228–83.

JAMES, William. *The Varieties of Religious Experience.* 1902. New York: Modern Library, 1936.

JAMESON, Fredric. *The Political Unconscious: Narrative as a Socially Symbolic Act.* London: Methuen, 1981.

————. *Postmodernism, or the Cultural Logic of Late Capitalism.* Durham: Duke University Press, 1991.

————. *Signatures of the Visible.* London: Routledge, 1992.

JARVIS, Charles. *Visions of Kerouac: The Life of Jack Kerouac.* Lowell, MA: Ithaca Press, 1974.

JEWINSKI, Ed. "James Joyce and Samuel Beckett: From Epiphany to Anti-Epiphany." *Re: Joyce'N Beckett.* Eds. Phyllis Carey and Ed Jewinski. New York: Fordham University Press, 1992, 160–74.

JOHNSON, Sandra Humble. *The Space Between: Literary Epiphany in the Work of Annie Dillard.* Kent, OH: Kent State University Press, 1992.

JOHNSTON, John. *Information Multiplicity: American Fiction in the Age of Media Saturation.* Baltimore: Johns Hopkins University Press, 1998.

JOYCE, James. *Dubliners.* 1914. New York: Bantam, 1990.

———. *Epiphanies.* Written 1990–1904. Ed. O. A. Silverman. Buffalo: University of Buffalo Press, 1956.

———. *A Portrait of the Artist as a Young Man.* 1916. New York: Bantam, 1992.

———. *Stephen Hero.* Written 1904–1905, pub. 1944. Norfolk, CT: New Directions, 1963.

———. *Ulysses.* 1922. Harmondsworth: Penguin, 1969.

KEATS, John. "Letter to Benjamin Bailey, 22 November 1817." *The Romantic Imagination.* Ed. John. S. Hill. London: Dent, 1975, 70–71.

KENNER, Hugh. *Dublin's Joyce.* Bloomington: Indiana University Press, 1956.

KELLER, Carl A. "Mystical Literature." *Mysticism and Philosophical Analysis.* Ed. Steven T. Katz. New York: Oxford University Press, 1978, 75–100.

KEROUAC, Jack. *Desolation Angels.* New York: Coward-McCann, 1965.

———. *The Dharma Bums.* 1958. Harmondsworth: Penguin, 1976.

———. *Good Blonde & Others.* San Francisco: Grey Fox Press, 1996.

———. *On the Road.* 1957. Harmondsworth: Penguin, 1991.

———. *The Subterraneans.* 1958. New York: Grove Press, 1981.

———. *Visions of Cody.* 1959. Harmondsworth: Penguin, 1993.

KITTLER, Friedrich A. *Discourse Networks 1800/1900.* 1985. Trans. M. Metter, with C. Cullens. Stanford: Stanford University Press, 1990.

———. "Technologies of Writing/Rewriting Technology: An Interview with Friedrich Kittler." 1995. With Matthew B. Griffin and S. M. Herman. http://www.emory.edu/ALTJNL/Articles/kittler/kit1.htm.

KLANCHER, Jon. "English Romanticism and Cultural Production." *The New Historicism.* Ed. H. Aram Veeser. New York: Routledge, 1989, 77–88.

KRAMER, Peter. *Listening to Prozac.* Harmondsworth: Penguin, 1994.

LACLAU, Ernesto and Chantal Mouffe. *Hegemony and Socialist Strategy.* Trans. Winston Moore and Paul Cammack. London: Verso, 1985.

LANDOW, George P. *Hypertext: The Convergence of Contemporary Critical Theory and Technology.* Baltimore: Johns Hopkins, 1992.

LANGBAUM, Robert. *The Word from Below: Essays on Modern Literature and Culture.* Madison: University of Wisconsin Press, 1987.

LANKSHEAR, Colin (ed.). *Critical Literacy: Politics, Praxis, and the Postmodern.* Albany: State University of New York Press, 1993.

LeCLAIR, Tom. *In the Loop: Don DeLillo and the Systems Novel.* Urbana: University of Illinois Press, 1987.

LEHMAN, Daniel W. "Raymond Carver's Management of Symbol." *Journal of the Short Story in English* 17 (1991): 43–58.

LEITCH, Vincent B. *Postmodernism: Local Effects, Global Flows.* Albany: State University of New York Press, 1996.

LENTRICCHIA, Frank. "*Libra* as Postmodern Critique." *The Fiction of Don DeLillo.* Ed. Frank Lentricchia. Special issue of *South Atlantic Quarterly* 89:2 (1990): 431–53.

———. "Tales of the Electronic Tribe." *New Essays on White Noise.* Ed. Frank Lentricchia. Cambridge and New York: Cambridge University Press, 1991, 87–113.

LEVERTOV, Denise. "The Secret." 1964. *Poetry.* Ed. Jill P. Baumgaertner. San Diego: Harcourt Brace Jovanovich, 1990, 411–12.

LEVIN, Harry. *James Joyce: A Critical Introduction.* 1941. New York: New Directions, 1960.

LOCKE, John. *An Essay Concerning Human Understanding.* 1690. London: Collins, 1964.

LOSEY, Jay. "'Demonic' Epiphanies: The Denial of Death in Larkin and Heaney." *Moments of Moment: Aspects of the Literary Epiphany.* Ed. Wim Tigges. Amsterdam-Atlanta, GA: Rodopi, 1999, 375–400.

LUKÁCS, Georg. *History and Class Consciousness.* 1923. Trans. Rodney Livingstone. London: Merlin Press, 1971.

LYOTARD, Jean-François. *The Postmodern Condition: A Report on Knowledge.* 1979. Trans. Geoff Bennington and Brian Massumi. Manchester: Manchester University Press, 1984.

MacCABE, Colin. "The Problems of Living in an Interpreted World." *Radical Philosophy* 1:2 (Summer 1972): 9–11.

McGANN, Jerome J. *The Romantic Ideology: A Critical Investigation.* Chicago: University of Chicago Press, 1985.

McGOWAN, John. "From Pater to Wilde to Joyce: Modernist Epiphany and the Soulful Self." *Texas Studies in Literature and Language* 32:3 (1990): 417–45.

———. "Postmodernism and Its Critics." *A Postmodern Reader.* Eds. Joseph Natoli and Linda Hutcheon. Albany: State University of New York Press, 1993, 203–222.

McKAY, George. "DiY Culture: notes towards an intro." *DiY Culture: Party & Protest in Nineties Britain.* Ed. George McKay. London: Verso, 1998, 1–53.

MAHAFFEY, Vicki. "Joyce's Shorter Works." *The Cambridge Companion to James Joyce.* Ed. Derek Attridge. Cambridge, UK: Cambridge University Press, 1990, 185–211.

MALTBY, Paul. "Self-Reflexive Fiction in the Age of Systemic Communication." *Centennial Review* 40:1 (Winter 1996): 49–68.

MANDEL, Ernest. *Late Capitalism.* 1972. Trans. Joris De Bres. London: Verso, 1978.

MANSFIELD, Katherine. "Miss Brill." *The Garden Party.* 1922. Harmondsworth: Penguin, 1951, 184–91.

MARSHALL, Paule. "An Interview with Paule Marshall." With Daryl Cumber Dance. *Southern Review* 28:1 (January 1992): 1–20.

———. "A *Melus* Interview: Paule Marshall." With Joyce Pettis. *Melus* 17:4 (Winter 1991): 117–29.

———. *Praisesong for the Widow.* New York: G. P. Putnam's Sons, 1983.

MARX, Karl. *Capital: Volume I.* 1867. Harmondsworth: Penguin, 1976.

———. "Theses on Feuerbach." 1845. *Early Writings.* Harmondsworth: Penguin, 1981.

——— and Friedrich Engels. *Basic Writings on Politics and Philosophy.* Ed. Lewis S. Feuer. Glasgow: Fontana, 1969.

MELEHY, Hassan. *Writing Cogito: Montaigne, Descartes, and the Institution of the Modern Subject.* Albany: State University of New York Press, 1997.

MENDELSON, Edward. "The Sacred, the Profane, and *The Crying of Lot 49.*" *Individual and Community.* Eds. K. H. Baldwin and D. K. Kirby. Durham: Duke University Press, 1975, 182–222.

MESSMER, Michael W. "'Thinking It Through Completely': The Interpretation of Nuclear Culture." *The Centennial Review* 32:4 (1988): 397–413.

MEYER, Michael (ed.). *The Bedford Introduction to Literature.* 5th Ed. Boston: Beford/St. Martin's, 1999.

MILTON, John. *Paradise Regained.* 1671. *The Portable Milton.* Ed. Douglas Bush. Harmondsworth: Penguin, 1976.

MORRISON, Toni. "Rootedness: The Ancestor as Foundation." *Black Women Writers (1950–1980).* Ed. Mari Evans. New York: Anchor Press, 1984, 339–45.

———. *Song of Solomon.* 1977. New York: Plume, 1987.

NAIPAUL, V. S. *A Bend in the River.* 1979. Harmondsworth: Penguin, 1980.

———. *In a Free State.* 1971. Harmondsworth: Penguin, 1973.

NICHOLS, Ashton. "Cognitive and Pragmatic Linguistic Moments: Literary Epiphany in Thomas Pynchon and Seamus Heaney." *Moments of Moment: Aspects of the Literary Epiphany.* Ed. Wim Tigges. Amsterdam-Atlanta, GA: Rodopi, 1999, 467–80.

———. *The Poetics of Epiphany.* Tuscaloosa: University of Alabama Press, 1987.

NICOSIA, Gerald. *Memory Babe: A Critical Biography of Jack Kerouac.* 1983. Berkeley: University of California Press, 1994.

NIETZSCHE, Friedrich. *The Portable Nietzsche.* Ed. and Trans. Walter Kaufman. New York: Viking Press, 1977.

———. *The Gay Science.* 1882. Trans. Walter Kaufman. New York: Vintage Books, 1974.

———. *On the Genealogy of Morals.* 1887. Trans. Walter Kaufmann and R. J. Hollingdale. New York: Vintage, 1969.

NILSEN, Helge N. "Saul Bellow and Transcendentalism: From *The Victim* to *Herzog.*" *College Language Association Journal* 30:3 (1987): 307–27.

NOON, William T. *Joyce and Aquinas*. New Haven, CT: Yale University Press, 1957.

O'CONNOR, Flannery. "A Circle in the Fire." *The Complete Short Stories*. New York: Noonday Press, 1993, 175–93.

———. *Collected Works*. New York: Library of America, 1988.

———. *The Complete Stories*. New York: Noonday Press, 1993.

———. "Everything That Rises Must Converge." 1961. *The Complete Stories*. New York: Noonday Press, 1993, 405–420.

———. "A Good Man Is Hard to Find." 1953. *The Complete Stories*. New York: Noonday Press, 1993, 117–133.

———. "Greenleaf." 1956. *The Complete Stories*. New York: Noonday Press, 1993, 311–34.

———. *Mystery and Manners*. New York: Farrar, Straus & Giroux, 1969.

———. "Parker's Back." 1965. *The Complete Stories*. New York: Noonday Press, 1993, 510–30.

———. "Revelation." 1964. *The Complete Stories*. New York: Noonday Press, 1993. 488–509.

O'NEILL, Eugene. *Long Day's Journey into Night*. 1940. London: Jonathan Cape, 1966.

PARKE, Nigel. "Stifled Cries and Whispering Shoes: Rites of Passage in the Modern Epiphany." *Moments of Moment: Aspects of the Literary Epiphany*. Ed. Wim Tigges. Amsterdam-Atlanta, GA: Rodopi, 1999, 207–232.

PASCAL, Blaise. *Pensées*. 1657–1658. Trans. A. J. Krailsheimer. Harmondsworth: Penguin, 1966.

PERLOFF, Marjorie. "Modernist Studies." *Redrawing the Boundaries*. Eds. Stephen Greenblatt and Giles Gunn. New York: The Modern Language Association of America, 1992, 154–78.

PETERSON, Linda H. "Newman's *Apologia pro vita sua* and the Traditions of English Spiritual Autobiography." *PMLA* 100:3 (1985): 300–314.

PETTIT, Norman. *The Heart Prepared: Grace and Conversion in Puritan Spiritual Life*. New Haven: Yale University Press, 1966.

PIFER, Ellen. *Saul Bellow Against the Grain*. Philadelphia: University of Pennsylvania Press, 1990.

POIRIER, Richard. *A World Elsewhere*. Oxford: Oxford University Press, 1966.

PORTER, Katherine Anne. "The Grave." 1944. *The Collected Stories of Katherine Anne Porter*. New York: Harcourt, Brace & World, 1965, 362–68.

PRESCOTT, Joseph. "James Joyce's Epiphanies." *MLN* 44 (May 1949): 346.

PRESCOTT, Lynda. "Past and Present Darkness: Sources for V.S. Naipaul's *A Bend in the River*." *Modern Fiction Studies* 30:3 (1984): 547–59.

PYNCHON, Thomas. *The Crying of Lot 49*. 1966. New York: Perennial Library, 1986.

———. *Gravity's Rainbow*. 1973. London: Picador, 1978.

————. *V.* 1963. London: Picador, 1975.

————. *Vineland.* 1990. London: Minerva, 1991.

REISING, Russell. *The Unusable Past.* London: Methuen, 1986.

RICH, Frank. "Disney's Bull Run." *New York Times,* 22 May 1994.

RORTY, Richard. *Contingency, Irony, and Solidarity.* Cambridge, UK: Cambridge University Press, 1989.

————. "Habermas and Lyotard on Postmodernity." *Habermas and Modernity.* Ed. Richard J. Bernstein. Cambridge, UK: Polity Press, 1985, 161–75.

ROSZAK, Theodore. *The Making of a Counter Culture.* London: Faber and Faber, 1970.

ROTH, Philip. *The Counterlife.* 1986. New York: Vintage, 1996.

ROUSSEAU, Jean-Jacques. *The Confessions.* 1765. Harmondsworth: Penguin, 1975.

————. "Essay on the Origin of Languages." Trans. John H. Moran. *On the Origin of Language.* Eds. John H. Moran and Alexander Gode. New York: Ungar, 1966, 5–74.

RUSSELL, Charles. *Poets, Prophets, and Revolutionaries: The Literary Avant-Garde from Rimbaud through Postmodernism.* New York: Oxford University Press, 1985.

SALTZMAN, Arthur M. *Designs of Darkness in Contemporary American Fiction.* Philadelphia: University of Pennsylvania Press, 1990.

SCHAFFER, Scott. "Disney and the Imagineering of Histories." *Postmodern Culture* 6:3 (1996): 1–18.

SCHOLES, Robert and Florence Walzl. "Notes, Documents, and Critical Comment: The Epiphanies of Joyce." *PMLA* 82, no. 1 (March 1967): 152–54.

SCHORER, Mark. *William Blake: The Politics of Vision.* New York: Henry Holt and Company, 1946.

SINCLAIR, Upton. *The Jungle.* 1906. New York: Bantam, 1981.

SMART, Ninian. *The Religious Experience of Mankind.* 1969. Glasgow: Collins, 1977.

SORRELL, Richard S. "The Catholicism of Jack Kerouac." *Studies in Religion* 11:2 (1982): 189–200.

SPIVAK, Gayatri Chakravorty. "The New Historicism: Political Commitment and the Postmodern Critic." *The New Historicism.* Ed. H. Aram Veeser. New York: Routledge, 1989, 277–92.

————. *In Other Worlds: Essays in Cultural Politics.* New York: Methuen, 1987.

SPOLSKY, Ellen. *Gaps in Nature: Literary Interpretation and the Modular Mind.* Albany: State University of New York Press, 1993.

STANGER, James. "The Power of Vision: Blake's System and Bellow's Project in *Mr. Sammler's Planet.*" *Saul Bellow Journal* 12:2 (1994): 17–36.

STEINBECK, John. *The Grapes of Wrath.* 1939. Harmondsworth: Penguin, 1976.

————. *The Log from the Sea of Cortez.* 1951. London: Pan Books, 1960.

STERNBERG, Robert J. *In Search of the Human Mind.* 2nd Ed. Fort Worth: Harcourt Brace College Publishers, 1998.

STRAUS, Roger A. "Religious Conversion as a Personal and Collective Accomplishment." *Sociological Analysis* 40:2 (1979): 158–65.

STROMBERG, Peter G. *Language and Self-Transformation: A Study of the Christian Conversion Narrative.* Cambridge, UK: Cambridge University Press, 1993.

TABBI, Joseph. *Postmodern Sublime: Technology and American Writing from Mailer to Cyberpunk.* Ithaca: Cornell University Press, 1995.

TANNER, Stephen L. "The Religious Vision of *More Die of Heartbreak.*" *Saul Bellow in the 1980s.* Eds. Gloria L. Cronin and L. H. Goldman. East Lansing, MI: Michigan State University Press, 1989, 283–96.

TANNER, Tony. *City of Words: American Fiction 1950–1970.* London: Jonathan Cape, 1971.

TEASDALE, Wayne. "Nature-Mysticism as the Basis of Eco-Spirituality." *Studies in Formative Spirituality* 12:2, May (1991): 215–31.

THOMPSON, E. P. *Witness Against the Beast: William Blake and the Moral Law.* New York: New Press, 1993.

TIGGES, Wim. "The Significance of Trivial Things: Towards a Typology of Literary Epiphanies." *Moments of Moment: Aspects of the Literary Epiphany.* Ed. Wim Tigges. Amsterdam-Atlanta, GA: Rodopi, 1999, 11–36.

TINKLER-VILLANI, Valeria. "'I Saw, I Felt, But I Cannot Describe': Demonic Epiphany in Gothic Fiction." *Moments of Moment: Aspects of the Literary Epiphany.* Ed. Wim Tigges. Amsterdam-Atlanta, GA: Rodopi, 1999, 101–114.

TSUR, Reuven. *What Is Cognitive Poetics?* Tel Aviv: Katz Research Institute for Hebrew Literature, 1983.

TYTELL, John. *Naked Angels: Kerouac, Ginsberg, Burroughs.* New York: Grove Weidenfeld, 1976.

ULLMAN, Chana. *The Transformed Self: The Psychology of Religious Conversion.* New York: Plenum Press, 1989.

VAN BIEMA, David. "Does Heaven Exist?" *Time,* 24 March 1997: 71–78.

VAN BOHEEMEN-SAAF, Christine. "Epiphany and Postcolonial Affect." *Moments of Moment: Aspects of the Literary Epiphany.* Ed. Wim Tigges. Amsterdam-Atlanta, GA: Rodopi, 1999, 195–206.

VAUGHAN, Henry. *The Complete Poetry of Henry Vaughan.* Ed. French Fogle. New York: New York University Press, 1965.

VESTERMAN, William (ed.). *Literature: An Introduction to Critical Reading.* Fort Worth: Harcourt Brace Jovanovich, 1993.

VISKER, Rudi. "From Foucault to Heidegger: A One-way Ticket?" *Research in Phenomenology* 21:1991 (Fall 1992): 116–40.

WALKER, Alice. *The Color Purple*. New York: Washington Square Press, 1983.

————. "Everyday Use." *In Love & Trouble*. San Diego: Harcourt Brace & Company, 1973, 47–59.

————. "Gifts of Power: The Writings of Rebecca Jackson." *In Search of Our Mothers' Gardens*. New York: Harcourt Brace Jovanovich, 1983, 71–82.

————. "A Name Is Sometimes an Ancestor Saying Hi, I'm with You." 1986. *Living by the Word*. Harcourt Brace Jovanovich, 1988, 97–8.

WALZL, Florence L. "The Liturgy of the Epiphany Season and the Epiphanies of Joyce." *PMLA* 50, no.4 (September 1965): 436–50.

WATTS, Alan. "Beat Zen, Square Zen, and Zen." 1958. Reprinted in *The Portable Beat Reader*. Ed. Ann Charters. Harmondsworth: Penguin, 1992, 607–614.

WEINREICH, Regina. *The Spontaneous Poetics of Jack Kerouac*. 1987. New York: Marlowe & Company, 1995.

WEISKEL, Thomas. *The Romantic Sublime: Studies in the Structure and Psychology of Transcendence*. Baltimore: Johns Hopkins University Press, 1976.

WELCH, Sharon. "An Ethic of Solidarity and Difference." *Postmodernism, Feminism, and Cultural Politics*. Ed. Henry Giroux. Albany: State University of New York Press, 1991, 83–99.

WELTY, Eudora. "A Still Moment." 1943. *The Collected Stories of Eudora Welty*. New York: Harcourt, Brace, Jovanovich, 1980, 189–99.

WEST, Richard. *Spectator* 245, 5 July 1980: 18.

WILCOX, Leonard. "Baudrillard, DeLillo's *White Noise*, and the End of Heroic Narrative." *Contemporary Literature* 32:3 (1991): 346–65.

WILLIAMS, Raymond. *Culture and Society 1780–1950*. 1958. Harmondsworth: Penguin, 1963.

————. *Marxism and Literature*. Oxford, UK: Oxford University Press, 1977.

WISE, Christopher. "The Garden Trampled: or, The Liquidation of African Culture in V.S. Naipaul's *A Bend in the River*." *College Literature* 23.3 (1996): 58–72.

WOLFE, Thomas. *Look Homeward, Angel*. 1929. New York: Scribner's, 1952.

WOOLF, Virginia. *Mrs Dalloway*. 1925. Harmondsworth: Penguin, 1964.

————. *The Waves*. 1931. Harmondsworth: Penguin, 1964.

WORDSWORTH, William. *Poetical Works*. Ed. Thomas Hutchinson. Rev. Ernest de Selincourt. Oxford, UK: Oxford University Press, 1969.

WRIGHT, Mary Anna. "The Great British Ecstasy Revolution." *DiY Culture: Party & Protest in Nineties Britain*. Ed. George McKay. London: Verso, 1998, 228–42.

WRIGHT, Patrick. *On Living in an Old Country*. London: Verso, 1985.

ZARETSKY, Eli. *Capitalism, the Family, and Personal Life*. London: Pluto Press, 1976.

Index

modernist poetry, 5
See also High Modernism
Modernity, 56, 119
Modernization, 36, 61, 68, 101, 115–119
 passim, 121
Morrison, Toni, 69, 143n.4, 144n.3
Mouffe, Chantal, 66, 67
Mr. Sammler's Planet (Bellow), 86–97 *pas-sim,* 139n.7
Mrs Dalloway (Woolf), 25, 27, 101
Murray, Albert, 142.10
Mysticism, 3, 31, 58, 62–63, 68, 70, 89,
 111, 123, 139n.4, 141n.4
 experience, 16, 19, 22–24, 48, 69,
  74, 84, 105, 106, 107, 122
 narrative, 3, 26, 105
 New Age, 3, 64
 union, 61–71, 123
Mystics, 19, 21, 23, 99, 105, 137n.2
 and African-American women, 112,
  114

N
Naipaul, V. S., 54–58, 136n.5
Narrative of the Life of Frederick Douglass,
 91
Narratology, 6, 93
Nation-state, 61, 67
Naturalist writers, 28, 94
Neoplatonism, 63–64, 105, 137n.2
Neoromanticism, 58–61 *passim*
New Deal, 117, 143n.7
New historicism, 8
New South, 116, 117–118
New Testament, 32, 85
 1 Peter, 86
 Acts of the Apostles 29, 32
 Mark, 85, 133n.5
 Matthew, 85, 138n.1
Newman, J. H. (Cardinal), 33
Nichols, Ashton, 1–2, 4, 11, 14, 35, 38,
 39, 43

Nicholson, Linda J., 130n.8
Nicosia, Gerald, 141n. 5
Nietzsche, Friedrich, 6, 60, 88
Nilsen, Helge, 139n. 4, 140n.13
Nirvana, 47, 63
Nkrumah, Kwame, 56
Noon, William, 14
Noumenon, 14
Nyerere, Julius, 56

O
O'Connor, Flannery, 4, 14–20 *passim,* 26,
 27, 48, 49, 50, 120, 133n.5, 134n.1,
 140n.8
O'Neill, Eugene, 63
Occult, the, 58, 82, 88, 118, 130n.5
 faculty, 3, 20, 23, 24, 89, 121, 123
Oceanic Feeling, 64–65, 136n.9
Oculocentrism, 32, 34, 130n.4
Of Time and the River (Wolfe), 42
Old Testament, 32, 86
 Daniel, 32, 86
 Ezekiel, 32, 86
 Genesis, 75
On the Road (Kerouac), 17, 20, 47, 102–
 107 *passim,* 141n.4
Origin, the, 76, 123
Oswald, Lee Harvey, 81–82

P
Paley, Grace, 28
Pantheism, 63, 64
Paradise Regained (Milton), 135n.3
Paralogy, 130n.9
Paranoia, 27
Paris Review, 22
Parke, Nigel, 2
Parody, 28–29, 31
Particularity, 54–61 *passim,* 70, 71
Particularization, 7
Pascal, Blaise, 87, 91, 139n.5